TEXAS GOVERNMENT

★★★

3RD EDITION

Tom Bass
University of St. Thomas

Nancy B. Kral
Tomball College

Gary Brown
Montgomery College

Scott A. Nelson
Kingwood College

James D. Gleason
Victoria College

James A. Puetz
North Harris College

Timothy G. Howard
North Harris College

David Robinson
University of Houston—Downtown

2000

DAME
Thomson Learning.

Australia • Canada • Denmark • Japan • Mexico • New Zealand • Philippines
Puerto Rico • Singapore • South Africa • Spain • United Kingdom • United States

Texas Government—Third Edition, by Tom Bass/Gary Brown/James D. Gleason/Timothy G. Howard/Nancy B. Kral/Scott A. Nelson/James A. Puetz/ David Robinson
Desktop Publishing: Sonda L. Frament
Cover Design: Andrea P. Leggett
Cover Photo: "Gary's Bluebonnets," by Carlos Landa (Carlos Landa is Professor of HRT at Montgomery College).
Printer: Mazer Corp.

Printed in the United States of America
1 2 3 4 5 02 01 00 99

For more information contact Thomson Learning Custom Publishing, 5101 Madison Road, Cincinnati, Ohio, 45227, 1-800-355-9983 or find us on the Internet at
http://www.custom.thomsonlearning.com

For permission to use material from this text or product, contact us by:
• **telephone: 1-800-730-2214**
• **fax: 1-800-730-2215**
• **web: http://www.thomsonrights.com**

ISBN 0-87393-889-5

This text is printed on acid-free paper.

Preface

The publication of *Texas Government* in 1995 marked a new concept in Texas government textbooks. The purpose of the book, then and now, is to provide instructors with a brief, up-to-date, and inexpensive resource emphasizing the nuts and bolts of how state government works and doesn't work. It is written for students who are seeking to find out what state government does to affect their daily lives and how they might in turn have a future impact on its policies.

The third edition, like the first two, has ten chapters covering the traditional subject to be discussed by an author who is an expert in that area. Though our fields of expertise vary, all of the authors regularly teach Texas government classes. The authors also have extensive backgrounds working in and with Texas government, including service as a county commissioner, state legislator, community college board of trustees member, MUD board president, president of the state's community college teachers association, board member of the Harris County 9-1-1 Emergency Network District, election precinct chairperson, and member of the Texas Democratic Party electoral college slate. The differing perspectives on the subject add strength to the overall approach and presentation, while differences in writing style have been smoothed out.

The material in *Texas Government* is current through 1998, though some new information was added in May, 1999, as the book was in galleys. Future editions of the book will continue to be published on a two year cycle.

The authors wish to thank Charles Pugsley Fincher for his generous donation of selected strips for use in this edition. Fincher, a full-time attorney, draws the popular Sunday newspaper strip, *Thadeus & Weez.*

Our ultimate hope is that the book will help students develop a better appreciation of Texas state government. We welcome your comments, criticism, and suggestions for improvement. Please contact us via e-mail.

garyb@nhmccd.edu

The Authors

Table of Contents

Chapter 1

The Texans: Geography, History, Demographics, & Culture

Learning Objectives:

After reading this chapter the student should be able to:

- ✪ Know the diverse geographic regions of Texas
- ✪ Understand the historical development of twentieth century Texas
- ✪ Describe the demographic, religious, and economic diversity of Texas
- ✪ Define and describe the cultural values of traditionalism and individualism as they have affected the institutions and branches of Texas politics

Texas Government didn't just "happen," but evolved as the embodiment of a population with a unique experience. Why do Texans have different political attitudes than, say, the people of New York? Why did Democrats lose their grip on virtually all state wide offices to the Republicans in 1998? Why does the Texas Legislature consist of part time "unprofessional" lawmakers, when the same institutions in other states are generally constructed quite differently? Why do Texans insist on *electing* judges, when most states have systems of *appointment*? Why does Texas lead the nation in the use of the death penalty and have the largest prison population? The answers to these questions are complex, but are rooted invariably in the attitudes, behavior patterns, and historical experience of the people of Texas. This chapter will explore these factors.

The Land

Texas has always been a land of immigrants. According to scholars, the "first Texans" were nomads who walked from Asia across the Bering Straits perhaps 30,000 years ago. These people gradually dispersed into a variety of tribes, the most prolific of which developed methods of agriculture in the fertile soil of what is now East Texas. The very name "Texas" derives from a Caddo Indian term for "friendship."

The Spanish explorers quickly discovered the principal feature of the Texas landscape: variety. This diversity spawned the sundry characteristics of the Texas population. Although scholarly observers have noted that Texas consists of four *principal* physical regions (the **Gulf Coastal Plains**, the **Interior Lowlands**, the **Great Plains**, and the **Basin and Range Province**), a casual inspection of the Texas landscape reveals more numerous and varied distinctions.

Starting at the very top of Texas in the Panhandle can be found a landscape flat as a pancake, but deceptively high in altitude at thousands of feet above sea level. The casual observer today notes the rich soil where corn, wheat, grain sorghum, soybeans, cotton, and other crops proliferate on gigantic farms—land where Commanches and Apaches once roamed in search of buffalo. Strikingly, the landscape here abruptly cleaves, revealing Palo Duro Canyon near Amarillo, reminding us that this area (which the Spanish called *Llano Esctacado*) is actually on the steppes of the Rocky Mountains to the northwest. Rainfall is in short supply, but just under the "Caprock" lies an ocean of fresh water, a natural reservoir known as the *Ogallala* Aquifer.

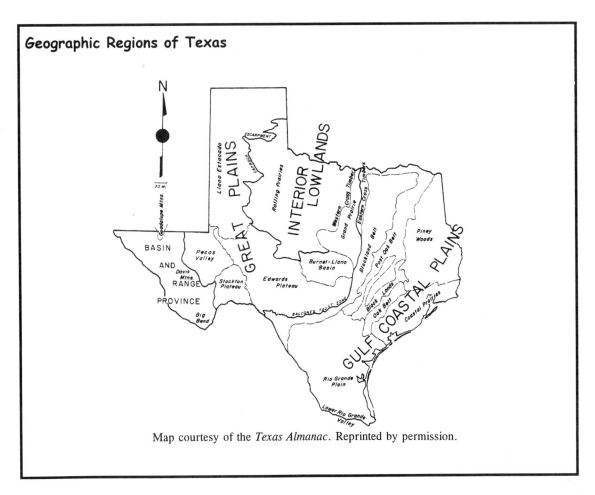

Geographic Regions of Texas

Map courtesy of the *Texas Almanac*. Reprinted by permission.

The extreme Western section of Texas is among the most sparsely populated areas in the United States. Breathtaking in its natural beauty, the "Big Bend" region along the Rio Grande includes the Davis Mountains and the rocky valley where the "Law West of the Pecos" of legendary Judge Roy Bean prevailed in the early 1800's. The area around the city of El Paso is so isolated from the rest of the state (Texarkana, Texas, for instance, is farther from El Paso than Chicago) that most folks in the region are more likely to identify with New Mexico's culture than that of Texas. Loving County, on the New Mexico border, boasts fewer than one hundred residents. Nearby Brewster County is larger in land area than Connecticut, but contains only a few small communities.

The central part of Texas is a confluence of geographic areas, the result of ancient seismic upheavals and extreme varieties in rainfall. The so-called "German Hill Country" between Austin and San Antonio sprouted into small self-sufficient farmland during the nineteenth century, attracting immigrants with few ties to the predominantly Southern culture of the rest of the state's population. The topography of central Texas is dramatically varied, with hills, valleys and, to the north, the windswept prairie and "cross timbers" area near what is now Dallas-Fort Worth.

South Texas has a distinctly Hispanic flavor, due largely to its proximity to Mexico. From the huge King Ranch west of Corpus Christi to the Rio Grande Valley, agriculture has been paramount. Indeed, the earliest cowboys, so much a part of Texas lore, were part of the *ranchero* culture of South Texas. "The Valley" is one of the foremost producers of citrus products and other commodities that require a warm climate and few harsh freezes in winter. The region is one of the most rapidly growing parts of the state due to rapid immigration from Mexico, Central, and South America. Many come to Texas for economic opportunity or, in some cases, to escape political repression. Business growth here has accelerated due to the controversial 1994 North American Free Trade Agreement, which eased tariff restrictions on commerce.

East Texas is typically labeled the "piney woods" region. Rainfall is generally abundant (notwithstanding recent devastating droughts), a quality that persuaded the earliest Anglo Settlers to clear timberland and establish farms. Nacogdoches, in East Texas, and Jefferson, in Northeast Texas, were once the state's principal urban centers. The people who migrated to this area were, for the most part, Southerners. While huge plantations were rare, the geography and climate of East Texas is very similar to the fertile farmland of the Old South. Today, timber, beef cattle, cotton, and soybeans are among the principal agricultural commodities. Not surprisingly, religious fundamentalism is more prominent here than in any other region of the state.

The Gulf Coast area of Texas is mostly flat with low altitude. Agricultural products include rice, which requires the large amounts of rainfall that people have learned to expect as one nears the Gulf of Mexico. While West Texans complain traditionally about the *lack* of rain, in the Coastal Plains the problem is often the reverse, particularly as metropolitan Houston has sprawled along the Upper Texas Coast. The principal rivers of Texas empty into the Gulf from higher latitudes—rivers which, when swollen with rain to the north and northwest, constitute a constant source of concern. Every now and then an enterprising politician proposes a "water plan" to somehow get water from the Coastal Plains—uphill—to the flatlands of the Panhandle, where underground water is quickly becoming depleted. Taxpayers are generally wary of such schemes, but grand ideas are consistent with Texas political tradition. The Gulf Coast region is heavily industrialized today, thanks to ready access to foreign shipping, especially since the Houston Ship Channel was enlarged in recent years to allow huge tankers and freighters to load and unload their goods.

Whatever labels geographers and other scholars use to characterize the impressive diversity of Texas, Texans themselves have grown accustomed to these rather distinct regions. Such categories are far too simple to fit the Lone Star

State's topography, altitude, climate, and size, and it has been mentioned more than once that Texas really should be *more* than just one state. Indeed, under the now-obscure terms of the Joint Resolution of Congress admitting Texas to the Union in 1845, some have argued that Texas could be partitioned into as many as five states—or even legally *secede* from the union. While such claims have no real validity except among fringe groups, the appearance of such sentiments on bumper stickers gives testament to the pronounced feeling of "separateness" found in the Lone Star State.

Twentieth Century Texas

Two events ushered in the new century in memorable fashion. The Galveston Flood, resulting from a terrible hurricane on September 8, 1900, brought nationwide attention. The tragedy of over 6,000 deaths and a once-thriving city in ruins held the country spellbound. Most impressive of all was the rebuilding effort by the rugged citizens of the Island, and the subsequent reshaping of the Gulf Coast into a commercial and tourist haven. Just a few months after the Galveston hurricane, the giant *Spindletop* oil well near Beaumont gushed over one hundred feet in the air. While oil was already being extracted and refined in other parts of Texas, the Spindletop strike made for a spectacular photograph, luring much-needed capital into Texas for further exploration and production. While the consumer market was not fully ready for the giant oil fields of Texas, a new era was dawning. Within a few decades, Texas became synonymous with oil. Petroleum replaced agriculture as the keystone of the Texas economy. Not surprisingly, oilmen replaced farmers as the chief political power as well.

One notable relic of the prior age was *James E. Ferguson*—elected Governor in 1914 and 1916—who loudly championed the cause of the "common man." "Farmer Jim" also made his share of enemies, as he urged Texans to put aside prominent issues of alcohol and race, infuriating prohibitionists and the Ku Klux Klan. Most significant of his adversaries, however, were the alumni of the University of Texas, upset with his veto of UT appropriations in 1917. Indeed, Ferguson was impeached and removed from office, charged with an assortment of corrupt and illegal acts. Not to be outdone, his wife, *Miriam A. ("Ma") Ferguson* was subsequently elected Governor in 1924 and later in 1932. Mrs. Ferguson was the first woman Governor elected in the United States. One campaign slogan read, *"I'm voting for Ma—and I ain't got a dang thing against Pa!"*

The rural society of Texas changed markedly during the twenties and thirties, with commerce and industry gravitating to the major cities. Oil booms contributed to the sudden growth of several communities such as Port Arthur in the east and Pampa and Borger in the Panhandle. In 1931, the giant *East Texas Boom*, boasting an oil field as large as Manhattan Island, transformed small, sleepy communities such as Kilgore into bustling centers of employment and commerce.

The Great Depression hit Texas hard, but much of the state was already in "depression" due to low cotton prices and years of severe drought. The New Deal programs of Franklin Roosevelt were popular with most Texans, particularly farmers, who were often able through federal relief to hold on to their land. Nevertheless, the monetary value of Texas farms fell 28 percent during the 1930's. The size of farms increased, but the number of Texans deriving their livelihood from agriculture shrank as the population migrated to the cities. Cities offered whatever scarce jobs existed, as well as the excitement of urban life, with electricity, movies, large churches, and transportation.

Politics also began to transform, particularly because of radio. Indeed, a Governor of the late 30's was a former radio star. W. Lee O'Daniel, also known as "Pappy," was overwhelmingly elected in the campaign of 1938, having no prior political experience. His radio show, sponsored by a flour company and accompanied by a "Hillbilly" band named the "Light Crust Doughboys," was a huge success. Music, homespun poetry and social commentary entertained devoted listeners. Letters flooded the station, convincing O'Daniel to run for office. Taking the Doughboys on the road, he attracted the largest crowds in Texas political history and won the Democratic Primary (which in those days meant victory was assured) by the largest margin ever. While his tenure as Governor was largely unproductive (his principal campaign pledge consisted of the Ten Commandments and the Golden Rule), O'Daniel represents the first "media" politician in Texas history—and a sign of things to come.

World War II provided a mixture of sacrifices and opportunities. On the home front, the Allies benefited greatly from the vast supply of Texas oil, which had been denied a market during the Depression. Numerous military bases, many of which were the product of nineteenth century crises with Mexico, provided training for hundreds of thousands of soldiers. Countless Americans had their first exposure to Texas while stationed in San Antonio, Abilene, Amarillo, or El Paso.

If Texas had a "great leap forward" economically, it was during the years immediately following the war. Prosperity was in the air, fueled by oil profits, military spending, interstate highway construction, and the rapid growth of the largest cities in Texas: Houston, Dallas, and San Antonio. The burgeoning oil business brought much needed capital and jobs into the state, as Texans invested profits in a variety of business activities.

Politically, the fifties provided a highly charged atmosphere. The Democratic Party, dominant since Reconstruction, began to show some wear. Conservatives, upset over the economic generosity and civil rights advocacy of the national Democrats, started to complain openly. When the national Democrats endorsed civil rights for blacks in 1948, it caused a Southern rebellion, as "Dixiecrats" walked out of the national Convention to nominate their own candidate for President. Four years later, with Dwight Eisenhower at the top of the Republican ticket, Texas voted

GOP for the first time since 1928. Eisenhower was born in Texas (though his family left for Kansas when Ike was an infant), and his states' rights position on the *Tidelands Question* (giving Texas off-shore petroleum royalties) were impressive to oil-rich contributors.

Generally speaking, the tendency of Texans to increasingly reject tradition and vote Republican parallels the infusion of money into the state. The oil business replaced cattle and agriculture as the political power base, with financial support flowing toward pragmatic politicians of both parties. Most, however, remained Democrats—for the moment. During the fifties, Senator Lyndon B. Johnson advanced quickly to the post of Majority Leader, ruling in tandem with fellow Texan Speaker of the House Sam Rayburn, placing Texas on the national political map.

Indeed, a new attitude was taking over. The federal government, seen as the enemy since the days of Reconstruction, was now viewed by pragmatists such as Johnson as a valuable source of revenue for jobs and prosperity. The myth of Texas "individualism" and independence still remained, but perhaps with less sincerity. Cold War military spending, highway construction, and projects such as the National Aeronautics and Space Administration pumped billions into the Texas economy.

By the 1960's, the days of "Pa" Ferguson and "Pappy" O'Daniel were a distant memory. Most Texans now lived in towns and cities rather than on the farm. Texans elected their first "urban Governor," *John B. Connally*, who became a national figure when wounded during the Kennedy assassination in Dallas. Under Connally (who later became a Republican), Texas devoted more resources to modernizing the state's system of higher education, which began to compete nationally for status and research dollars. Petroleum, banking, health care, space technology, and tourism replaced farming as the principal employers.

In the 1970's Texas found itself the beneficiary of a national dilemma: the Energy Crisis. After the Arab Oil Embargo of 1974, crude oil prices nationwide shot upward, as lines of cars waiting for precious fuel were prominent on the evening news. While the rest of the nation suffered, another Oil Boom was on in Texas. Hundreds of thousands of job-seeking Americans from northern "frost-belt" states flooded across the Red River hunting opportunity. Houston became synonymous with traffic and congestion, as money flowed into the pockets of the lucky and the bold. In many ways, the boom of the 1970's resembled the land rush of previous centuries, when fortune-seekers of European ancestry journeyed to "Tejas" amidst countless personal obstacles.

But soon the party was over. The Oil Boom became the Oil Bust, as world supplies of petroleum increased prodigiously in the 1980's, driving crude prices downward. The Texas energy industry experienced layoffs and rusting oil rigs, while the nation—on the surface—enjoyed the Reagan and Bush years in relative prosperity. While oil and gas companies went through hard times, other sectors showed amazing versatility, and even growth. "High-technology" became the new buzzword, as companies found Texas to be a good place to invest. Foreign imports flowed through the Houston Ship Channel, employing thousands.

Economically, the close of the twentieth century has brought a mixture of uncertainty and opportunity to Texas. In the mid-90's oil prices plunged downward once more. The abrupt end of the Cold War resulted in military cutbacks nationwide, including Kelly Air Force Base in San Antonio, one of the largest employers in that city. On the other hand, in Central Texas, *Fort Hood*, the largest military base in the world, *gained* personnel from closings elsewhere. While Congress voted in 1993 to scrap the *Superconducting Supercollider* south of Dallas (an ambitious scientific project involving billions), in 1998 it appropriated much more for Texas highway expansion to accommodate the congestion spawned by a booming economy. So despite a recession (and many would call it depression) in the oil industry, Texas has exhibited amazing resilience and diversity in its economy, pumping extra billions into the state's treasury.

While the federal government's role in the Texas economy is important, it must be remembered that most jobs remain in the private sector. Investors still find Texas an attractive place to take risks—a tradition that goes back to the early explorers and land speculators. Texans have always seen themselves as different from other Americans—a legacy that has certainly affected its politics.

The Texans Today

One way scholars attempt to understand the political environment of a population is to study various "demographic" characteristics. *Demographics* means, literally, "a picture of the people," and attempts to present a statistical portrayal of social traits. Common demographic characteristics include age, income, religion, gender, and educational level. Factors such as these are important because such traits are strongly linked to political behavior. How someone votes, for instance, is often very predictable if one knows a few important statistical "variables," that is, traits which vary from population to population.

At the beginning of the 21st century, the *population* of Texas is slightly short of 20 million, according to the Comptroller of Public Accounts. By 2020 it will exceed 25 million. Texas several years ago surpassed New York as the second largest state in the United States, making California the only state with more people. Despite its rural heritage and large land mass, Texas today is decidedly urban and suburban in nature, with over ninety percent of its residents living in large communities rather than small towns or on farms. Texas also has three of the ten largest metropolitan areas in the United States: Houston, Dallas-Fort Worth, and San Antonio. Greater Houston contains approximately 4 million people—a figure larger than many entire states. Harris County, which contains Houston, has around six times the population of Alaska, and is more populous than Arkansas.

Ethnicity. During the 1980's and 90's, over a million people came to Texas to live. Almost half these new immigrants were born outside the United States. Hence the "new" arrivals reflect a striking racial and ethnic diversity. Whether recent immigrants or native Texans, there are two readily identifiable ethnic categories of great political and social significance at the close of the twentieth century. According to the 1998 *Texas Almanac*, almost 30 per cent of Texans are *Hispanic*. Most are Mexican by heritage, though there are increasing numbers from Central and South America as well. (It is a matter of great dispute as to the number of *non-citizens* who have immigrated to Texas. By law non-citizens cannot vote but are nonetheless counted in the census whether they are here legally or not. According to the Comptroller of Public Accounts, the figure is approximately 8 per cent.) 12 per cent of the Texas population is *African American*.

The African American population has remained relatively constant in its proportion of the population for the past several decades. These Texans of course reflect the legacy of slavery, with East Texas counties registering higher proportions than Central and West Texas. It must be remembered, however, that urban migration of African Americans is a nationwide phenomenon of the twentieth century. Hence it should come as no surprise that the majority reside in the three principal urban areas. Politically, African Americans constitute a sizable voting "bloc" that has attracted the attention of numerous elected officials. Voter turnout (the percentage of eligible voters who actually vote) is somewhat lower than that of whites, but political studies have confirmed that this trait is probably due to differences in income rather than race. In the nineteenth century, African Americans nationwide supported the party of Emancipation, the Republicans. Since around the 1940's, however, they tend to vote Democratic in all regions of the country, including Texas.

Hispanic Texans constitute the largest and most rapidly growing ethnic minority. Proximity to Mexico is an obvious factor in this development. Indeed, as might be expected, the Hispanic proportion increases the closer one gets to the Rio Grande, and some counties in the border regions are over 95 per cent Hispanic. Although their lower voter turnout rate mirrors that of other racial minorities, the sheer size and volatility of the Hispanic population makes it a formidable political force in almost all regions of the state. Recently, Hispanic organizations such as the League of United Latin American Citizens (LULAC) and the Mexican American Legal Defense Fund (MALDEF) have been very active in the courts, filing lawsuits to help address the historic inequities in the distribution of resources such as school funding.

In a relatively new development, the state's Asian population has grown to two per cent, consisting mostly of recent immigrants from China and Southeast Asian countries such as Vietnam. New "Chinatowns" have abruptly sprung up in the major urban centers, reflecting an economic—and political—presence. Other nationalities can also be detected, some with ancient Texas roots such as Native Americans, and others more contemporary, such as those from Middle Eastern countries. All in all, ethnic minority groups constitute 44 per cent of the population of the state. It is easy to predict that early in the next century Texas will become "majority minority." Indeed, in the urban centers, this is already the case. Hispanics and African Americans make up over 60 per cent of Houston's population, for instance. The recent election of Lee Brown as Houston's first African American mayor is an obvious example of this shift in voting strength.

For the ethnic minorities of Texas, the chief policy issues have involved education at all levels, which is rightfully seen as the key to narrowing the gap in incomes and opportunity between whites and non-whites. In K-12 education, a longstanding controversy continues over the funding of public schools with a local property tax , which discriminates against property-poor areas—including those with high concentrations of minorities. In higher education, a fierce debate rages over the recent *Hopwood* decision in the federal courts, which banned all race-based affirmative action programs at Texas colleges and universities.

Religion. While the United States Supreme Court has recognized the tradition of "separation of church and state" since the 1950's, religion is an important demographic variable in explaining political behavior. Most denominations in America are not "political" in an active sense, but whether one is Catholic, Baptist, Jewish, or Hindu occasionally says much about one's politics.

According to the respected Texas Poll, 60 per cent of Texans say they belong to a Protestant denomination. Nearly a third of the population calls themselves Baptists. Twenty-five per cent of Texans identify with the Catholic faith, largely reflecting the huge Hispanic population of the state. Almost 80 per cent say they attend religious services at least twice a month, a figure higher than responses given by the nation as a whole. Religious belief occasionally becomes manifestly political. Southern Baptists, for example, have been very vocal in their opposition to horse race betting, the state lottery, and proposals for casino gambling. It is unclear whether the state's recent approval of various forms of gambling such as the lottery reflect a weakening of the "Baptist factor" or whether it merely displays a national trend by states to find new ways to raise money in an anti-tax atmosphere. At any rate, Texans take their religion seriously.

Economic Status. One very useful statistical indicator for social and political scientists is the income level of a given population. Wealthy people, as one might expect, behave different politically than poor people. They are more likely to vote, for instance. People of higher income also tend to be more conservative in their political opinions, to give another example. How wealthy are Texans? The stereotypical Texan is, of course, a wealthy oil man or rancher who owns vast amounts of land. Hollywood has helped perpetuate this myth. Sure enough, Texas consistently ranks near the top in *total* personal income. It is important to emphasize, however, that Texas ranks close to the top of the fifty states in virtually *every* social category, simply because Texas is second in population. Hence Texas is at or near the top in numbers of farms, licensed drivers, AIDS cases, social security recipients, and vegetarians. *Total* wealth—total *anything*—is rarely a valid measurement when ranking states.

A better way to determine economic status is to look at *per capita* income, which is an average, or *mean*. (Using average incomes involves problems as well, however. For instance, it can be very misleading if the mean reflects *extremes,* as averages tend to do. If a hypothetical community contained only rich and poor folks—with no middle class—the average would be somewhere in the middle.) As for Texas, not only is the stereotype of wealthy oil men blatantly wrong, a picture of a middle-American population is also misleading. Annual *per capita* income in Texas since the 1980's has consistently been *below* the national average. Likewise, this is also true with another statistical measurement, *median household income.* Furthermore, these numbers in no way indicate that Texas incomes are evenly distributed. Indeed, they are not.

Contrary to stereotype, a higher proportion of Texans live in poverty than in most other states. Currently, according to the Comptroller, 17 per cent of Texans live below the official poverty line, which is approximately $14,000 a year for a family of four. 13 per cent receive food stamps. Poverty is found disproportionately among racial minorities. African Americans, as noted earlier, constitute 12 per cent of the population, but 28 per cent of the poor are black. Hispanics account for 40 per cent of the poor, though they represent less than 30 per cent of the entire population. Welfare benefits in Texas are historically among the lowest in the nation, perhaps reflecting the frontier legacy of individualism and resistance to taxes. A new development in this area concerns the potential impact of the "Welfare Reform" bill passed by Congress in 1996 and signed by President Clinton. At the heart of the new law is a program of "block grants" to the states, with a mandatory exclusion of non-citizens from health, education, and welfare benefits. As in the rest of the country, welfare rolls are declining sharply, probably due to the strength of the economy in the 1990's. However, it is much too early to measure the new law's impact upon poverty in Texas. The unequal distribution of wealth has many social consequences. There is a high correlation between low socioeconomic status and most criminal behavior, for instance. Hence it is not surprising that the Texas prison population is the highest among all the states. This is not to say that poverty *causes* crime (crime rates occasionally go up in *good* times rather than bad), but that unequal distribution of resources contributes to the social situations that breed criminal activity. Tax dollars that could go to education, for example, are diverted into prisons. It is worth noting incidentally that, for whatever reasons, most categories of crime in the United States and Texas have dropped dramatically during the 1990's.

Wide disparities in income may be partially a result of the system of taxes in the Lone Star State. Texas is one of only seven states with no *personal income tax*. Consequently policy makers are forced to rely upon *sales* and *property* taxes as the main sources of revenue. Sales taxes, and especially property taxes, are *regressive*, *i.e.*, they tend to fall hardest upon those of lower income. A higher proportion of a poor person's income will be devoted to property taxes than that of wealthy people. Income taxes, on the other hand, are usually based on the ability to pay. A person with very little income will pay little or no income tax. However, this person will be paying sales taxes on purchased items and property taxes as well (renters pay property tax "hidden" in the rent). Even the Texas State Lottery has a tendency to take money from those who can least afford it. Those of lower incomes and educational levels bet a higher proportion of their incomes than wealthy people do. It is important to note, however, that Texans of *all* income levels have fiercely resisted a personal income tax. Indeed, Texans voted overwhelmingly in 1993 for a Constitutional Amendment requiring direct public approval before the Legislature can enact an income tax. Furthermore, with current forecasts of unprecedented budget surpluses, it is unlikely that state leaders will impose any new forms of taxation.

Education. Linked closely with income, educational level is a very valuable measurement for social scientists. The level of educational advancement, for instance, is the strongest statistical "predictor" of voting. In other words, the higher the educational level of a population, the greater the likelihood of a high voter turnout. Not unexpectedly, Texas ranks below most other states.

The level of education can be measured a number of ways: dropout rates, scores on standardized tests, pupil/teacher ratios, money spent per child in school, *etc.* The relatively poor standing of Texas in all these categories is obviously linked to incomes and a host of other demographic variables. Southern states tend to fare worse in such measurements, with some exceptions. Furthermore, the dropout rate among Hispanics is consistently over 50 per cent, reflecting language deficiencies and the historical lack of educational opportunity to Mexican Americans in the history of Texas, particularly along the border.

Since the Texas school system relies heavily upon the local property tax, poor areas of the state such as the Rio Grande Valley have always operated at a distinct disadvantage. As will be discussed in a later chapter, recent court cases such as the *Edgewood I.S.D. v. Meno* decision have attempted to address the inequities, but school districts with a great deal of property wealth are reluctant to send money to poorer schools, calling such plans "Robin Hood" arrangements. There is no statistical proof that money alone will solve the lower educational level of Texans, but all observers agree the available funds have been distributed unequally.

Occupations. Farming was the only occupation of any real political importance until well into the twentieth century. When the Texas Constitution was written in 1875, a farmers' organization called the National Grange was the most powerful faction. Later, politicians such as "Pa" Ferguson and "Pappy" O'Daniel made successful appeals to the "farm vote" during their careers. These days are clearly over. Agriculture is still a vitally important component of the Texas economy, and Texas has more acreage in farms than any other state, but farmers constitute only one per cent of the population.

The job picture today is more complex. A wide assortment of manufacturing industries remains significant, particularly the petrochemical firms and refineries along the upper Texas coast. These jobs represent the traditional "blue collar" occupations, though their ranks have dwindled in recent years as foreign oil became cheaper than domestic. Indeed, Texas never experienced the heavy industrialization of other big states such as Pennsylvania, New York or Ohio. The labor movement in Texas has also traditionally been weak politically, hindered by a *"right to work" law* forbidding union membership as a requirement for employment.

While manufacturing continues to be a significant employer of Texans, the principal growth in recent years has been in two principal sectors: the *"service" economy* and *"high-tech"* industries. "Service" industries range widely from banking, insurance, entertainment, transportation, medicine, education, and a host of others. One of the distinguishing characteristics of the service economy is the striking variety of wages and salaries it offers. Jobs can be very high paying—or very low. Consider the difference between the income of a medical specialist at the Texas Medical Center in Houston and the wages of people working in a fast food franchise. Not surprisingly, educational level is the most important factor in whether an individual is well paid or not.

Texas has also become a leader in a variety of "high-tech" industries. While these are too varied to describe in detail, they would include numerous computer firms that have gravitated to the "I-35 Corridor" since the 70's and the relatively new field of Biotechnology, which has attracted a great deal of attention and capital, especially in San Antonio and Houston. Biotechnology involves such exotic fare as the industrial use of bacteria and genetic engineering, frontiers of science that hold promise for future progress—and jobs.

Politically, it is still uncertain whether these new kinds of fields will produce any surprises. It does seem clear that old traditions will be less important. Political parties will not hold peoples' loyalty as much in the future, a trend that has already begun. Most political activism will probably find its way into special interest groups, as the members of these new industries "find each other" and form alliances to protect and advance their interests.

Political Culture

The mass media usually portrays the beliefs of Americans in terms of "liberal" or "conservative." The trouble with such labels is that, while many people certainly fit such ideological descriptions, Americans tend to be inconsistent in their beliefs and behavior patterns. Categorizing Americans, and Texans, is very difficult. In terms of social class, for instance, the vast majority of Americans tend to think of themselves as "Middle Class," whether they are very wealthy or barely making it.

One of the most influential attempts at making sense of the way Americans interact with government was formulated by political scientist Daniel Elazar in an influential book entitled *American Federalism: A View from the* States. Elazar attempted to evaluate the political *culture* of Americans, which relates to their most fundamental attitudes and behavior. Why would a farmer in Minnesota with a high school education and earning $30,000 per year vote for a Democrat, while a farmer in Oklahoma or Texas with the same income and educational level support a Republican? It may have something to do with the *culture*, which relates to ancestral roots and experiences.

Elazar writes that there are three principal American political cultures: *moralistic, individualistic,* and *traditionalistic.* The moralistic culture has its roots in the New England of the early Puritan settlers. These people were deeply religious and socially conscious, and wanted to establish a political society that embraced everyone. Their descendants, along with Scandinavian and immigrants who came to America in the nineteenth and early twentieth centuries, settled in the upper Midwest, the Great Lakes region and into such locales as Iowa, Oregon, Washington, and a few other western states. Moralists believe that politics is a healthy enterprise and everyone's duty. Politicians, who are considered to be public servants, enjoy high status. Government can—and should—be used as a positive force to improve society. High voter turnout and a willingness to pay taxes to solve problems are traits of this culture in modern political life. Interestingly, Elazar does not find the moralistic culture to any significant degree in Texas.

The individualistic political culture has its roots primarily in the non-Puritanical English and Germanic settlers. With these people, the pursuit of individual opportunity had a higher priority than the goals of the community. As this culture migrated westward, its people found a home in more or less the middle third of the nation. Americans in this category view government as having a limited role in society. Basically, government should stay out of the way, unless it can help enhance economic success. An individualistic person is not a "do-gooder," but rather sees the political arena as a marketplace. Politicians are "errand boys," as Elazar describes them, sent to fetch desired goods and services for interested parties. Mass participation by citizens is allowed, but not particularly encouraged. The participation of special interest groups fits in nicely with the individualistic culture. People combine in political organizations merely to pursue common economic interests. A certain level of corruption is also assumed to be the natural order of things. Texas, particularly West Texas, became fertile ground for people of the individualistic political culture.

A final grouping of Elazar's is the traditionalistic political culture. The key to understanding this category is the realization that its origins lie in the plantation system of the Old South, dating back to America's founding era. With these people, the principal function of government is to preserve the existing social order and "way of life" of the social elites of the community. Leaders tend to come from "old families" in traditionalistic areas. Obviously, this characterization for Elazar is related to the practice of racism, whereby blacks were kept in "their place" not only by social custom, but also by government policy. But other issues come to mind as well. A traditionalistic community would tend to favor rigid zoning practices—legal restrictions on certain types of business or residential housing in particular areas. Keeping in mind that early Texas was settled principally by Americans from Southern states, it is no surprise that Elazar finds the traditionalistic culture quite prominent in Texas. East Texas is particularly dominated by this culture. Naturally, as immigrants from other areas of the country (and world) have populated the Lone Star State, the culture has been partially diluted by more individualistic Texans.

If Elazar is correct, the political behavior of Texans over the years is clarified substantially. As we have seen repeatedly in this chapter, Texans tend to take a rather unfavorable view toward government, particularly efforts to "reform" society or help those less fortunate. When it comes to welfare, public education, and other such policies, Texans can be downright stingy with tax dollars compared with other Americans. On the other hand, if it's highway construction, the space station, or military bases with a large payroll, Texans are all for it, sometimes regardless of cost. Such an attitude is consistent with Elazar's individualistic political culture. Couple this with the basic conservatism of the Texas political system when it comes to preserving the existing social order of society (as expressed in the traditionalistic culture), and you have at least a partial explanation of the Texas political experience.

While the culture of a given society is the product of long-term experience, it is also very fragile. Due to the projected changes in the demographic picture of Texas over the next few decades, it is extremely likely the two predominant cultures of the state will become more difficult to trace and identify. Scholars have argued for years whether America is a "melting pot," with its diverse cultures and ethnic groups blending together, or a "salad bowl," into which they are tossed together yet remain distinct. Either way, "Texans" will become increasingly difficult to categorize in the future.

On-Line: The Texans: Geography, History, Demographics, and Culture

Interested in learning more about Texas on the Internet? Here is an overall reference to Texas-related Web sites, provided as a cooperative service of the Texas Department of Information Resources and the Texas State Library and Archives Commission:

http://www.texas.gov/

Chapter 2

The Texas Constitution

Learning Objectives:

After reading this chapter, the student should be able to:

- Describe the historical development of the Texas Constitution of 1876
- Compare and contrast the structure and content of the U.S. and Texas constitutions
- Describe the restraints upon public policy found in the Texas Constitution and how the document promotes limited government in Texas
- Review the attempts to replace the Texas Constitution of 1876

Introduction

Constitutions perform important functions for government. First, they **outline the structure** of government, establishing how authority is to be organized. The U.S. Constitution, for example, establishes the legislative, executive, and judicial branches of government in Articles I, II, and III. Second, constitutions **grant power** to public officials. The U.S. Congress, for example, has the enumerated power to declare war, granted in Article I, Section 8. Third, constitutions **place limits on the power** of public officials. The Texas legislature is required by its constitution to operate within the framework of a balanced state budget after its two year session. In other words, the legislature is limited to spending only what revenue is available. Last, a constitution serves as a **symbol** of our country or of our state. The United States Constitution, which established a federal system of government, has served as a model for the governments of Canada, Mexico, Germany, and Australia. Conversely, the Texas Constitution of 1876, a poorly organized and terribly written mishmash of specific laws, is hardly inspiring to any developing country.

Historical Development

Texas has had six constitutions since 1836; the most recent constitution was ratified in 1876. Each of the five earlier constitutions was the product of the state's political instability from its early days as a republic to its acceptance as a state through the Civil War and the Reconstruction era.

The first constitution established the Republic of Texas in 1836. This document was the product of a convention that assembled during the course of the war for independence from Mexico. The government created under the constitution resembled that of our national government in structure and processes: it consisted of executive, legislative, and judicial branches, but instead of a governor, Texas had a president and a Congress. The 1836 Constitution guaranteed basic rights for its citizens while maintaining the existence of slavery.

Texas was sovereign, that is, self-governing, from 1836 until 1845, when the republic was admitted into the Union. The second constitution, written in 1845, was concerned with Texas statehood and resembled the lengthy constitutions of other southern states.

The third constitution, written in 1861, was a modification of the 1845 constitution. The rewrite was necessitated by the secession of Texas from the United States and its admission into the Confederate States of America. This document also guaranteed the institution of slavery.

Following the defeat of the Confederacy in the Civil War, Texans wrote their fourth constitution, in 1866, to establish a government and gain the approval of President Andrew Johnson for readmission to the Union. The 1866 document nullified the existence of slavery, but retained the length and form of the 1845 constitution.

As in other confederate states, the Reconstruction era was a period of instability in Texas as well as in other Confederate states. During this period, radical leaders in Congress passed the Reconstruction Act of 1867 which voided the 1866 constitution. The state government was rendered powerless and martial law imposed.

The fifth state constitution (and second Reconstruction constitution) was adopted in 1869 and met the conditions set by Congress for Texas to be readmitted to the Union. This constitution was influenced by radical Republicans in conflict with Confederate sympathizers (Democrats), and it created a strong state government. When military rule ended in 1870, the radical Republicans gained control of the state legislature. Edmund J. Davis, a former commander of Union forces in Texas during the Civil War, was elected governor.

The reign of Governor Davis and the Republican-dominated legislature (1870 until 1874) was characterized as oppressive, fiscally irresponsible, and corrupt. During this period, the state was policed by a militia that flagrantly abused the liberties of the citizenry. Local governments became subservient to the state, as the governor controlled the electoral process and appointed supporters to municipal positions. Mandatory public school attendance was initiated, with schools paid for by property taxes. The state debt was increased while the state subsidized the growth of corporations, particularly railroads.

In the election of 1873, the Democrats, weary of the Davis regime, regained control of the state legislature, and Governor Davis was defeated by Democratic challenger Richard Coke. This marked the beginning of the end of Republican-inspired policies in Texas for the next hundred years. All that remained of their reign was the 1869 constitution. A convention was called in 1875 to rewrite the document once again.

The Texas Constitution of 1876

The Texas Constitution of 1876, the state's sixth in nearly 40 years, has been described as a "perpetual product of Reconstruction".[1] The intent of the framers attending the 1875 convention in Austin was to write a document designed to replace the 1869 Reconstruction Constitution and its salient features: centralized authority resting with the state government, high property taxes, mandatory public school education, and the perceived abuse of power by the governor, legislature, and courts.

When analyzing the content of the Texas Constitution, context is crucial. The 83 men who actually attended the convention (90 were invited) were influenced by rural, agrarian interests with a unifying link of fiscal conservatism. Nearly half of the delegates were members of the National Grange of the Patrons of Husbandry, better known as the Grange, a national farm movement that claimed 800,000 members, including 45,000 members in Texas. The national goal of the Grange was to improve the lot of farmers. Twenty of the delegates had been officers in the Confederate Army, while 75 of them were Democrats. The delegates wanted a reversal of the government that had been forced upon them during Reconstruction. Changes were written to limit the power of the executive, legislative, and judicial branches. The philosophical foundation of the Texas Constitution of 1876 was that the power of government should ultimately lie with the people as a counterweight to the excess and abuse of power by elected officials. Most of the important features of the document were written in direct response to the Davis administration.

In the area of public policy, the framers targeted the state's compulsory attendance school system. By 1875, the government was carrying a heavy $4 million debt, and requiring a free public school system proved financially ruinous. Although a public school provision was included in the new constitution, restrictions were also imposed.

Students today who are native Texans or have lived in Texas since the late 1970s are in the best position to notice changes in the social and economic environment of the state. Many recent changes were responses to the restrictions imposed by the framers that have altered the social and political culture of Texas for the past one hundred years. Consider these provisions contained within the 1876 Constitution:

1. Community property for wives and husbands (Article XVI, Section 15)
2. Regulation of alcoholic beverages (Article XVI, Section 20—amended in 1970)
3. Prohibition against branch banking (Article XVI, Section 16—amended in 1986)
4. Protection of homesteads against forced sale (Article XVI, Section 50)
5. Prohibition against general home equity lending, or borrowing all or part of an individual's equity in their home.(Article XVI, Section 50—amended in 1997)
6. Prohibition against lotteries (Article III, Section 47—amended in 1991)
7. Guarantee of mechanics' liens against property on which work is performed (Article XVI, Section 37)
8. Garnishment of wages for court-ordered child support payments (Article XVI, Section 28)
9. Local tax limitations (Article VIII, Section 9)
10. Debt limitations of state government (Article III, Section 49)
11. Pension benefits for schoolteachers and other public employees (Article XVI, Section 67)
12. Provision for an income tax on personal income, though this measure was severely restricted by constitutional amendment in 1993 (Article VIII, Section 1)
13. Limitations on state welfare spending (Article III, Section 51-a)

14. Property tax benefits for lands in agricultural production (Article VIII, Section I-d)
15. Ban against imprisonment for debt (Article 1, Section 18)
16. The right to bear arms, but the state can regulate the wearing of concealed handguns. (Article I, Section 23)

Texas and U.S. Constitutions Compared

Similar Structure

The U.S. Constitution and the Texas Constitution of 1876 have a similar structure. The organization, subject matter, and parts of the two documents are compared in Figure 2-1.

Figure 2-1. The United States and Texas Constitutions Compared

United States Constitution	Subject or Part	Texas Constitution
Preamble	Preamble	Preamble
Amendments I-X	Bill of Rights	Article I (30 sections)
	Separation of Powers	Article II (1 section)
Article I (10 sections)	Legislative	Article III (62 sections)
Article II (4 sections)	Executive	Article IV (26 sections)
Article III (3 sections)	Judicial	Article V (30 sections)
Amendments XV, XIX, XXIV, and XXVI	Suffrage	Article VI (5 sections)
	Education	Article VII (17 sections)
	Taxation and revenue	Article VIII (23 sections)
	Counties	Article IX (12 sections)
	Railroads	Article X (1 section)
	Municipal corporations	Article XI (12 sections)
	Private corporations	Article XII (3 sections)
	Land titles	Article XIII (0 sections)
	Public lands	Article XIV (1 section)
	Impeachment	Article XV (9 sections)
Article IV (4 sections)	Federal relations	
Article V (1 section)	Mode of amending	Article XVII (2 sections)
Article VI (1 section)	General provisions	Article XVI (53 sections)
Article VII (1 section)	Ratification	
17 (since 1791)	Amendments	376 to 1998
7 articles, 24 sections		17 articles, 287 sections

Source: Pettus and Bland, *Texas Government Today* (Homewood, II: Dorsey Press, 1986), p.56 (updated by author).

Both documents contain a Preamble, Articles, and Amendments. Each protects the rights and liberties of its citizenry through a Bill of Rights. One critical difference between the two documents is that there is no Equal Rights Amendment forbidding gender discrimination in the U.S. Constitution; the measure was defeated as the then-proposed twenty-seventh amendment in the early 1980s. The Texas Equal Rights Amendment was added as section 3-a of Article I by constitutional amendment in 1972.

The U.S. Constitution contains 7 articles and 24 sections, while the Texas Constitution has 17 articles and 287 sections. The difference in length is largely due to the excruciating detail with which the Texas Constitution defines public policy matters. Railroad regulation, education, welfare and taxation are defined in explicit terms, thus restricting the ability of public officials to act outside constitutional mandates. Although the framers intended for these provisions to protect Texas citizenry, they presently serve as a structural impediment to popular government.

Age of Documents

The Texas Constitution, was drafted in 1875 and submitted to a ratification vote of the people in February, 1876. The new constitution was approved by a more than 2-to-1 margin. Of the then-150 counties in Texas, support came from the state's rural counties and its small towns, while opposition centered in several of the larger cities. Perhaps this explains why almost 120 years later many of the political battles that take place in the state's legislature and courtrooms have their roots in the rural-urban conflict that exists in Texas still today. The constitution, with its rural, agrarian influence and bias, has worked to the detriment of metropolitan government.

The U.S. Constitution is now over 210 years old. It was written first as a revision, then as a replacement for the Articles of Confederation. Other countries such as the Soviet Union and its 15 republics, France, Italy, and Yugoslavia have experienced upheaval and collapse of their political systems. The United States and its constitution have served as an icon for durability and stability.

Length

The Texas Constitution is now more than 80,000 words long, four times the size of the original document, and exceeded in length only by the constitutions of Alabama, Georgia, and Oklahoma. Putting it into perspective, the Holy Bible has 773,000 words. The length of the Texas Constitution is attributed to its detailed restrictions on legislative action because redundant and outdated verbiage remains that should have long ago been removed. Article XVI—"General Provisions"—serves as the best example. Featured in this article are sections that pertain to fence laws (section 22), livestock laws (section 23), and the provision of convict labor for laying out and working public roads (section 24). Section 47, "Scruples Against Bearing Arms", reads as follows: "Any person who conscientiously scruples to bear arms shall not be compelled to do so, but shall pay an equivalent for personal service". Dueling was prohibited (Section 4) until 1969, when the ban was deleted by constitutional amendment. Article V, Section 24 provides for the removal of local government officials for habitual drunkenness. Not to be outdone, the framers gave similar treatment to state judges in Article XV, Section 8. Until 1982, the constitution provided for pensions for Confederate veterans and their widows (Article VII, Section 17), all of whom were deceased.[2] Political incorrectness still survives in the document: Article VI—"Suffrage" in Section 1 prohibits "idiots and lunatics" from voting. The longest provision, Article IX, Section 12, "Establishment of Airport Authorities", goes for 765 words before ending a sentence with a period!

Conversely, the U.S. Constitution contains approximately 8,700 words. It is characterized as a fundamental set of laws—general nonspecific, and brief. It is a flexible document, easy to interpret and adaptable.

Separation of Powers

Both documents establish a separation of powers system with checks and balances. Both establish legislative, executive, and judicial branches of government and a bicameral legislature. The difference between the two documents lies in the elaboration. Article II of the Texas Constitution makes explicit the doctrine of separation of powers— "Departments of Government to be Kept Distinct", while the concept is only implied in the U.S. Constitution in Article I (Legislative), II (Executive), and III (Judicial).

The Legislative Function

The Texas Constitution of 1876 was written with the underlying philosophy that "The government that governs least, governs best". An obvious example lies with the legislature, a direct target of the framers. An impediment to legislative authority is the limited legislative session: the Texas legislature meets in regular session every two years, beginning on the second Tuesday of January in the odd-numbered year. These sessions are limited to 140 consecutive calendar days, concluding in May. Legislators are part-time and paid $7,200 per year. Conversely, the U.S. Congress meets in general session during the entire year, except for recesses, and their compensation ($136,700 per year) reflects their full-time status.

Legislature - meets every 2 years for 140 cons. days

Article III of the Texas Constitution established a bicameral legislature: The Senate, consisting of 31 members who serve four year terms, and the House of Representatives, which "shall never exceed 150" members, who serve two year terms.

The Texas legislature's authority is limited by the 287 sections of the constitution. There are no implied powers in the document. The legislators do not have the same "Necessary and Proper" clause of Article I, Section 8, Subclause 18 of the U.S. Constitution that grants a blank check of legislative power to the Congress.

How spending is handled also varies between the two documents. As amended in 1942, the Texas Constitution states "...no appropriations (spending) in excess of the cash and anticipated revenue of the funds from which such appropriation is to be made shall be valid" (Article III, Section 49-a). In other words, deficit spending is not encouraged or allowed, except casual deficits can be carried after the first year of the two-year budget. Texas has a "pay as you go" system, and state spending now and in the future will be handcuffed by this reality. Yet Texas has incurred over five billion dollars of long-term bonded debt to finance prison construction, college student loans, farm and ranch development programs, and even an ill-fated superconducting supercollider research facility. Article III, Section 49 of the Texas Constitution requires the legislature to submit bonded debt questions to the voters in proposition form.

The U.S. Congress has no such restriction. Instead, the Congress takes advantage of Article I, Section 8, Clause 2, "To borrow money on the credit of the United States." If spending exceeds revenue, as it has every year since 1969, Congress raises the debt ceiling and carries the country further into debt—$5.6 trillion as of 1999!

Both the U.S. Congress and Texas legislature have the constitutional power to override an executive veto of a bill. To do so requires a two-thirds vote of both the House and Senate.

The Executive Function

If the primary mission of the delegates to the 1875 convention was to revise the 1869 Constitution, the secondary mission was to design the structure and authority of the executive branch to prevent the recurrence of the regime of Governor Davis. Article IV, Section 1 of the 1876 Constitution diluted the power and authority of the governor's office. It established the "plural executive", an executive department of seven officers, all but one of whom were elected by the people (the secretary of state is appointed by the governor). Along with electing the governor, the people also elect the lieutenant governor, the comptroller of public accounts, the land commissioner, and the attorney general. The treasurer's position was removed by constitutional amendment in 1995. Other executives established by legislative statute, such as the agriculture commissioner, are also elected by the people.

Initially, the length of the governor's term of office was cut back from four years to two. This was amended in 1972 when the term of office was again returned to four years. There is no limit on the number of terms that a Texas governor may serve.

The governor was still left with some significant executive powers. Like the president, the governor has a legislative veto. The governor enjoys the power to veto bills passed by the legislature, as well as individual items in the appropriations bill, (the so-called "line-item veto"). In 1996, Congress passed a line-item veto bill that would give the president authority to veto certain parts of a spending bill without invalidating the entire measure. The presidential line-item veto went into effect on January 1, 1997. It took only four months for a federal district judge to declare the presidential line item veto unconstitutional, a decision upheld in 1998 by the U.S. Supreme Court.

The governor can call the legislature into thirty day special sessions and establish the agenda for these sessions. This power is the sole authority of the governor, whereas in numerous other states a legislature can both call itself back into special sessions and establish the agenda.

Unlike the president, who has true chief executive authority in directing the federal bureaucracy, the governor must direct the state bureaucracy through appointive "citizen" boards and commissions. The framers of the Texas Constitution intended for the day to day administration of state government to remain in the control of the people by having "citizens" appointed to oversee each state agency. These "citizens" often prove to be cronies of the governor, political party loyalists, or contributors to the governor's election campaign.

Article IV, Section 12 gives the governor the power to fill vacancies in these boards and commissions, with confirmation by the Senate. A new governor has to contend with the boards and commissions of nearly two hundred agencies dominated with hundreds, perhaps several thousand appointees of his predecessor. These boards provide oversight of the state's social service programs, highways, public safety, mental health and mental retardation facilities, universities, and have the responsibility to oversee the licensing and regulation of many professions and occupations such as barbers, nurses, cosmetologists, morticians, and acupuncturists.

One such board is the Texas Board of Criminal Justice, restructured in 1989 to bring the state's probation, parole, and prison functions under a centralized administrative system. The board has nine nonsalaried "citizen" members appointed by the governor with Senate approval for six-year, staggered terms. Three appointments are made every two years, so it is impossible for a governor to "clean house" and replace all of the board members at one time. The Criminal Justice Board has the responsibility to oversee the operations of the state's prison system, including the power to hire and fire the TDCJ executive director.

Further, the governor lacks budget-making power. The state budget, which serves as the roadmap for state spending priorities, is largely a legislative function through the Legislative Budget Board (LBB). As you can see, the governor of Texas ranks low in terms of constitutional powers in contrast to the governors of the other 49 states. The constitutional framers accomplished their mission.

The Judicial Function

To diminish the power of the judiciary, the Texas Constitution creates two Supreme Courts for separate classes of litigation. The nine member Texas Supreme Court is concerned with civil litigation. The nine member Texas Court of Criminal Appeals, established by constitutional amendment in 1891, deals solely with criminal litigation. In the United States, only Texas and Oklahoma have two branches of courts, both independent of each other.

Texas judges are elected by the people in partisan elections. Trial court judges are elected for either two-year or four-year terms and appeals court judges serve six-year terms. Vacancies in state court positions are filled by the governor with Senate confirmation and eventual election by the people. This is indicative of the framers' intention to keep the judiciary accountable to the people. The United States judiciary, on the other hand, has a unified judicial structure with one Supreme Court which considers both civil and criminal litigation. Federal judges are appointed to life terms by the President with Senate approval.

The Texas Constitution also creates "inferior" courts, that is municipal courts (two-year terms); justice of the peace courts (four-year terms); county courts (four-year terms); and state district courts (four-year terms). Below the Supreme Court and Court of Criminal Appeals are the intermediate Courts of Appeals, with judges serving six-year terms.

During the Davis regime, judges were appointed by the governor. Many of them proved to be incompetent, so the power of the court was weakened by the constitution. Further, the power of the state judiciary is narrow in its interpretation of the constitution, so there has been little or no growth in constitutional authority by means of judicial interpretation. Constitutional change has come about largely through the formal amendment process.

The Amendment Process

In order for a constitution written many years ago to survive and grow, it has to adapt to the changing times. For instance, when the framers penned the second amendment of the U.S. Constitution, "...the right of the people to keep and bear arms," did they envision the lethal potential of the AK-47 semi-automatic assault rifle in an urban society? Being of such a general nature, the major means of changing the U.S. Constitution has been through judicial interpretation. The framers were suspicious of radical change of the U.S. Constitution and impediments were placed to slow the rate of change. Amendments, which change the words in the document, must be initiated or proposed by a two-thirds vote of both chambers of the Congress and ratified or approved by the legislatures of three-fourths (38 of 50) of the states. To date, the U.S. Constitution has been amended 27 times, the most recent in 1992.

The Texas Constitution is another story. Texas judges do not necessarily interpret the constitution. Instead, they apply it. The Texas Constitution is so long and detailed there is little room for judicial interpretation. The chief means of changing the Texas Constitution has been the formal amendment route.

An amendment to the Texas Constitution is proposed in a bill before the legislature which must pass by a two-thirds vote in both the House of Representatives and Senate. Ratification of the proposed amendment is by a majority vote (50 percent plus one vote) of the people in a regular or special election. This procedure, outlined in Article XVII of the constitution, reflects the intent of the framers to retain control of the state's governing document in the hands of its people. This amendment process as envisioned by the constitutional framers was great in theory but in fact has proven less than successful. In general elections when candidates are on the ballot, many voters ignore the amendments. Reasons given for skipping the amendments section of the ballot might include (1) **oversight** (amendments are listed in the trailer section of the ballot); (2) **intimidation**, because of the wording used in describing the amendments (amendments often read like the subclauses in your automobile insurance policy); (3) **time limitations** (people want to cast their vote for the big races and cut out back to work or the poolhall from whence they came) and (4) **exhaustion**, as voters asked to read, digest, and comprehend the intricacies of 14 amendments (as in November, 1997) might be stretched to their limits.

A major part of the problem is that the state does not effectively publicize the amendments. Article XVII requires that the proposed amendments must be printed twice in a newspaper in each county of the state, the first notice to be published not more than 60 days before the date of the election, and the second to be published on the same day in the succeeding week. Reality sets in when the state has to pay rather high rates for advertising per square inch of newspaper space. Official notices of the amendments end up among the classified advertisements and legal notices. One such public notice appeared in the Texas A&M University student newspaper, *The Battalion*, underneath a pizza parlor coupon and an advertisement for a nail salon.

Figure 2-2 is evidence of the increased pace by which Texas has amended its state constitution. Only 44 amendments were added in the first 50 years following ratification in 1876.

Figure 2-2. Rate of Constitutional Amendments in Texas

Time Period	Amendments Proposed	Ratified	Amendment Rate per year	Adoption Rate % (proposed/ratified)
1876-1926	117	44	0.9	37.6%
1927-1951	102	66	2.6	64.7%
1952-1977	174	122	4.7	70.1%
1978-1985	62	54	6.8	87.1%
1986-1997	113	90	8.2	79.6%
Totals	568	376	3.1	66.2%

Remember that oil was discovered at Spindletop in 1901, and the state's economy has shifted from agriculture to manufacturing to a services-oriented economy clustered in the state's three metropolitan areas. The stress of population growth has produced a greater number of proposed amendments over time with a larger adoption rate. During the half century from 1927 to 1977, 188 amendments were ratified. From 1978 to 1997, 144 amendments were approved, three times the number added in the first 50 years. There are now a total of 376 amendments through 1997. As veteran political journalist Felton West observed, "Isn't it amazing that at a time when voters appear to be less inclined to vote that they are being asked to approve more and more constitutional amendments?"[3]

With a mostly disinterested and uninformed voting electorate to contend with, how do we know which amendments will pass and which ones won't? It is safe to say by looking at the data in Figure 2-3 that the odds are a measure will pass. Voters tend to approve amendments that they perceive will work to the benefit of the state as a whole and not raise taxes.

In 1997, statewide turnout for 14 proposed amendments averaged a little more than 10%. Harris County, boosted by Houston city elections, recorded the highest turnout (20.60%) while Starr County in South Texas recorded the lowest (1.27%).

Figure 2.3 summarizes the results of all 14 measures in the 1997 election.

By far the most salient issue was Proposition 8, the amendment that would allow homeowners to use the equity in their homes as collateral for loans. True to its conservative nature, the 1876 Texas Constitution went to extraordinary lengths to protect family homesteads from debt collectors. The home equity measure, strongly supported by banks and other financial institutions, passed by a 3 to 2 margin.

Figure 2.3 summarizes the results of all 14 measures in the 1997 election.

Figure 2-3. 1997 Constitutional Amendment Election

	Votes	Percent		Votes	Percent
Prop. 1 Municipal Court Judges to hold more than one office			**Prop. 8** Expand types of liens for home equity loans		
In Favor	423,793	36.69%	In Favor	698,870	59.56%
Against	731,044	63.30%	Against	474,443	40.43%
Race Total	1,154,837		**Race Total**	1,173,31	
Prop. 2 Limit increases in residence homesteads for ad valorem tax			**Prop. 9** Authorize ad valorem tax rate in rural fire prevention districts		
In Favor	852,031	75.66%	In Favor	558,400	53.12%
Against	273,957	24.33%	Against	492,666	46.87%
Race Total	1,125,988		**Race Total**	1,051,06	
Prop. 3 Granting exemption on property for water conservation initiation			**Prop. 10** Compensation to victims of crime fund and crime auxiliary fund		
In Favor	681,060	61.80%	In Favor	763,646	68.84%
Against	420,923	38.19%	Against	345,563	31.15%
Race Total	1,101,983		**Race Total**	1,109,20	
Prop. 4 Eliminate duplicate numbering in Constitution			**Prop. 11** Limiting amount of state debt payable from general revenue fund		
In Favor	865,397	78.83%	In Favor	742,798	67.95%
Against	232,350	21.16%	Against	350,317	32.04%
Race Total	1,097,747		**Race Total**	1,093,11	
Prop. 5 Supreme Court to sit anywhere in Texas			**Prop. 12** Deadline for Supreme Court on motion for rehearing		
In Favor	655,617	59.19%	In Favor	858,513	77.22%
Against	458,791	40.80%	Against	253,254	22.77%
Race Total	1,124,408		**Race Total**	1,111,76	
Prop. 6 Allow Texas Growth Fund to continue to invest without disclosure			**Prop. 13** Establish Texas tomorrow fund as protected trust fund		
In Favor	562,535	49.93%	In Favor	811,873	72.07%
Against	564,070	50.60%	Against	314,516	27.92%
Race Total	1,126,605		**Race Total**	1,126,38	
Prop. 7 Texas Water Development to transfer bonds for water supply, etc.			**Prop. 14** Legislature to prescribe qualifications of constables		
In Favor	707,498	63.95%	In Favor	869,156	78.04%
Against	398,795	36.04%	Against	244,472	21.95%
Race Total	1,106,293		**Race Total**	1,113,62	

Source: Texas Secretary of State Website.

Time for a new Constitution?

In the sixth edition of the classic *Texas Government* by MacCorkle and Smith, written in 1968, the authors write: "...it seems evident that the constitution of 1876 has not been altogether a successful document. In fact, there has been considerable dissatisfaction with it from the beginning, and many efforts have been made in the legislature to call a convention for drawing up a new fundamental law".[4] Six years later the legislature convened to write a new constitution. A parliamentary procedure required that a two-thirds vote of the legislators was necessary for the new document to pass. For all of the time and money spent, no new document emerged. Texas is a diverse state with legislators representing diverse interests, and the entire effort collapsed in stalemate. The following year, embarrassed legislators tried to salvage their effort by offering voters a revised, shortened, and modernized constitution of 17,000 words in the form of eight constitutional amendments. All measures were defeated by a better than two to one margin.

What happened? Not having the support of then-Governor Dolph Briscoe, a rancher from Uvalde, certainly hurt the cause for a new constitution. Yet the new document was supported by Lieutenant Governor Bill Hobby and Attorney General John Hill. There was mention of the conservative, business-oriented "elite", the corporate and banking sectors of the state in Houston and Dallas, opposing the measure because of their fear of higher taxes, legislative meddling, increased regulatory oversight by state agencies, and repeal of the state's *right-to-work law*. A right-to-work law makes it illegal to require a worker to join a labor union as a condition of employment. Criticism of the new document also centered on the legislature and the belief that appointed framers would write a better document than elected representatives. Perhaps the conservative political culture of Texas, with people suspicious of sweeping changes, will continue to prohibit constitutional revision in the foreseeable future.[5]

Constitutional revision reared its head in 1998 when a veteran legislator, Texas Senator Bill Ratliff, announced a plan to rewrite the Texas Constitution in the 1999 legislative session.

Two major targets of the shortened document would be in the executive and judicial branches. The number of statewide elected executives would be trimmed while the governor's executive powers would be expanded.

As proposed, state judges would be appointed by the governor and subject to non-competitive retention elections. Theoretically this would eliminate the controversial practice of judges soliciting campaign contributions from trial lawyers and other parties with pending litigation.

Where constitutional revision is going is anybody's guess. Introduced as this book was heading to press, the language contained in Senate Bill 670 offers a clue. If signed into law, the bill would create a Constitutional Revision Commission to rewrite the document over a six-year period. This would give the governor, legislature, and special interests enough cover to place the issue on the proverbial "back burner."

On-Line: The Texas Constitution

The Constitution of the State of Texas is the entire text of the state's constitution on the Internet, article by article, with a helpful index. Including the document as an appendix would have added at least 100 pages to the length of this book!

http://www.capitol.state.tx.us/txconst/toc.html

U.S. State Constitutions and Web Sites provides access to the complete constitutions of 43 states, including Texas. It is a useful site to compare good documents with bad.

http://www.constitution.org/cons/usstcons.htm

Endnotes

1. Beryl Pettus and Randall Bland, *Texas Government Today* (Homewood, Il: Dorsey Press, 1986), p. 61.

2. Felton West, "Texas Badly Needs a New Constitutional Convention," *Houston Post*, 1 November 1991, p. A-37.

3. West, "Texas Badly Needs a New Constitutional Convention."

4. Stuart A. MacCorkle and Dick Smith, *Texas Government* (New York: McGraw-Hill, 1968), p. 25.

5. West, "Texas Badly Needs a New Constitutional Convention."

Chapter 3

Local Government

Learning Objectives:

After reading this chapter, the student should be able to:

- ✪ Describe the organizational structure of the city, county, and several special districts
- ✪ Describe the functions of the major policy makers and administrators of the city, county, and special districts
- ✪ Describe the major policy issues facing the city, county and special districts
- ✪ Describe the financing of the city, county and special districts

The study of local government has not traditionally generated much interest for students. Examination of contemporary American government topics such as Social Security, elections, or foreign policy tends to be more exciting. This seems to be the case despite the fact that during their lifetime students will have far more contact with local government officials and are more likely to be affected by local government issues than by any other level of government. Local governments provide public school and community college education, sanitation, water and sewage disposal, police and fire protection, road construction and maintenance, welfare, health care and hospitals, parks and recreation, airports, tax appraisal, and professional sports, among other services. Most of us take these services for granted, yet a temporary disruption often brings much attention and derision.

The U.S. Census Bureau recognizes the existence of municipalities, villages, townships, counties, and special districts as forms of government at the local level. Texas has municipalities and a few villages, but townships exist mainly in the Northeastern U.S. There are 254 counties in Texas, and two types of special districts: the school district and non-school special district. This chapter will examine municipalities, counties, and special districts.

On November 19, 1863, President Abraham Lincoln, in his Gettysburg Address, referred to "government of the people, by the people, and for the people." By voting, attending meetings, donating to local campaigns, working in local campaigns, signing petitions and writing letters to the newspaper editor, the average citizen can achieve more "clout" than at other levels of government. It is at this level citizen involvement in government is achieved or lost.

County Government

The Texas Constitution of 1876 provides for the organization of the county and the functions of the elected county officials. Counties in Texas serve as the administrative arm of the state, performing local services to those areas of the state not in a city's boundary. There are 254 counties in Texas, ranging from Harris County with nearly three million residents to rural Loving County in West Texas, with a population of only 141.

What do counties do? Here is a partial list of services:

1. Issue license plates and certificates of title for autos.
2. Enforce the state's criminal laws.
3. Record vital statistics, i.e., births, deaths, marriages, divorces, deeds of property.
4. Enforce the state's health laws, operating public health clinics.

5. Provide local government services:
    -Road and bridge construction and maintenance
    -Environmental pollution control
6. Operate public hospitals.
7. Operate parks and other recreational facilities, including sports stadiums.
8. Operate libraries.
9. Operate airports.
10. Provide local welfare services.

Today's county judge and commissioners face problems that did not face their counterparts over a hundred years ago. Expanding transportation, emergency medical services, and criminal justice facilities lead the list. Sometimes the county commissioners face an unusual issue. In January 1999 the Comal County commissioners had to decide whether a "wolf-dog" mixture would require a variance from the county's wild animal ordinance.[1]

Dillon's Rule, although less applicable today, basically states that local units of government are state creations and can only perform powers granted by the state constitution and laws. Local units lack the sovereignty that the federal and state governments possess. The state authorizes cities with more than 5,000 population to adopt home rule status for greater flexibility of government services. Counties in Texas have no home rule authority, limiting them to what is provided in the constitution. Unlike municipalities, which have a home rule option, the 254 counties of Texas have an identical government structure. This is done despite the fact that 48 of the state's 254 counties contain over 80% of the state's population. Each county has a **commissioner's court**, comprised of a **county judge**, elected at large and serving the entire county. The county judge presides over the commissioners court. There are four **commissioners** who are elected from four equally populated **precincts**, though the Texas Constitution provides for as many as eight commissioners. Figure 3-1 shows the organization for a typical county.

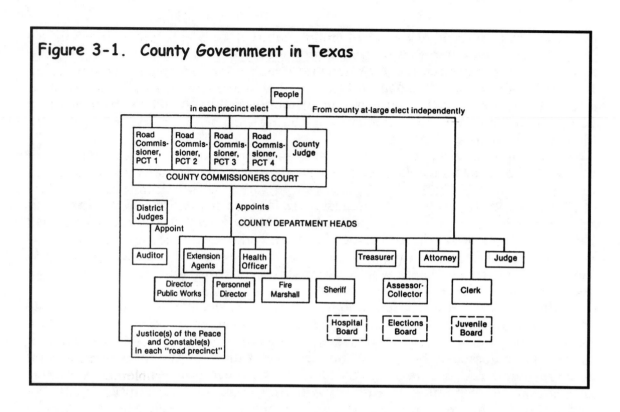

Figure 3-1. County Government in Texas

The commissioner's court is the identical form of government for both Harris and Loving counties, the extremes of urban and rural counties in the state, despite the fact that Harris County has its own unique set of urban problems that cannot be effectively addressed with such inflexibility. Add to this that under the Texas Constitution, counties are denied ordinance-making power, which limits their responses to crises such as flooding, transportation gridlock, and the AIDS epidemic. A list of county officials does not necessarily mean that one can find each office filled in all of the 254 counties. While some small counties and some large populated counties have both a district and county attorney, some counties, like Victoria, pay a salary supplement to the district attorney to perform the duty of the county attorney.

County officers are elected in **partisan elections** which means they run for office with a political party label. Elections are held in even-numbered years, countering municipal elections held in odd-numbered years. County elections feature what is called the **long ballot**, meaning that the constitutionally-based office holders are accountable to the public via the ballot box. Voters, not normally attentive to most local political issues, might know the name of the county judge and the commissioner in their home precinct. They might also know the name of the justice of the peace who presided over traffic court, that is the extent of their political knowledge of county government affairs. When they see the names of all of the county officials listed on a ballot, many voters experience information overload and either skip that portion or go the safe route and vote a straight party ticket. The state of Texas has a system that provides for tied runoff elections to be decided by a coin toss. Chambers County had a commissioner's race decided by a coin toss in May 1998 after a runoff primary showed a 669 tie between two candidates. David "Bubba" Abernathy, who lost the election, said "This is no way to decide an election."[2]

Besides having the county judge preside over the commissioner's court, Article V, Section 15 of the Texas Constitution also makes the same individual a judge on the county court. Section 15 only requires the judge be "well informed in the law of the State." The demands of being perceived "county leader" has led many of the office holders to forego any judicial functions. The county judge is also recognized as the county spokesperson and ceremonial leader. His duties also include administering applications for beer and wine licenses. The county judge can fill a vacancy in the office of commissioner. In February 1999, Galveston County Judge Jim Yarbrough named a replacement for Precinct 3.[3]

Because each county commissioner is elected from his own precinct, countywide concerns may not receive all the attention they deserve. While it is the responsibility of the county judge to coordinate policy between the four precincts, it does not always occur successfully. Just as the commission form of municipal government suffered coordination and cooperation problems between commissioners, some county governments experience the same difficulties. The power of a commissioner was illustrated in January 1999, when Wharton County Judge Lawrence Naiser, after two employees were dismissed when a new commissioner took office, stated that new elected commissioners may choose to hire and fire employees "at will," with or without valid reason.[4]

In rural and lesser populated Texas counties, road and bridge construction is the chief responsibility of each commissioner. That is why commissioners in rural counties are called "road commissioners."

Urban counties have different spending priorities: law enforcement, court administration (especially in Harris, Dallas, and Bexar counties), health care, welfare, parks and recreation, flood control, along with the traditional road and bridge construction and maintenance function. In urban counties, health care costs have skyrocketed because of AIDS, increased hospital costs, a large number of people with no or inadequate health care insurance, and drug abuse. Law enforcement costs have escalated because of the higher crime rate.

Although television westerns and paperback novels have created legendary figures of Texas county **sheriffs**, the real office holders are modern law enforcement officials. The county sheriff is the county's chief law enforcement officer. He also directs the operation of the county jail facility. As a practical illustration, the Harris County Sheriff manages 3,400 employees, is responsible for law enforcement in unincorporated areas, serves as bailiff process server for the county and state courts, and operates four jail facilities. An issue that will need to be resolved is the low pay of West Texas sheriffs. In October 1998, a sheriff in Briscoe County made $18,643 while the Harris County Sheriff was paid $95,280. With the two recent and devastating droughts in West Texas, farming communities are reluctant to support raising taxes. Low pay can lead to high turnovers.[5]

The **district attorney** is responsible for prosecuting felony and high misdemeanor crimes in state district and county courts. The **county attorney** serves as the legal counsel for the commissioner's court and represents the county in civil cases. The county attorney also prosecutes misdemeanor cases in JP and county courts, and handles juvenile crime cases.

Some counties are using tougher tactics to combat juvenile crime. Construction of local juvenile detention centers are allowing authorities to have more local control over juvenile offenders. Several counties, Harris included, instituted teen curfews to keep children off the city's streets from midnight to six a.m.

The **tax assessor-collector** collects property taxes and handles motor vehicle registration. Victoria County appointed the county tax assessor-collector to calculate the effective tax to support the budget. The job of being a tax assessor-collector can be very demanding. The Harris County officeholder has a budget of $23 million and a staff of over 500. This office collects property taxes, sells motor vehicle inspection stickers, and registers voters[6] To assist the county tax assessor-collector, a countywide appraisal district has been created by the legislature. Every year, a homeowner receives a notice from the tax appraisal district informing him of the appraised value of his property. The homeowner is given a certain date, usually May 31, to protest the appraisal. It is not uncommon to see a wealthy property owner armed with a lawyer, real estate appraiser/consultant, and tax accountant marching in to see the appraiser. Yet it is the average taxpayer who often succeeds. The successful protest of a county appraisal could result in hundreds, perhaps thousands, of dollars in property tax savings to the homeowner.

Justices of the peace serve on the lowest level courts involving Class C misdemeanor cases and small claims lawsuits. A county may have as many as eight JP precincts with each precinct electing one or two JPs. If you are stopped for a traffic violation in the unincorporated area of the county, your case will be heard by a JP. With a court atmosphere reminiscent of television's "People's Court," neighborhood disputes involving up to $5,000 will also be heard by a JP. Because the complaints heard are common and reoccurring, many JP courts struggle under a six to eight month backlog of cases.

A 1971 law requires annual training for the justices of the peace. In 1973, the Texas Legislature required the counties to start paying a salary to these office holders. This is good because a justice of the peace handles traffic tickets, hot checks, evictions, lawsuits, truancies, theft and assault. He also can issue emergency commitment warrants and almost all of the search warrants requested by law enforcement agencies throughout the county. Age is not a barrier to holding this office. Comal County Justice of the Peace Fred Stewart began his seventh term at age 91 in January 1999.[7]

A **constable** is a licensed law enforcement officer. The constable is elected to a constitutionally created office (Article XVI, Section 65) for a term of four years within each justice of the peace precinct. He is both a Texas peace officer and chief process server for the justice of the peace. A constable and his deputies can provide patrols beyond local police and sheriff's patrols to fight crime and traffic control. In Harris County, for instance, the constable's office contracts with homeowner's associations of residential neighborhoods to patrol their subdivision areas.

The **county clerk** is the county's chief record keeper, responsible for maintaining the county's vital statistics records on births, deaths, marriages, divorces, and registration of deeds of property, mortgages, and contracts within the county. In many counties they also serve as the person in charge of elections, while in other counties the tax assessor-collector assumes this role. Harris County employs the tax assessor-collector to be in charge of voter registration as a check and balance to the clerk, who is in charge of the overall election process. Montgomery County, on the other hand, turns the election responsibility over to an appointed election administrator.

The **district clerk**, often confused with the county clerk, maintains legal records for the county and district courts. Your anxiously awaited jury summons will probably come from this person. Even Governor George W. Bush honored a Travis County court jury summons in 1996–no one is above the law! An additional duty of the district clerk is to collect child support payments in the county.

The **county treasurer** receives and disburses funds and manages the county's money. Several Texas counties in the past decade have abolished this office by having the state legislature propose a constitutional amendment. The county then transfers the duties of treasurer to a **county auditor**, who is appointed by the district judge or judges. Although the auditor is paid a salary approved by the commissioners court, the auditor reports the county's financial standing directly to the district judges. A county treasurer, in addition to investing county funds, receives revenues, disperses accounts payable belonging to the county and handles the payroll for a county. Sometimes the county treasurer, auditor and others are trained to be a county investment office (CIO) to maintain and invest public accounts. Nine counties had abolished the office of county treasurer. Their functions were then transferred to the county auditor. Comal county commissioners began the effort in December 1998, when they passed a resolution which asked the 76th Legislature to abolish the county office. A constitutional amendment with statewide voter approval would be necessary.[8]

Several counties still have the office of county surveyor, who maintains the survey records of the county plain surveyor. Some in 1998 were contested (Travis) while others were uncontested (Williamson).

To promote health, many counties have a health department or a joint city-county health department. These health departments provide medical services (child health clinics, sexually transmitted diseases, tuberculosis, diabetic screening, pregnancy testing, dental clinics, communicable disease surveillance, and HIV services to name a few). This same department must inspect food establishments, hospitals, schools, foster homes, day care facilities, public swimming pools, on-site sewage systems, water wells and produce stands. It can conduct county-wide rabies vaccination programs, food sanitation training, rabies and mosquito control.

Where does a typical Texas county get its revenue? The major source of funds is the ad valorem property tax, however, state law limits the tax rate to a maximum 80 cents per $100 valuation. Counties are empowered to assess a maximum 15 cents per $100 valuation on top of this for roads and bridges, as well as to assess a maximum 30 cents to construct and maintain farm-to-market (FM) roads. Counties also receive revenue from the state, federal aid, service charges, sports stadiums, and issuing bonds.

The adoption of the county budget is a significant undertaking. After public hearing and work session by the county commissioners court, they will pass a budget which will probably include a cost-of-living raise for county employees and officials and set the tax rate.[9] A sample county budget is found in Figure 3.2. Compare the priorities, amounts and percentages with another county that is on-line: Harris (www.co.harris.tx.us).

Figure 3-2. 1998 Victoria County Revenues and Expenditures

Revenues		Expenditures	
Taxes	47.7%	Criminal Justice	39.7%
Fees & Fines	9.0%	Road & Bridge	10.4%
Contract Revenue	14.8%	Admin/Internal Services	20.6%
State & Federal	6.2%	Airport & Health	11.3%
Airport and Health	10.1%	Long term Debt	4.7%
*Other	12.2%	Capital	4.6%
		**Other	8.7%

*Includes interest earned, transfers, and miscellaneous revenues.
**Includes maintenance, transfers out, intergovernmental functions.

(1998 Victoria County Annual Budget)

County government in Texas is in need of reform. The archaic structure features a long election ballot, a spoils system with most county commissioners having their own staff and road crews, the proverbial "good ol' boy" image of doing business, inflexible organization, limited powers of taxation, and virtually no power to pass ordinances. The latter is particularly significant given that the county cannot pass zoning ordinances or comprehensive future development plans.

One available avenue of reform is to adopt a county manager form of government. This would bring a needed professionalism to county government and lessen the image of the county as a province of "good ol' boys" who only pave roads.

Another avenue of reform is to create an elected executive position (equivalent to a strong city mayor) for the county. Most citizens already believe a present county judge "runs" the county by means of his veto, appointment, and removal powers. Although this is erroneous, a constitutional amendment would legitimize what voters already expect.

Nationwide, many states are moving towards the consolidation of city and county governments when large cities are involved. The origin of this concept, called *Unigov* or *Metro* (for Metropolitan), took root in Toronto, Ontario in 1954 by establishing the Metropolitan Government of Toronto. The province of Ontario merged the city of Toronto with its suburbs as a metropolitan corporation. Separate corporations were then established to provide regionwide local government services and public schools. Montreal, Calgary, and Vancouver have followed with similar Metro governments.

City-county consolidation in the United States originated in Nashville-Davidson County, Tennessee, Indianapolis-Marion County, Indiana, and Miami-Dade County, Florida. Other cities which followed suit include Jacksonville, Florida, Portland, Oregon, and Seattle, Washington.

Consolidation of Texas cities with their surrounding counties, given constitutional restrictions, requires legislative action to offer state voters the opportunity to amend the Texas Constitution to establish a unified metropolitan government. Voters in the cities/counties must then approve the combined governmental charter. Two previous attempts in Bexar County and San Antonio failed.

Houston and Harris County are the most likely future target for the establishment of a metropolitan government consolidating city and county operations. The key component of such a movement is water. The city of Houston owns the rights to the area's water supply in Lake Houston. At the same time much of Harris County is under a mandate which forces the city and water districts to convert from using well water from the Evangeline and Chicot aquifers to using surface water available from Lake Houston. Compliance is scheduled in phases beginning in the year 2002.

Supporters of a Houston/Harris County metropolitan government would point out that there would be substantial taxpayer savings from improved economies of scale. Major problems such as transportation needs, economic development, and public safety concerns could be addressed more effectively and efficiently with one unified government. They would argue, for example, that law enforcement in Harris County is currently provided by multiple governments at state, city, county, special district, and school district levels. Establishment of a metropolitan police through consolidation would remove the duplication of services among local area governments.

On the downside, critics point out that city dwellers would benefit from the establishment of a regional government at the expense of county residents. For example, they believe local area equity in the provision of services would fall short. Politically, county residents do not want to pay for city services.

Counties in Texas face significant changes if two bills are passed by the 76th Legislature. Senator Drew Nixon's SB586 prevents cities from annexing areas outside of their home counties without a vote by the affected commissioners. The city of Houston spills over into Fort Bend and Montgomery counties.[10] Another bill would require counties to provide water and sewer services to residents lacking them in unincorporated areas. Representative Kevin Bailey introduced the bill which Harris County Commissioner Steve Radack called "extremely ridiculous" and would cost hundreds of millions of dollars.[11]

A concern for Texas citizens is that the state of Texas has 225 county courthouses that are in serious need of repair and restoration. The Texas Historical Commission and the Office of Governor are working to accomplish this. Richard Moe, president of the National Trust for Historic Preservation, has stated we must rally "behind these temples of democracy to ensure that they continue to serve as symbols of community pride."[12]

Municipalities

Whether you live in a rural area or an urban setting, chances are good you either work in a city, travel there to do your shopping or occasionally take advantage of the amenities and conveniences a city can offer.

Students are often confused by the term "incorporated" as it applies to municipalities. There are over 4,500 unincorporated towns in Texas, places like "Klein," "Spring," "Fred," "Fink," "Dime Box," "Ding Dong," and "The Woodlands." As an unincorporated town, they have no legal status other than as a place on the map. Contrary to popular belief, there is no Spring, Texas–as a city, that is. "Spring" is a place that serves as a mailing address to thousands of suburban residents in Harris County. Back in the 1970s, Waylon Jennings and Willie Nelson sang about a place called Luckenbach ("Let's go to Luckenbach, Texas . . ."). Luckenbach was nothing more than a collection of three buildings: a general store/post office, a honkytonk saloon, and a souvenir shop. Located in Gillespie County in West Central Texas, Luckenbach, population 25, was not incorporated, but that did not stop the thousands of tourists from around the world in search of the city of Luckenbach. Imagine a group of Japanese tourists, dressed in western garb, sitting out back on picnic benches, eating barbecue and drinking *Shiner Bock* beer! One overzealous fan, wanting a souvenir of his sojourn, decided to liberate the "Luckenbach" sign from the front porch of the general store. Without the sign, people were driving aimlessly around on Hill Country ranch roads asking farmers, "Where's Luckenbach?"

An **incorporated municipality** has legal status as a city under the laws of the state of Texas. Conroe is an incorporated municipality, as are Houston, Tomball, Magnolia, Oak Ridge North, Victoria, Humble, and believe it or not, Cut and Shoot!

How does a municipality come into being? A municipality is formed, or **incorporated**, when at least two hundred people living in a contiguous, unincorporated area not in another city's extraterritorial jurisdiction obtain enough signatures on an incorporation petition. The petition is presented to the county judge, who calls for an election in which voters may choose to incorporate, remain unincorporated, or dissolve an existing municipality. The beach community of Crystal Beach, located on the Bolivar Peninsula in Galveston County, disincorporated when citizens felt that maintaining a municipal government was unnecessary and a property tax expense they did not wish to pay. Conversely, the farming community of Anderson, the county seat of Grimes County, disincorporated their municipal government in the late 1980s, only to reincorporate in 1995. Why? The residents of Anderson discovered that in order to procure a federal grant of over one million dollars to renovate the failing sewer system of their county courthouse, they had to be incorporated as a municipality. Money talks in this state!

One of the most useful documents to gain an understanding of municipal government is the **city charter**. A charter is written when a municipality has incorporated. The city charter is like a local government constitution; it is a governing document defining the incorporation status of the municipality, the form of government, and its powers.

The state of Texas has 1,175 incorporated municipalities and 294 **home rule** cities. The Texas Constitution provides that cities with a population of 5,000 or less may be chartered as **general law** cities. They are called general law because they operate under the general laws of the state of Texas, with limited powers and services. More than 800 municipalities in Texas are of the general law variety, which shows that despite growing urbanization, Texas remains a state of many small towns.

Once a city reaches 5,000 or more in population and residents vote to do so, a city may adopt its own **home rule** charter. In 1986, the cities of Jersey Village and Tomball in Harris County reverted to home rule status when both cities reached a population of over 5,000. A home rule city is afforded a stronger form of government by the state, and can offer more city services and levy a higher property tax rate than its general law counterpart. Just as important, a home rule city in Texas has stronger annexation powers which allow it to add unincorporated property to its boundaries without a popular vote of the people being annexed. The issue of annexation will be addressed later in the chapter.

Forms of Municipal Government

The state of Texas employs three forms of municipal government: (1) the **mayor-council** form with two subtypes, the **strong mayor-council** with an elected mayor serving in a dual capacity of chief policy maker and chief administrator, or the **weak mayor-council** with an elected or appointed mayor who is first among equals with a city council; (2) the **council-manager** form with an elected city council employing a professional trained administrator; and (3) the **commission** form with an elected council and each member serving in a dual capacity of policy maker and a department administrator. Figure 3-3 shows typical organization charts for the three forms of municipal government.

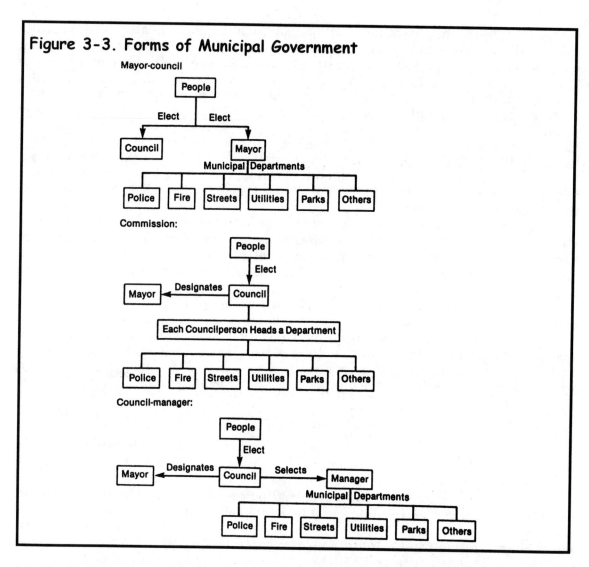

Figure 3-3. Forms of Municipal Government

Mayor-council

People

Elect — Council

Elect — Mayor

Municipal Departments

Police | Fire | Streets | Utilities | Parks | Others

Commission:

People

Elect — Council

Designates — Mayor

Each Councilperson Heads a Department

Police | Fire | Streets | Utilities | Parks | Others

Council-manager:

People

Elect — Council

Designates — Mayor

Selects — Manager

Municipal Departments

Police | Fire | Streets | Utilities | Parks | Others

The largest city in the state, Houston, utilizes the **strong-mayor council form** as do the five largest cities in the country (New York, Los Angeles, Chicago, Philadelphia and Detroit). In Houston, the mayor serves a dual role: he is both the city's most identifiable political leader and the city's chief administrator. As a full-time administrator, the mayor has the power to name and/or remove department heads, prepare the budget, preside over city council meetings, and in essence run city government operations on a day-to-day basis. The mayors of our larger cities find that foreign trips are important to make contact with foreign officials and to demonstrate a city's interest in establishing business ties. In early February, Mayor Lee Brown of Houston joined seven members of the city council on a trade mission to Japan, China and Taiwan.[13] The salary of the mayor of Houston exceeds $100,000 per year, indicative of his full-time status and authority. City council members earn a salary exceeding $30,000 per year. For some council members, this is their sole source of income, while others supplement their income from businesses or law practices they operate.

The **weak mayor-council form** is the most popular in general law municipalities in Texas. In it the mayor is a figurehead political leader, since government services tend to be limited. The mayor presides over council meetings, which are usually held on a weekly or monthly basis. Official acts of government might be limited to events like the ribbon cutting ceremony at the opening of the new *Walmart* store on the outskirts of town. Salaries are quite small, perhaps no more than a couple thousand dollars a year, reflecting the part-time status of the position, or the mayor and council members may be paid meeting fees ranging from $50 to $100 for each city council meeting.

The most prevalent form of government in home rule cities is the **council-manager form**, employed in over 200 Texas cities. Under it the mayor and city council appoint a professional administrator, most commonly known as a city manager, to run city government operations on a day-to-day basis. It is a prototype of the private sector model in which the board of directors of a corporation hire a chief executive officer (CEO) to run the corporation. When things are going well, the city manager stays on the job, earning a salary in larger cities exceeding $100,000 per year plus benefits. When things are not going well, the city manager sees the writing on the wall and either resigns "to pursue other opportunities" or is fired by the mayor and city council. In 1995, for example, the Galveston city manager was fired for shortcomings in the city's financial operations. Many city managers spend their careers settled in one city, fitting into the community as nicely as a high school principal.

Dallas is the largest city in the United States (and Texas) to employ the council-manager form of government. San Antonio, Austin, Fort Worth, Corpus Christi, Victoria, Beaumont, Conroe and Tomball also use it. In the 1980s, many people thought that popular mayor Henry Cisneros ran the city of San Antonio. In reality, Cisneros was a college professor who earned only several thousand dollars a year as the figurehead mayor, while Lou Fox, the city manager, actually ran the city on a day-to-day basis. Few people knew Fox's identity or that there was a city manager. The theory behind the council-manager form is that by hiring an outsider as a city's administrator, much of the politics is removed from city hall and city services can be provided more efficiently. Occasionally a reform movement emerges in Houston to make that city a council-manager form of government, but it never really gets anywhere. A popular mayor such as Bob Lanier achieved national recognition when he was identified as President Clinton's "favorite big city mayor" and was rumored to be on the short list as a replacement for the President's cabinet at the beginning of his second term. It would be difficult for a mayor such as Lanier, yielding the substantial power that he has, to give it up, though he did step down in 1997 after serving three two-year terms due to term limits.

The duties of a city manager include: (1) presides as chief administrator and executive officer of the city; (2) presents annual balanced budget proposal to City Council; (3) follows policies set by the City Council; (4) supervises all city departments; (5) attends all City Council meetings; (6) must operate the city within its budget; (7) serves at the will and pleasure of the City Council; and finally, (8) executes all authorized city deeds, contracts, agreements or franchises. The selection of a new city manager is one of the more difficult tasks for a city council. Candidates are usually chosen for "their financial expertise, team building skills, and personality."[14]

The third and least popular form of government is the **commission form**. After the devastating hurricane that hit Galveston in 1900, civic leaders created the commission form as an expedient means of restoring city services. Each commissioner was an elected council member who in turn served as a department head over finance, police and fire, water and sewers, streets, and public improvement services. The commission form caught on like wildfire, with nearly 500 municipalities utilizing it by the year 1920. Due to corruption, inefficiency and lack of cooperation, the commission form with the passage of time has dropped off to the point where only a handful of municipalities in the state still use it. Galveston, its originator, dropped the form in 1960 and today employs the council-manager form.

Fiscal Policy

City governments, like the families they serve, conduct their financial affairs with a sharp eye on income and expenses. Just as a family borrows money in the form of a mortgage to purchase a home, a city government has the authority to borrow money by issuing bonds to finance long-term capital expenditures. Two key principles to govern city government fiscal policy: (1) where does the money come from (revenue) and (2) where does the money go (expenditures).

Sources of Revenue

The primary source of revenue for Texas cities is the **ad valorem property tax**. A city has the authority to assess a tax on the appraised value of real property such as homes, commercial businesses, and land within its boundaries.

An annual property tax rate is expressed in terms of dollars per $100 of property value. For instance, the 1997 property tax rate of Conroe in Montgomery County is 42 cents per $100 of appraised value (or .42000), whereas the 1997 property tax rate of Houston is 66 ½ cents per $100 valuation (or .66500). A city like Houston will generate more than 40% of its revenue base from the ad valorem property tax, making it the largest source.

The Texas Constitution authorizes cities to grant a **homestead exemption**, which lowers the amount of the appraised value subject to the property tax, to its residents. A government entity in Texas, be it a city, county, or special district, has the option to offer a homestead exemption to lower the tax burden to property owners, the elderly, or disabled. The underlying philosophy is that Texans could not be foreclosed out of their home due to an inability to pay property taxes. Taxing entities may grant a homestead exemption in amounts ranging from a minimum of $5,000 to a maximum of 20% of the property value. The taxing entity also has the option of restricting homestead exemptions to all but the elderly or disabled.

Calculate a typical property tax bill for a residence in the city of Conroe. Assume that the appraised value of the home is $100,000 and that the city does not offer the homestead exemption. Assuming the tax rate is .42000 per $100 of appraised value, the annual tax bill for a $100,000 home is $420. In a hypothetical situation, if the city offered a 20% homestead exemption, the tax rate would be applied to $80,000 of appraised value, then the annual tax bill would be $336. Before our homeowner jumps at the prospect of a lower tax bill, remember that the city would probably raise the property tax rate to offset the homestead exemption in order to get its $420!

The property tax is an item which city governments may use as an enticement to attract new manufacturing or commercial development to move into the city. Cities across the country and within the state compete with each other for conventions, sports franchises, and industry. The theory is that for every one basic employee with a job in a chemical plant, two non-basic jobs are generated in a grocery store, dry cleaners, or other facility to support the basic worker. **Property tax abatement** is the carrot dangling on a stick which cities may offer to lure new industries to their area. In 1993, MCI Communication Corporation struck a deal with the city of Sugar Land and Fort Bend County to locate a new small business customer center in Sugar Land. It was estimated the center would represent over 1,000 new jobs in Texas and pump more than $200 million into the economy. As part of the deal, MCI would have received a property tax abatement of $434,000 for its facility over six years. Unfortunately, the best laid plans of mice and men often go astray, and MCI's recent takeover by a British communications company forced it to shut down the center, only two years after its undertaking.

A sample city budget is included in Figure 3-4. Compare the priorities, amounts & percentages with several other cities that are on-line: Austin (www.ci.austin.tx.us); Alvin (www.ci.alvin.tx.us); Brownwood (www.ci.brownwood.tx.us); and Houston (www.ci.houston.tx.us).

Figure 3-4. 1998-1999 City of Victoria Budget

Revenues			Expenditures		
Property Taxes	$13,024,128	13.42%	Public Safety	$14,601,982	15.04%
Water & Wastewater Fees	14,320,000	14.75%	Development	15,475,365	15.94%
Sales Tax	8,487,440	8.74%	Debt Service	8,386,364	8.64%
Intergovernmental & Grants	3,763,569	3.88%	Water and Wastewater	45,780,207	47.16%
Franchise Fees & Other Taxes	3,840,355	3.96%	Solid Waste	2,866,810	2.95%
Solid Waste Fees	3,103,200	3.20%	Recreation	4,212,556	4.34%
Interest Income	2,526,500	2.60%	General Administration	2,880,632	2.97%
Use of Fund Equity	22,059,935	22.72%	Public Health	0	0.00%
1999 Sewer Revenue Bonds	15,000,000	15.45%	All Other	2,869,619	2.96%
1998 C.O. Bonds	6,200,000	6.39%			
All Other	4,748,408	4.89%			
Totals	$97,073,535	100%		$97,073,535	100%

Another major source of revenue for a city is the **sales tax**. Wherever you are in Texas, the state's general sales tax rate on the retail sale of taxable items is 6.25% per dollar. The state allows a city to supplement the state sales tax rate with a legal maximum of two cents per dollar. Conroe utilizes the full two cents, so the purchase of a shirt from *Walmart* would cost the customer a sales tax of 8.25%. Houston merchants also apply the full two cents, with one penny going to the city government and one cent going to the Metropolitan Transit Authority (Metro), the special district which provides mass transit in Harris County. Conversely, a *Walmart* shopper in The Woodlands, which is unincorporated, only pays a sales tax of 6.25% in the absence of a city government or transit authority, while The Woodlands Mall Town Center, a special district formed to provide water and sewer service to the huge Woodlands Mall, has a sales tax of one cent. Merchants send sales tax revenue to the state comptroller, who in turn returns the city's share to the city government as a source of revenue. One can measure the health of the state's or a city's economy by monitoring its sales tax revenue. When things are going well, people tend to buy merchandise, which adds money to a city's coffers. Sales taxes generate as much as 25% of a typical Texas city's revenue base.

Cities also charge **utility franchise fees** to electricity, telephone, natural gas, and cable television providers. The theory is that the city maintains the rights-of-way on a homeowner's property. Fees are assessed to utility companies for the privilege of bringing a service, for example, cable television, into the home. The cable television company pays the city a franchise fee, but in reality passes its cost to the customer in the form of a higher bill. Franchise fees in some cities generate more than 10% of their revenue.

Another source of revenue is **intergovernmental aid**, most often in the form of federal grants. Grants are available in areas of crime prevention, clean air and clean water, community development, transportation, and public housing. Cities also generate revenue from **licenses and permits** for businesses, ranging from Floyd's Barber Shop to *Rick's Cabaret*. Building permits and construction inspections provide revenue, especially during building booms. A city also derives income from **service charges**, such as utility tap fees, water and sewer service, the cost of having a softball team in a city-run softball league, charging for the use of lights at tennis courts in a city park, and in some cities, sanitation fees for trash pick-up.

Those of you who have been stopped by a city patrol officer for a traffic violation or a parking ticket take heart: you have contributed to a major source of city revenue, **municipal court fines**. The great majority of municipal cases deal with traffic violations, though there will be the occasional public intoxication case, along with city ordinance violations. A typical city can derive as much as 5% of its revenue from speeding tickets, though the legislature has clipped the wings of many speed trap towns by limiting the contribution of moving violations to their revenue base. Many smaller municipalities circumvent state law by not reporting traffic violations to the DPS in Austin, which spares the unfortunate motorist from having his already high automobile insurance increase, but he is still out the $40 or so that he paid on the ticket.

A source of income for a city with a healthy economy is the city's sales tax rebate. The City of Victoria collected $7.8 million in rebates from November 1998 through May 1998. The city receives rebates on sales taxes totaling 1.5 cents per dollar.[15]

For the really big improvements, like sewer system renovation, building a new municipal airport, or the construction of a wastewater treatment plant, a city can raise money by borrowing. If a city does not have the cash on hand, it can issue either **general obligation bonds** or **revenue bonds** to deal with capital expenditures. A **bond** is defined as a long-term debt or IOU, such as an individual financing the purchase of a home with a 15 year or 30 year mortgage. Investors, either individuals or large financial institutions, loan money to the city. The city pays off the bond with interest, and the attractiveness of municipal bonds for investors is that the interest earned is tax-free, increasing its effective yield. A general obligation bond is paid off with income generated from collecting property taxes. A revenue bond is paid off with user fees, like money spent by drivers on toll roads or by spectators purchasing tickets to sports events at city-operated stadiums or arenas. Revenue bonds are considered more risky of the two types, since motorists have the choice of not driving on a toll road, while it is difficult to evade paying property taxes. Congress is taking a long hard look at the tax-exempt status of many recently issued revenue bonds, which should slow down the boom in sports facilities construction across the country.

Expenditures

Where does the money go? Using Houston's general fund statement as an illustration, the largest expenditure supports the city's public safety function. Outlays for police and fire protection amount to 41% and 22%, respectively, of the budget. Obviously, this is a testament to the concern city officials and community members have about crime and safety.

In Houston's budget, public works and engineering (the city's water and sewer department) is the third major spending priority, followed by public health, solid waste management, and parks and recreation. A growing number of cities, most recently Conroe, have rid themselves of the city's sanitation function, by contracting the service to private trash collection companies. Trash collection typically generates the most complaints about service, and private companies have proven much more effective and efficient in many communities. This practice, known as **privatization**, is a movement spreading throughout the country at different levels of government. For instance, many states contract with private firms to operate corrections facilities, and from time to time Congress debates the idea of turning over First Class mail delivery to private carriers like UPS. The debate will no doubt continue over whether equitable service of government functions can be provided as effectively by private companies with a profit motive attached, or whether these companies take shortcuts to trim expenses and increase profits.

Contemporary Urban Issues

Some of the problems faced by modern Texas cities include: (1) solid waste disposal; (2) population concentrations putting a strain on municipal resources for police, fire, water supply, an sewage disposal; (3) traffic congestion; (4) assimilation of different nationalities; (5) rivalry between the downtown and suburban shopping centers; (6) air and water pollution; (7) a shortage of parks and recreation areas; (8) the rise in crime; (9) adequate public housing; and finally (10) the loss of industry.

Annexation and Extraterritoriality

Annexation is perhaps the most controversial contemporary issue facing Texas cities and their surrounding suburban areas. For a city to annex means it adds an adjoining unincorporated area to its existing incorporated boundary. Texas cities, led by Houston, Dallas, and San Antonio, have been aggressive annexers. Why? A city annexes for the same reason a corporation merges with or takes over another corporation. If a corporation can't whip another in the competitive marketplace, than it might as well eliminate it as a competitor by making a lucrative financial offer to buy it. The board of directors of that corporation have a fiduciary responsibility to look out for the interests of the stockholders, delivering to them the greatest return on their investment. If the stock price reaches a high enough price, the board of directors will decide to sell out. The corporation making the acquisition buys all of the assets, right down to the paper clips, and assumes the outstanding debts of the other corporation. It is very likely that many, if not most of the employees in the corporation being acquired will lose their jobs. Why pay two employees to do the work of one?

When a city annexes an unincorporated area, it is annexing the municipal utility districts, or MUDs, that are already in place to provide water and sewer service to that area. Many MUDs are developed with tax-exempt general obligation bonds. As investments they are thought of as stable but not necessarily secure. During the glory days of Texas real estate development in the 1970s and early 1980s, municipal utility districts were popping up like daisies in suburban areas surrounding the larger cities. Several of the more speculative developments never got off the ground, which increased the chance that the MUDs would go bankrupt and default on their bonds. This scared away the more cautious water district bond investors. Annexation of a utility district proves to be a financial boon to these investors, because their bonds are assumed by the annexing city. The bonds, which were speculative and non-rated, are in turn backed by the financial rating of the annexing city. This increases the likelihood the bond will be paid off for its face value, at an even higher interest rate. Risky bonds are suddenly much more lucrative. Although a small cabal of people stand to make big financial gains, this is secondary to those residents annexed, many of whom would prefer to be left alone.

The process of annexation is governed by the Municipal Annexation Act of 1963. The day after then-Governor John Connally signed the bill into law, the city of Houston went on a land grab the likes of which had not been experienced since the land rush in Oklahoma in the 1890s. Houston proceeded up the median of the area's highways, the so-called "umbilical cord" approach, and declared substantial tracts of land part of its extraterritorial jurisdiction and subject to future annexation. Those tracts included The Woodlands, Kingwood, the property now containing Intercontinental Airport, and Clear Lake.

The traditional purpose of annexation is to add to a city's tax base. For example, the city of Houston, with a tax base exceeding $65 billion, stands to add billions of dollars of appraised property value to its tax base through annexation. In return, Houston provides the annexed area police and fire protection, garbage pickup, street maintenance and construction, health services and other amenities, plus the opportunity to participate in city elections. A city also stands to gain population, which can lead to greater city representation in the state legislature and Congress, as well as more federal grant money.

Some cities, such as Houston, have used annexation to reverse the social trend of "white flight," in which predominantly white residents abandon the city for more affluent suburbs. Although many of these residents work in the city and use its services during the day, they escape any financial obligations when they return in the evening to their suburban homes. For instance, the declining tax base due to the white flight to suburban Henrico and Chesterfield counties has left Richmond, Virginia, in financial straits, with a deteriorating inner city that harbors poverty and crime.

Another goal of annexation is to allow a city like Houston to protect themselves from being hemmed in by smaller incorporated municipalities. There are a collection of enclave cities, places like Bellaire, Piney Point, South Houston, and West University Place, that incorporated years ago when they were on the periphery of the Houston city limits. Through the use of annexation, Houston leapfrogged the enclave cities and added the adjacent property to its territory. Dallas has not been as fortunate. Dallas' move beyond its northern boundaries has been stopped by a gauntlet of incorporated suburban bedroom communities, like Garland, Richardson, and Plano.

In 1996, Houston tackled its most controversial annexation to date, that of the affluent Kingwood area. Kingwood, a 20 square mile planned urban community of Exxon's Friendswood Development Corporation, has homes with values exceeding $100,000, and over 41,000 residents in 14 different villages. Houston encroached ever so close to Kingwood in 1995 when it annexed two unpopulated municipal utility districts adjacent to Kingwood in northeast Harris County.

Undeterred by the rather vocal opposition of Kingwood residents and local area chambers of commerce, Houston Mayor Bob Lanier pushed annexation through the Houston city council and set a target date for December 1996. Almost immediately, a federal lawsuit was filed by representatives of Kingwood and two Houston residents claiming the annexation violated the spirit of the Voting Rights Act of 1965. The suit's basic argument was that adding the predominantly white population of Kingwood would dilute the voting strength of the minority population in the city. Ultimately, the federal judge who heard the case ruled against Kingwood and the annexation process continued.

After several near-deals and compromises, the city of Houston annexed Kingwood and five other areas. Much to the consternation of Kingwood residents, the Houston Police Department began a show of force that very day by patrolling

Kingwood's major thoroughfare. Additionally, ten municipal utility districts and the private companies which provided water and sewer services were forced to turn their financial records over to the city of Houston. The Kingwood annexation appears to be complete, so now Houston will turn its attention to future annexation targets, namely the FM 1960-area in Northwest Harris County and The Woodlands in South Montgomery County.

The annexation of Kingwood continues to plague the City of Houston. Although the city dissolved the utility districts and assumed their assets and obligations, Mayor Brown contends that these districts violated state law by spending $675,000 on lawyers challenging the annexation or by making illegal contributions to volunteer fire departments and annexation strategy committee.[16] The war over the annexation continues in the 76th Legislature when state Representative Joe Crabb, R-Kingwood, filed a bill to allow Kingwood residents to break away from Houston by December 11, 2000. A similar bill failed in the 1997 Legislature.[17]

Under Texas law, incorporated cities with more than 5,000 people may claim **extraterritorial jurisdiction** (ETJ) beyond their annexed areas and city limits. Any development taking place in the ETJ must comply with city building codes, because it eases the process for future annexation. Cities can therefore influence the development in the immediate areas around them. Many are under the mistaken notion a city cannot annex beyond the boundary lines of its county. Wrong! The boundary of Houston already extends into Montgomery and Fort Bend Counties, and its ETJ extends well out into Waller County near Hempstead on Highway 290. As of December 1996, the city of Houston encompassed an area of 617 square miles, along with 1,310 square miles in its ETJ. The largest city in the country, Jacksonville, Florida, has an area of 760 square miles due to the fact that the city consolidated its government with that of Duval County. The potential size of Houston will easily surpass that of Jacksonville, and will be almost twice that of the state of Delaware!

Putting it in simpler terms, Texas annexation law encourages geographically larger cities. Attempts have been made to amend the Municipal Annexation Act in the legislature to allow for a popular vote by the people in the unincorporated areas within a city's ETJ as to whether they want to be annexed. Without question, weakening a city's power to annex is a legislative football that will be tossed about in many years to come.

Zoning and Deed Restrictions

Future land use regulations will undoubtedly transform the urban Texas landscape. In the past, land owners were given unbridled authority regarding use and industrial, commercial, or residential development. The only restriction was the availability of water and sewer services, and other infrastructure requirements, such as the provision of electricity and roads. The negative results of limited regulations are obvious: land use in growing urban areas resulted in a hodgepodge of disjointed developments built one next to the other without any semblance of order.

With the passage of time, community groups and other activists have been far more vocal about a city's appearance. Residents, too, are more concerned about quality of life issues as it pertains to urban development. Many Texas municipalities now have **zoning ordinances**, allowing citizens to decide how land is used. Zoning policies dictate where light and heavy industries may locate, the placement of business districts, and the types and locations of housing developments.

The origin of zoning in Texas dates to 1927, when the Texas legislature authorized municipalities to adopt zoning ordinances. Most of the larger cities in Texas implemented zoning, beginning with Dallas, Fort Worth, San Antonio, and Austin. Only Houston remains unzoned. Two referendums attempting to approve a comprehensive zoning ordinance in Houston have both been defeated, the first time in 1962, the second in 1993.

Practical examples illustrate the importance of zoning: in Dallas, "Property For Sale, 10.2 Acres, Zoned R-4, 214-555-1212" signs advertise that the tract of land has been zoned by the local zoning board as a residential property allowing construction of as many as four homes per acre on a parcel of vacant property. A similar tract of land in Houston, which is unzoned, would simply state, "Property For Sale, 10.2 Acres, Utilities Available, 713-555-1212." The only limitation to development is the availability of water and sewage disposal service. Imagine building a 4,000 square foot, single family house, only to discover that no water and sewer service is available from the nearby municipal utility district! It would be difficult to resell an expensive home with only a water well and septic tank system. This is precisely what a group of medical doctors and other wealthy investors learned when they discovered that the car wash they built on Stuebner-Airline Drive just north of FM 1960 in Harris County was not serviced by any nearby municipal utility district. A car wash uses thousands of gallons of water every day, and the water well the doctors drilled was inadequate. Not surprisingly, the car wash closed down within a week.

Besides controlling land use patterns and building density, zoning also has other devices to regulate urban development. **Set-backs** require a commercial establishment, such as a strip shopping center, to be developed a certain number of feet away from major traffic thoroughfares. The widening of the thoroughfare is kiboshed when builders in years past built a commercial establishment ever so close to the road, so as to take advantage of every square foot of property. Recently an unfortunate motorist in Northwest Harris County misjudged the turn into a shopping center entrance and careened his pickup truck into the dining room of a Burger King restaurant on Louetta Road. And who happened to be in the dining room at the time, "having it their way," but two off-duty Harris County sheriff's deputies!

Another zoning restriction is the **off-street parking** requirement, which mandates that commercial establishments furnish a certain number of parking spaces for customers. This limits the practice of drivers blocking driveways in adjacent residential areas or obstructing city services by parking in alleys.

The **height limitation** regulation restricts the height of buildings. For instance, the city of Austin restricts the height of buildings in its downtown central business district so as not to obscure the view of the state capitol dome from the I-35 overpass. In Houston, however, the Transco Energy Company decided to build its impressive Transco Tower building at the juncture of the 610 loop and the Southwest Freeway, one of the worst traffic areas. The Transco Tower, in the absence of a height limitation ordinance, gives Houston the dubious distinction of having the tallest building in the world not part of a city's central business district (CBD).

Although several cities in Harris County, including Baytown, implement land-use zoning, Houston and its surrounding suburban communities use deed restrictions. **Deed restrictions** are private covenants in subdivisions which control what residential property owners can and cannot do with their property. Enforcement of the deed restriction is usually the responsibility of the subdivision homeowner's association. Normally the purchaser signs a deed restriction agreement at the closing of a sale of residential property. Months pass, and the new homeowner, who parks his Winnebago camper in the driveway, discovers via the U. S. Postal Service that this practice violates a deed restriction. If he continues, the homeowner's association may contact the city attorney, who can summon the violator into court.

The underlying rationale of deed restrictions in lieu of zoning is that it forces homeowners to keep up the appearance of their property, thus enhancing its value. Because the biggest investment a typical individual makes in his lifetime is the purchase of a home, homeowners like the benefits deed restrictions offer, namely: visually appealing neighborhoods. Additionally, builders and developers favor deed restrictions because they don't want to be encumbered with zoning restrictions and regulatory red tape.

On the downside, deed restrictions are limited in their power to influence development outside the boundaries of the subdivision. If a field of vacant property lies just outside a residential subdivision, in the absence of zoning restrictions the developer can build virtually anything on the land, including a solid waste landfill. In this case, zoning might not necessarily provide the answer either: a typical zoning board is comprised of members appointed by a mayor and city council. Because members usually have ties to the real estate industry, either as developers, architects, builders, or commercial property brokers, the industry essentially polices itself. Still, zoning affords property owners the democratic means of redressing land use grievances, a far cry over deed restriction limitations.

The ongoing tension between zoning and deed restrictions policies is perhaps best illustrated by examining the dissimilar treatment *sexually-oriented businesses* (or "SOB" as they are often referred) receive under each. Dallas, a zoned city, clusters all SOB in a single "red light" business district. Houston, on the other hand, has sexually-oriented businesses scattered throughout its city proper, some in clear proximity to schools and churches. In an effort to achieve "zoning" in an unzoned city, the Houston City Council recently passed a restriction mandating that all SOB locate a minimum of 1,500 feet from schools, churches, and residential subdivisions.

Municipal Elections

Elections for most municipal officials take place in odd-numbered years so as not to conflict with state and national elections. Although municipal elections generate less interest and participation among rank-and-file voters, the issues and personalities have the potential to generate very exciting elections. Teen curfews, cable television regulation, gang violence and crime, stadium referendums, and taxes are just some of the issues included on municipal ballots. Personalities, too, play an important role, especially when minority or special interest group representation is an issue. For example, the special election in January 1997, to fill the unexpired term of former Houston City Council member John Peavy drew 16 candidates, ranging from a gay rights activist to a tax relief advocate.

Municipal elections in Texas are conducted on a **nonpartisan** basis, that is, an election in which candidates run without a political party label. An election for a city council position will feature, for example, Joe Smith versus Jane Doe, as opposed to listing Joe Smith, Republican versus Jane Doe, Democrat on the ballot. The rationale is: (1) restrict the local campaigns to local issues, minimizing the influence of national and state political parties; and (2) put a candidate's individual qualifications and experience forward rather than his party affiliation.

What is the appropriate geographic configuration for a city council seat? Actually, configuring boundary lines for a city council position is tremendously complicated. In an ideal setting, city council members should represent roughly equal numbers of residents, boundaries should be relatively compact, and drawn to reflect the racial/ethnic composition of the area so as to maximize the power of the minority groups located there.

Traditionally, Texas cities used **at-large elections** to choose city council members. An at-large election allows every citizen in a geographical area to select a public official. In essence, the entire city becomes the council member's district. In the 1950s, voters in Houston city elections tended to elect wealthier Anglo males who had the financial resources to run expensive campaigns and gain name recognition throughout the city. This resulted in severe under-representation for minority citizens.

The Voting Rights Act of 1965 greatly impacted at-large municipal elections. Under the Act, an at-large election was deemed invalid and unconstitutional if it was demonstrated that minority groups lost their right of equal representation.

In the 1970s, minority-rights groups won federal rulings that forced cities like Houston, Dallas, and San Antonio which relied entirely on at-large election systems, to revert to a *combination system* of at-large and district council seats. **District** seats represent a smaller geographic area with a more homogeneous population. In 1979, Houston, which had its eight city council members elected at-large, changed to its present geographic configuration of nine district seats, labeled "A" through "I," and five at-large seats, numbered one through five. San Antonio went to a system electing all council members from districts, while Dallas adopted a system of eight district positions and two at-large. In 1991, Dallas reverted to an entirely district-based system of 14 council positions, with only the mayor elected at-large. In Summer 1989, Houston voters rejected a proposition to expand its city council from a 9-5 election system to a district-based system of 17 council positions. Voters were evidently satisfied with the 9-5 combination system, and believed the enlargement of the city council's membership an unnecessary expansion of government.

The last election for Mayor of Houston is memorable for two reasons: (1) the election of the first black mayor to serve the city; and (2) campaign record spending of more than $7.6 million for that office. Vince Ryan, former council member, said "Something is out of balance when that much money is spent on a mayor's race." Lee Brown, former police chief, defeated Rob Mosbacher with 53% of the vote in the runoff election.[18]

Municipal elections are often very frustrating to analyze. In February 1998, only 600 of the nearly 8,000 eligible voters in a single member district in Victoria voted (7.5%) with the result that none of the five candidates was able to prevent a runoff by receiving 50% of the vote.[19] A number of municipalities close to Houston saved the expense of municipal elections because no candidate drew challengers. Texas law allows a city to simply declare the candidates as winners. 1998 examples include Needville, Hitchcock, Tiki Island, Dayton, Devers, Hedwig Village, Jacinto City, Jersey Village, Cut and Shoot, Brookshire, and Hempstead.[20]

The use of an **initiative**, **referendum**, or **recall** gives city voters the direct opportunity to make or repeal *ordinances* (a local law or regulation), as well as to replace unacceptable council members and mayors before they can complete their terms of office. For instance, in 1985, then-city council member John Goodner promoted a referendum in which city voters repealed a gay-rights ordinance which protected gay city employees from job discrimination.

The special election in January 1997, featured an initiative petition as to whether the city of Houston should adopt a citywide ordinance establishing a minimum wage of $6.50 per hour, nearly $1.50 above that of the federal minimum wage. This initiative went over like a lead balloon with the voters, 77% *Against* to 23% *For*. Only 4% of the affluent River Oaks/Tanglewood-area residents supported the measure.

Another initiative on the January 1997, ballot dealt with tax reform. A proposed amendment to the city charter, "Proposition A," would have required a citywide election to increase taxes, fees, or charges, a decision historically left to the city council. Organized opposition to the initiative, led by Mayor Lanier, helped defeat "Proposition A" but by a closer margin than anticipated, 61% *Against* to 39% *For*.

In the past decade mayors of Del Rio and Port Arthur were subjected to recall elections by local voters. Both officials successfully held on to their positions.

Professional Sports and Stadiums

One of the hottest issues facing large and medium-sized cities across the country is having professional sports teams. Those who support the idea of city-sponsored teams and stadiums argue they generate substantial revenue, civic pride, and national recognition. Detractors, on the other hand, complain that such support is frivolous in the wake of crumbling infrastructures and increasing public service needs.

Recent examples illustrate both sides of the argument: two cities, Baltimore and Cleveland, constructed new state-of-the-art baseball stadiums, Camden Yards for the Baltimore Orioles and Jacobs Field for the Cleveland Indians. The success of these two facilities, situated in downtown locations, spawned a nationwide building boom of sports stadiums and arenas in cities like Arlington, Texas, Atlanta, Georgia, Nashville, Tennessee and Charlotte, North Carolina. The city of San Antonio, on the other hand, passed a bond referendum authorizing the expenditure of $150 million to construct the Alamodome, a domed stadium, in the hope of attracting a National Football League franchise and to date, that effort has been unsuccessful. The NBAs San Antonio Spurs remain the Alamodome's only tenant. Playing in a cavernous atmosphere with curtains drawn to block the half-empty stadium, the Spurs have been unhappy since leaving the downtown Freeman Coliseum, oftentimes playing before more Houston than San Antonio fans when the

Rockets are in town. Obviously, San Antonio taxpayers are still paying for the Alamodome and will for many years to come.

Many teams today have outgrown their host city's capacity to pay for them. Houston, for example, lost the Houston Oilers football team to Nashville, Tennessee in 1996. Although the Oilers were one of the original members of the American Football League, Nashville offered Oilers team owner, K. S. "Bud" Adams, something he could not resist: a superstadium which seats 66,000 fans, with 120 luxury boxes.

Playing in a facility geared for baseball rather than football, Adams in 1994 went to the city of Houston with a proposal for a 70,000 seat domed facility (facetiously labeled the "Bud Dome") that could field his football team, as well as accommodate the NBA Rockets and a National Hockey League franchise. The projected construction cost of the stadium was $245 million, of which Adams offered to contribute $65 million. The city, led by Mayor Bob Lanier, was none-too-enthusiastic for diverting city funds for a venture that would allow a professional football team to play ten games a year at the expense of city services and a crumbling infrastructure.

Concerns of Municipal Government

Concerned about water resources, electric deregulation, and military base closings, cities like San Antonio, have entered into contracts with a Washington law firm to lobby and protect the city's interests.[21]

Citizens everywhere expect their city and county officials to be honest and have integrity. On December 14, 1998 former Houston City Councilman Ben Reyes and former Houston Port Commissioner Betti Maldonado were found guilty of a "cash for vote" scheme to influence a city contract. A first trial had ended in a hung jury. The second trial found them guilty and they were sentenced February 24, 1999. A U.S. District Judge said these two engaged in a pattern of "pervasive corruption in government" resulting in a "loss of public confidence in government."[22]

The Year 2000 computer bug, known as Y2K, has cities working to make sure the city's crucial services are ready. Steve Collier, director of Austin's Office of Emergency Management, is sure they are ready to provide electricity, water, fire, police and emergency medical care without disruption.[23]

An interesting development in municipal government is the possibility of a lawsuit over firearms. The U.S. Conference of Mayors, with 300 mayors, met in Reno, Nevada in the summer of 1998. Some want a joint suit against gun makers while a majority prefer to work with the gun industry to reduce gun violence. With the tobacco case as a precedent, a suit would be more than just interesting.[24]

Special Districts

We know that in Texas there are 254 counties and over 1,100 incorporated municipalities. But what about the "hidden governments" of Texas, better known as **special districts**? There are many more thousands of special districts in Texas providing local government services. Most of you reading this textbook attended a public school that is neither an enterprise of the city or county. For years, many Houstonians have been under the mistaken notion that the Houston Independent School District (HISD) is operated by the city of Houston. This is not the case. HISD is a separate entity of government, a *special district*, the same as Conroe ISD or Tomball ISD. Additionally, taxpayers obtain daily drinking water in their home not from a city government, but from a special district of government called a *municipal utility district*, or MUD for short.

There are three criteria necessary to distinguish a special district: (1) a special district performs a service of government not readily available from general purpose (county or city) government; (2) a special district has an elected or appointed governing board which oversees its operations; and (3) a special district has taxing authority (property taxes or sales taxes) to help pay for its services and retire its debt. When analyzing an entity of government, if it meets all three of these criteria, you have a special district. In Texas, there are two varieties of special districts: (1) **school districts** and (2) **non-school districts**.

Public School Districts

The Texas Education Agency reported in 1994, the latest figures available, that there were six common schools and 1,051 independent school districts with 3.7 million students enrolled in public schools. A public school district in the state of Texas is charged with the responsibility of educating the children of Texas, including the children of illegal aliens.

The governing board of school districts, better known as an **Independent School District** (ISD), is called the Board of Trustees. To be a trustee, for instance, in the Victoria Independent School District, one must possess the following qualifications: (1) be a qualified voter; (2) take the official oath of office; (3) serve without compensation; and (4) reside in the district.

The *common school district*, very common in the past when the state was predominantly rural, is almost obsolete. Usually a five member board of trustees, one elected at-large and one from each of the county commissioners precincts, served as the policy making group. They would hire teachers, apportion the school funds, run a bus program, and create the boundaries for the various schools in the county. All of these elected officials were elected in partisan elections with four year terms.

Most of the state's public schools operate under the *independent school district* form. Residents elect the members of the school board, also known as the board of trustees, who oversee the general operation of the school district. An important function of the board is to select a superintendent, who is much akin to a city manager. The superintendent is the person responsible for the day-to-day operation of the schools within the district and represents the interests of the school within the general community and the state. He hires and fires school principles, deals with personnel matters, handles the fiduciary matters of the district, and helps establish a property tax rate. Superintendents in the larger or more suburban areas earn compensation packages approaching $150,000 per year. Remember, the state's governor is earning only $115,000 per year!

In the state of Texas, members of a school board are not paid. It is frequently a thankless job and a political hot seat. A school trustee sometimes wins his position with a voting turnout less than the school district employees. Running for the school board at one time meant the successful candidate must be in his thirties or older. In 1994, a 19 year old won a seat in West Oso Independent School District and in 1998, another 19 year old won in the Robstown Independent School District.[25] Goose Creek Consolidated School District (Baytown), for instance, has over 2,000 personnel, yet little more than 600 voters participated in the last school board election. Because of the problematic considerations like budgets, long meetings, attendance boundaries, calendars, busing, salaries, property taxes, facilities, violence, state mandates, and student drug use, the job demands a volunteer with courage and "thick skin." A typical school budget is shown in Figure 3.5.

Figure 3-5. 1998-1999 Victoria Independent School District

Official Budget for 1998-1999	
Revenues	**General Fund**
Local and Intermediate	$38,423,768
State	31,447,908
Federal	173,785
Total	70,045,461
Expenditures	
Instruction	43,722,100
Instructional Resources	1,263,896
Staff Development	867,687
Instructional Administration	1,189,094
School Administration	3,701,093
Guidance & Counseling Services	2,706,127
Social Work Services	242,429
Health Services	461,397
Pupil Transportation	1,809,077
Food Services	123,427
Co-Curricular Activities	2,268,461
General Administration	2,373,999
Plant Maintenance & Operations	8,537,456
Security and Monitoring Services	294,980
Data Processing Services	443,594
Community Services	71,706
Debt Service	201,938
Facilities ACQ/Construction	92,000
JUV Justice Alt Ed	0
Total	$70,370,461

Two items of importance come from Figure 3-6. First, note that the local contribution to the revenue base from the school property tax is 54.8%, while the state contribution is only 44.8%. The Federal contribution is 0.2%. Prior to the 1990s, those numbers were reversed. The larger local contribution is testament to the enormous increase in property taxes, while the state's contribution has remained stable. Second, the instruction expenditure of 62% is not out of line with other districts. Teachers feel, however, that top heavy administration and staff personnel are siphoning funds that should go towards teacher salaries and providing more money for instructional resources. The rationing of teaching supplies like pencils, paper, and chalk, serves as an impediment to the learning process.

Problems facing Texas educators today include: (1) inadequate teacher salaries; (2) lack of classroom space; (3) taxpayer revolts; (4) low student achievement; (5) busing; (6) the role of religion in education; (7) school dropouts; and (8) meeting the technical/vocational needs of students in an ever changing global economy.

As public education heads into the 21st century, perhaps its greatest challenge is how to guarantee each student an equal learning opportunity. Because funding plays such a substantial role in achieving this goal, the Texas Supreme Court's 1995 decision in *Edgewood v. Kirby* is especially noteworthy. The ruling in this case challenged the method by which public schools are funded. Subsequent legislative and judicial action refined the ruling such that in January 1995, the Texas Supreme Court in a 5-4 majority opinion ruled that Texas school districts which enjoy huge property tax bases must share their wealth in one of five ways or face state-imposed sanctions. No doubt, the tension between the governor and the legislature, the rich and the poor school districts, state income tax proponents versus property tax supporters will ensure this issue a long, volatile life.

School trustees face the explosive issue of adopting school boundaries. The Austin ISD allowed residents to comment on the boundary maps by calling the district, attending meetings, or by e-mail after viewing the boundary maps (www.austin.isd.tenet.edu). Redrawing the boundaries can eliminate crowded schools and shorten commuter time but it can also alter ethnic and racial diversity at some schools.

School boards face the challenge of hiring district administrators (superintendent, business manager, athletic director), approving the district calendar, hiring teachers, deciding the use of school property for nonschool use, having closed sessions for a conference with an employee or student appeal, and the yearly budget.

The lawmakers in the 76th Texas legislature meeting this spring have numerous education issues: (1) teacher pay; (2) school vouchers; (3) social promotion; and (4) changes in the Texas Assessment of Academic Achievement test (TAAS).

The first issue, teacher pay, involved a $6,000 raise to put Texas teachers at the national average. Texas legislators want salaries to meet the national average to help recruit and attract more teachers and maybe bonuses for qualified teachers in shortage disciplines.[26] The public school teachers in Texas do not have an organization that speaks in one voice, even on pay. The four major groups are the various affiliates of the American Federation of Teachers, Texas Classroom Teachers Association, the various affiliates of the National Education Association, and the Association of Texas Professional Educators.

The second major issue is school vouchers. This may involve a broad program or a pilot project to allow tax dollars to be used to send children to private, including religious, schools.[27] "School Choice" versus "Public School Funding" is the debate. The fear of vouchers is that when a district loses students to state voucher-sponsored schools, the public school district loses state money which is tied to student attendance.[28] Dolores Munoz, Edgewood Independent School District superintendent, has been critical of a privately funded school voucher program that caused a loss of $4 million in state funding and 700 students.[29] Some are very opposed to tax dollars to pay for a pupil to attend a school that has religious teachings that parents might disagree with. Some Texas supporters of vouchers fear that vouchers could provide an opportunity for the state to gain control over a private school's curriculum, qualifications of personnel, and selected admission. School vouchers has its proponents and opponents. The Texas Association of Business and Chambers of Commerce have announced support for voucher legislation while opposition comes from most education associations, PTAs, and civil rights groups like MALDEF. Jacqueline Lain, assistant director for the Texas Association of School Boards (TASB) and an opponent of vouchers has said vouchers are "syphoning" money out of the public schools. "We're for school choice, too; that is, choice with the public schools."[30] The school voucher and charter school concepts are rapidly becoming a battle between the public and private schools. Whether or not it is settled this legislative session remains to be seen. Some educational reformers want to use the charter school concept to invigorate a failing public school system. The data from the pilot school programs is just now becoming available and the results will need to be analyzed. Setting up an "almost private" school that is exempt from many of the usual school regulations does not make for a level playing field with the public schools.

The issue of vouchers and school financing is complicated by lower gas prices, which may sound good, but local Texas public school districts have been hurt by the loss of tax revenue by dropping land values. The Texas Comptroller's Office projects Refugio and Victoria Independent School District losses will be at $852,183 and $100,957, respectively.[31] West Texas school districts face massive layoffs, programs and salary cuts because of the low oil prices with the result of less tax revenue for school districts. "This is the worst crisis education has had in this state in my memory," and "Do you know of any business that could stand to lose one-third of its operating budget and still open its doors the next year?" said David Goodman, Andrews Independent School District superintendent.[32]

The third major issue facing the 76th Legislature concerns "social promotions." Will eliminating the promotion of students that are not ready to advance lead to more teacher pressure to "teach the test (TAAS)" and more minority students being held back?[33]

Fourth, the TAAS is the mainstay of the school accountability system in Texas. There is mounting pressure to raise scores and add algebra exams to exit-level tests for seniors. The Texas Education Agency accountability ratings are based primarily on student scores on the Texas Assessment of Academic Skills (TAAS). Texas school rankings are available on the TEA web site (www.tea.state.tx.us).

Although a new state constitution will probably not be completed this session, some legislators are suggesting that the state board of education be appointed rather than elected to eliminate the fierce battles over the direction local districts should take.[34]

Homeschooling is a concern the legislature needs to address. In June 1994 the Texas Supreme Court affirmed a decision by both the trial court and Texas Court of Appeals. *Leeper et al. v. Arlington ISD et al.* held that the Texas Education Agency had no legal basis for prosecuting homeschooling families. There is presently no registration or testing of the pupils.

Education for Texans is our key for opening the door to participate in the global economy. New skills (computer, foreign language) will be required. The new worker will have to be better educated than his parents with more salable skills as he or she will re-enter the job market several times due to technological change or "downsizing." Training for jobs that do not yet exist is difficult. Who would have thought in the 1970s that IBM punch cards would fade away so fast and be replaced by personal computers. Texans should be thankful that the state views public school funding as an investment in the future. The 76th session of the Texas legislature is the last session, barring a special session called by the governor, of this century. The new millennium will require that the state legislators address the problems of an education system under attack.

Community Colleges

Community college districts have a seven- or nine-member board of trustees, serving six year overlapping terms, elected by the voters residing within the district. The trustees serve without pay. The President, or Chancellor, is the chief administrator selected by the trustees to oversee the operation of the college or college district with multiple campuses. Each college district may have different missions ranging from academic to technical-vocational. Community college districts do not have to be countywide. In Harris County, for example, community college education is provided by four separate community colleges: the Houston Community College system, North Harris Montgomery Community College District, San Jacinto College District, and Lee College in Baytown.

Community colleges in Texas seek to: (1) offer academic courses that can transfer to four year colleges and universities; (2) offer technical and vocational programs; and (3) offer continuing education to the community. A typical budget to accomplish this goal is found in Figure 3-6.

Figure 3-6.

1998-1999 VICTORIA COLLEGE OPERATING BUDGET

Income

	Amount	Percent
State Funds	$ 6,743,217	32.13%
Federal Funds	2,024,261	9.65%
Tuition and Fees	2,837,256	13.52%
Ad Valorem Taxes	3,220,000	15.34%
Miscellaneous	895,194	4.27%
Student Aid	1,599,321	7.62%
Auxiliary Enterprises	2,321,800	11.06%
Debt Service	1,343,625	6.40%
Total	20,984,674	100.00%

Expenditures

	Amount	Percent
General Administration	$ 578,112	2.75%
Student Services & Admissions	981,061	4.68%
General Institutional Expense	887,540	4.23%
Staff Benefits	1,088,199	5.19%
Instruction	7,557,717	36.02%
Library	474,397	2.26%
Instructional Media Services	39,837	0.19%
Public Service	46,000	0.22%
Physical Plant Operation & Maintenance	1,985,064	9.46%
Federal Funds	2,024,261	9.65%
Student Aid	1,662,521	7.92%
Auxiliary Enterprises	2,321,467	11.06%
Debt Service	1,318,625	6.28%
TOTAL	20,964,801	99.91%
Reserve for contingencies	19,873	0.09%
	20,984,674	100.00%

Two items of importance are apparent in Figure 3-6. First, students should note that tuition and fees contribute only 13.52% toward the cost of education. State funds and district property taxes are the largest sources of revenue. Second, far less expenditure is allocated to instructors' salaries in the community college system than for public schools. Administrative costs for community colleges also tends to be less top heavy than that for public schools.

Community colleges can now save the college district voting costs by canceling trustee elections when there are candidates facing no opponents.

Rather than raising students fees, raising property taxes, or opting for bond issues, Del Mar College is exploring enlarging the college's taxing district beyond the five Corpus Christi schools now served.[35]

Non-School Special Districts

The second special district is the non-school type. These units of government operate hidden from the public eye, yet still enjoy the privilege of eminent domain and limited immunity from legal lawsuits. There are nearly 15,000 school districts and more than 33,000 non-school districts in the United States.

Non-school districts provide a variety of government services to citizens. The most common form is the **municipal utility district**, or MUD, which provides water and sewer service to residential subdivisions and commercial developments in unincorporated areas surrounding cities. There are over 1,100 MUDs in Texas.

A major criticism of operating water districts is the lack of awareness of their existence by the general citizenry. One of the textbook authors is an elected member of the Rolling Creek Utility District, a district located in West Harris County beyond Beltway 8. This district with over $15 million of appraised property value and a tax rate of $1.45 per $100 (this equates to a yearly tax bill of $1,450 for a $100,000 home), more than twice the county rate, has very little participation by district residents. A 1995 change in the Texas Election Code allows a water district to forego the elections for its directors when no one has filed to oppose an incumbent running for reelection. Foregoing elections saves the district more than a thousand dollars in expenses. The author was unopposed and automatically reelected to a four year term. The bimonthly board meeting, with five elected directors, by law open to the public, is rarely attended by any of the district's residents. Conversely, the author's father ran for the water district board of the Freshwater Supply District (FWSD) #52 in the Champions subdivision in Northwest Harris County. Nearly 500 votes were cast by the residents, and despite receiving over 180 votes, he still lost the election!

Other non-school special districts include **housing authorities, flood-control districts, groundwater subsidence districts, transit authorities, hospital districts, noxious weed control districts, navigation districts, river authorities, airport authorities**, and **mosquito control districts**. We will analyze the criteria of a non-school special district using Metro, Houston's transit authority, as an example. First, Metro provides a service of government, in this case mass transit service, that is not readily available from the city of Houston, Harris County, or the 14 enclave cities that comprise the Metro service area. Second, Metro has a Board of Directors, several of whom are appointed each by the mayor of Houston, the Harris County Commissioners Court, and the other enclave cities in the Metro service area, to oversee its daily operations. Third, Metro imposes a one cent sales tax as part of its taxing authority to help pay for its services. By meeting these three criteria, we distinguish Metro as a special district.

The method of selection for special district board members depends on how the original state statute creating them was written. In Victoria County, the navigation district's board of directors is appointed, while the drainage district board is elected. Victoria County does not have a hospital district, but it does have a county hospital whose board is appointed by the county commissioner's court. There is no law that requires those with the authority to spend taxpayers money and make decisions affecting taxpayers to be elected.

Special districts perform functions that some feel could be better accomplished by strengthening the county. But the reality is that counties cannot or will not perform some of the tasks needed. These special districts can be formed to: (1) bypass old and obsolete tax limits; (2) enlarge the tax base; (3) avoid the politics seen in existing governments; and (4) solve pressing problems quickly. The Metropolitan Transit Authority of Harris County (Metro) was established by a referendum in 1978 and given the authority to be funded with a one cent sales tax. Prior to that time, transit service had been operated by the city of Houston. Because Houston was experiencing dramatic growth, officials realized that effective mass transit and overall transportation policy could only be achieved through the creation of a regional transit authority which had to be authorized by the voters. The city of Houston was only too happy to be rid of a major policy burden.

River authorities are also special districts. The Guadalupe-Blanco River Authority (GBRA), created by the state in 1935 by an act of the Texas legislature, is a typical example. Established to develop, conserve, and protect the water resources of the Guadalupe River Basin, there are ten counties within the district. Similar to some types of special districts, the GBRA cannot levy or collect taxes or assessments, or in any way pledge the general credit of the state. Revenue is provided chiefly from water sales and lake operations, power sales, and sewage services. The GBRA is governed by a board of nine directors appointed by the governor. Each director serves a six-year term with three directors appointed every two years.

Although local non-school special districts serve the general public with more efficiency and faster delivery than those of the state or national levels, many of these non-school districts are less "visible" to the general public. Annual reports or newsletters to the taxpayers would improve the public awareness of these districts.

The October floods in Central Texas will long be remembered. The Guadalupe-Blanco River Authority (GBRA) is currently in the process of evaluating lakes for water safety and the removal of debris (houses, houseboats, refrigerators). Airboats, photographs, and global position finders will be employed for debris removal.[36]

Regional Planning Commissions

Regional Planning Commissions are voluntary associations of local governments. The local governments include cities, counties, hospital districts, soil and water conservation districts, municipal utility districts (MUDs), independent school districts, river authorities, and others. Additionally, the Regional Planning Act of 1965 authorized regional councils. There are presently 24 regional **councils of governments** (COGs) in the state of Texas. These regional councils go by a variety of names but all are basically voluntary associations of local units of government. Their primary responsibility is to plan and help implement regional development plans. Membership in a typical regional planning commission is shown in Figure 3-7.

The Councils of Governments are political subdivisions of the state and therefore subject to laws governing open meetings, open records, and conduct of public officials. One of the great drawbacks of a COG is that they have no regulatory power over member governments. These COGs have no taxation, law-making, regulation making or law enforcement authority. Rather, the purpose of these COGs is to encourage regional planning and cooperation.

Funding for COGs comes from federal, state, and local governments. Federal funds are channeled through the state and local funding is composed of dues paid by members.

Councils of government administer funds for many programs including senior citizen assistance, job training, regional economic development, solid waste planning, rural transportation, housing programs, and 911 planning and implementation. Each Council of Government is made up of elected officials from city and county governments, school districts, and other governing bodies. The Houston-Galveston Area Council has 13 counties, 106 cities, 19 school districts, and 11 soil and water conservation districts in 1999. In 1973, the Texas Association of Regional Councils was formed. Each COG provides one representative to a board which meets on a quarterly basis. The TARCs home page is www.txregionalcouncil.org.

Figure 3-7. Golden Crescent Regional Planning Commission

Membership List
Fiscal Year 1999

MEMBER COUNTIES

Calhoun   Jackson
DeWitt   Lavaca
Goliad   Victoria
Gonzales

MEMBER CITIES

Cuero   Point Comfort
Edna   Port Lavaca
Ganado   Seadrift
Goliad   Shiner
Gonzales   Smiley
Hallettsville   Victoria
LaWard   Waelder
Moulton   Yoakum
Nixon   Yorktown
Nordheim

HOSPITAL DISTRICTS

Cuero Community Hospital
Jackson County Hospital

WATER RELATED DISTRICTS

Calhoun County Drainage District #11
San Antonio River Authority
Lavaca Navidad River Authority
Guadalupe-Blanco River Authority

SOIL & WATER CONSERVATION DISTRICTS

Copano Bay SWCD #329
DeWitt County SWCD
Goliad County SWCD
Gonzales SWCD
Lavaca County SWCD
Victoria County SWCD

MUNICIPAL UTILITY DISTRICT/ DRAINAGE DISTRICT/WATER CONTROL & IMPROVEMENT DISTRICT

Calhoun County Drainage District 11
Quail Creek Municipal Utility District
Victoria County WCID2

INDEPENDENT SCHOOL DISTRICTS

Bloomington I.S.D.
Calhoun County I.S.D.
Cuero I.S.D.
Edna I.S.D.
Nixon-Smiley C.I.S.D.
Nursery I.S.D.
Victoria I.S.D.
Waelder I.S.D.

OTHER

Bloomington Volunteer Fire Department
Gulf Bend Center
Region III
South Texas Zoological Society
Weesatche Fire Association

Source: 1999 Annual Board and Membership Training Manual, January 27, 1999, page 6.

On-Line: Local Government

City of Houston is the site of the state's largest city. Of particular interest is the financial statement showing revenue and expenditures linked through "Monthly Financials."

http://www.ci.houston.tx.us/

City of San Antonio is the site for the state's third largest city. It offers a very good diagram showing the organization of a council-manager form of government

http://www.ci.sat.tx.us/

State of Texas City information contains Web site addresses for several dozen Texas Municipalities.

http://www.state.tx.us/cities.htm/

Harris County, Texas is the Web site showing the operations of Harris County government and its various elected officials.

http://www.co.harris.tx.us/

Harris County Appraisal District takes you through the basic steps of the property tax appraisal process and filing for a Homestead Exemption.

http://www.hcad.org/

The Port of Houston Authority is an overview of the Harris County special district for the world's largest inland port facility.

http://www.portofhouston.com/

Wells Branch Municipal Utility District is a water district in the Austin area which has gone into Cyberspace. It offers a good overview of a utility district's background and operations.

http://www.know.com/wbmud/home.htm

HISD is the home page of the Houston Independent School District, the state's largest ISD.

http://www.houston.isd.tenet.edu/

ENDNOTES

1. Roger Croteau, "Commissioners delay vote on pet's status," *San Antonio Express-News*, Friday, January 15, 1999, 7B.

2. Cinday Horswell, "Heads, she wins, but coin toss in election runoff disputed," *Houston Chronicle*, Saturday, May 2, 1998, 33A.

3. Kevin Moran, "Commissioner position filled in Galveston," *Houston Chronicle*, Friday, February 5, 1999, A29.

4. Scott Reese Willey, "Wharton County upholds dismissal of two employees," *The Victoria Advocate*, Wednesday, January 13, 1999, 4A.

5. Chris Newton, "Sheriffs fretting about low pay in West Texas," *Austin American-Statesman*, Wednesday, October 14, 1998, B3.

6. Alan Bernstein, "Second time a charm: Democrats confirm tax assessor nominee," *Houston Chronicle*, Tuesday, August 25, 1998, 14A.

7. Roger Croteau, "JP continues to serve Comal at 91," *San Antonio Express-News*, Friday, January 1, 1999, 1B.

8. Roger Croteau, "Comal commissioners aim to abolish treasurer's office," *San Antonio Express-News*, Thursday, December 24, 1998, 3B.

9. Tim Delaney, "Victoria County adopts '99 budget," *The Victoria Advocate*, Thursday, September 10, 1998, 2A.

10. –, "Legislation would limit annexations," *Houston Chronicle*, Friday, February 19, 1999, 23A.

11. July Mason, "Proposal would make county provide water, sewer services," *Houston Chronicle*, Friday, February 19, 1999, 23A.

12. Nicole Fay, "225 county courthouses endangered," *San Antonio Express-News*, Tuesday, June 16, 1998, 9A.

13. Matt Schwartz, "Mayor joins 7 on council on Asia trip," *Houston Chronicle*, Wednesday, January 27, 1999, 17A.

14. James A. Suydam, "Council to interview city manager candidates May 26," *Corpus Christi Caller-Times*, Monday, May 18, 1998, B1.

15. Andrea Jares, "City's sales tax rebate shows economy healthy," *The Victoria Advocate*, Wednesday, May 13, 1998, 4A.

16. Matt Schwartz, "Council vote on Kingwood suits delayed," *Houston Chronicle*, Thursday, January 28, 1999, A17.

17. Julie Mason, "Bill puts new life in Kingwood deannexation," *Houston Chronicle*, Wednesday, February 10, 1999, 35A.

18. —, "Houston's mayoral candidates set spending record," *The Dallas Morning News*, Saturday, January 17, 1998, 17A; —, "Houston elects first black mayor," *The Victoria Advocate*, Monday, December 8, 1997, 2A.

19. —, "City will call a runoff election," *The Victoria Advocate*, Thursday, February 26, 1998, 2A.

20. —, "Canceled municipal election," *Houston Chronicle*, Sunday, April 26, 1998, 44A.

21. Christopher Anderson, "Council awards contract or Washington lobbying," *San Antonio Express-News*, Friday, January 22, 1999, 8B.

22. Ed Asher, "Judge throws book at Reyes," *Houston Chronicle*, Thursday, February 25, 1999, A1, 12.

23. Dick Stanley, "Key services safe for Y2K, city says," *Austin American Statesman*, Thursday, January 21, 1999, B1, 6.

24. Melanie Eversley, "Mayors will hold off on suit over firearms," *Houston Chronicle*, Monday, June 22,1998, 2A.

25. Ron George, "Teen hopes school board win leads to higher office," *Corpus Christi Caller-Times*, Tuesday, May 5, 1998, B2.

26. Terrence Stutz, "The Texas Agenda," *Dallas Morning News*, Sunday, January 10, 1999, 24A.

27. Kathy Walt, "School voucher program to be tested in Legislature," *Houston Chronicle*, Friday, January 15, 1999, 31A.

28. Anastasia Cisneros-Lunsford, "Voucher debate back on the table," *San Antonio Express-News*, Thursday, January 14, 1999, 5A.

29. Kathy Walt, "Voucher foes take case to Austin," *Houston Chronicle*, Thursday, February 4, 1999, 32A.

30. Jamie Castillo, "Groups stake ground in voucher debate," *San Antonio Express-News*, Friday, January 15, 1999, 2A.

31. Robert Schoenberger, "Schools hit by drop in price of oil," *The Victoria Advocate*, Wednesday, February 10, 1999, A1.

32. "Low oil prices mean layoffs, cutbacks for school districts," *The Victoria Advocate*, Friday, February 12, 1999, 10A.

33. Editorial, "Education issues," *Corpus Christi Caller-Times*, Sunday, January 17, 1999, A10.

34. Dave McNeely, "Appointed school boards looking smarter," *San Antonio Express-News*, Tuesday, January 5, 1999, 13A.

35. Heather Howard, "Del Mar wants to expand tax district," *Corpus Christi Caller-Times*, Sunday, January 17, 1999, B1.

36. Roger Croteau, GBRA on mission to find lake debris," *San Antonio Express-News*, Wednesday, January 20, 1999, 3B.

Chapter 4

Interest Groups

Learning Objectives

After reading this chapter, the student should be able to:

- ✪ Explain the functions of interest groups, lobbyists, and political action committees
- ✪ List important lobbies and identify their major interest
- ✪ Identify the different kinds of interest groups and the concerns they represent
- ✪ Identify and discuss the different techniques used by interest groups to achieve their political goals
- ✪ Describe and illustrate the different kind of lobbying activities
- ✪ Discuss the role of interest groups in elections
- ✪ Summarize the impact of interest groups on democratic institutions and public policy

Public Interest For Sale?

In an incident that has entered the annals of Texas political lore, "Bo" Pilgrim (the self-professed "chicken man" and owner of Pilgrim's Pride Chicken) appeared on the floor of the Texas Senate to talk to his "friends." Checkbook in hand, Pilgrim began to write $10,000 "campaign contributions" to legislators who were interested in making changes in the workers' compensation law. The Workers' Compensation Insurance Program is a state-run but privately financed insurance program. Employers in Texas pay insurance premiums for their employees who are then eligible to receive financial benefits should they become injured while on the job. Like all insurance programs, the annual WCIP premium for employers is determined by the total payments paid out by the fund to injured workers. In 1989 the legislature was considering new rules that had been recommended to them by industry lobbyists. If enacted these changes would have altered the procedures for determining eligibility for compensation and imposed limits on the total amount of compensation workers could draw from the fund. Supporters of the proposed changes wanted to impress on legislators the seriousness of the matter, and thus Pilgrim appeared on the floor of the House with his checkbook poised to help "help" his supporters.

In defending his actions, Pilgrim later claimed that even though he was writing $10,000 checks on the floor of the legislature, he was not violating existing state law or commonly held moral prohibitions about "buying influence." Indeed, he chaffed at the suggestion that he was engaged in any action that was illegal or even remotely unethical. He defended his actions by claiming that he was doing what business and industry leaders always do—offer campaign contributions to politicians and decision-makers (their "friends") who are sympathetic with their causes. Pilgrim believed that he was not violating any legal standards because his "campaign contribution" was available to both supporters and opponents of the changes he wanted. And by not agreeing upon any *specific* promise of receiving a special favor in return for the contribution, Pilgrim and the legislators who accepted the "contribution" avoided violating any ethics laws regarding conflict of interest.

What is remarkable about this case? Was it the amount of money Pilgrim was cavalierly brandishing about? Was it the sheer Texas-size brashness of Pilgrim? Was it the absence of laws preventing such an egregious case of influence peddling at the heart of government? Or was it remarkable that this incident created only a *public relations* embarrassment for politicians and lobbyists? After all, Pilgrim was doing in full view of the public and the media what usually takes place secretly behind closed doors. Eventually, the legislators did enact workers' compensation "reform" and, in a gesture towards good government, made it illegal for elected officials to accept campaign contributions on the floor of the legislature (sometimes referred to as "Pilgrim's Law").

The Public Interest and Special Interests

Bo Pilgrim's "lobbying" on the floor of the Texas Senate illustrates one of the central issues of governing in a free and open political system. Because government is a public authority, most citizens believe that public officials should serve the public interest. But our system of self-government is also based on the belief that individuals should be free to pursue their self-interest. Citizens have a right to organize and defend their private interests and to present their views to officials. In a democracy all citizens have the right to participate in an effort to influence government. In order to run effective campaigns most candidates for public office seek campaign contributions from private interests like Bo Pilgrim. A fundamental question of political legitimacy is thus raised. Do the laws and policies of the State of Texas serve the public interest or do they reflect the needs and interests of the well-organized and influential?[1]

The *public interest* is the aggregate of economic, social, and moral conditions that, ideally, enhance the *general welfare* of all citizens of a political community. In a perfect world, people would generally agree on their common interests and governing officials would concern themselves with protecting the public interest and the good of the community. *Special interests* are groups of individuals bound together to pursue their *particular goals*. These goals may be publicly spirited or they may be rooted in the desire to advance the group's financial interest. An **interest group** is an organization of individuals (a) who are committed to a common agenda and (b) who attempt to influence the decisions of officials who make public policy. The purpose of an interest group is to shape the conditions of public life in a manner that reflects the values and interests of the group. To comprehend the immense scope of actions used by interest groups it is important to define public policy in the broadest possible manner. Legal statutes, regulatory decisions, agency budgets, case law, and even corporate policies can be influenced by interest group actions. Sometimes groups determine that in order to change public law they must first change the public opinion on which the government policy rests. Changing *attitudes* about drinking and driving, for example, has been a tactic employed by Mothers Against Drunk Driving (MADD) as part of their overall strategy to combat injury and death on the highways. Other groups focus on altering corporate actions. Members of some environmental groups have chained themselves to trees in order to raise public awareness about clear-cutting logging practices in virgin forests.

Political Functions of Interest Groups

Interests groups assume important roles in democratic politics. These activities include:

- ✪ Gather and Share Information.
- ✪ Linkage To and Check On Government Power.
- ✪ Promote Participation in Democratic Elections.
- ✪ Representation.

Information Sharing. Information is a critical resource in modern societies. Interest groups are one of the principal sources of information in Texas politics. Well-financed groups can gather and distribute information to the group's membership, the media, and government officials more effectively and efficiently than an individual acting alone. Public officials frequently have a need for information that only groups can provide. Well-financed organizations often hire researchers, lawyers, and other experts in their fields to assist in the task of gathering facts and making a case for the group.

Linkage. Interest groups create the opportunity for citizens to organize and promote their common beliefs, interests, and ideals. The ability of citizens to organize and petition their government is a hallmark of a free and open democracy. Interest groups serve the vital role of connecting the values and interests of the citizens with the actions of officials. Interest groups also provide an institutional basis for citizens to organize for their common interest. Interest groups thus function as monitors of government action and help to prevent the abuse of power. An open political process protects the ability of citizens to "network" and to promote their views to officials.

Electioneering. Interest groups try to influence public policy by supporting candidates for public office. Groups gather and distribute information on the personal background of candidates, publicize voting records, and make campaign contributions. One of the most important election activities occurs when a group recruits volunteers for a candidate and generally promotes a candidate (or slate of candidates) with the group's membership. The goal of electioneering is to promote the careers of decision-makers whose values and views are supportive of the group's agenda.

Representation. Representation is a fundamental value of democratic politics. Article I of the Texas Constitution and the First Amendment of the U.S. Constitution protect the right of citizens to organize and to petition the government.

Lobbying is the activity of communicating a group's goals to the officials with the legal authority to make decisions. Lobbying thus gives expression to the values and interests of the individuals in the group and protects the hard-won democratic right of citizens to represent their views in the decision-making process.

Types of Interest Groups

It is useful to classify interest groups according to the general purpose the group seeks to advance.

Economic Groups. The father of the U.S. Constitution, James Madison, believed that economic differences and controversies were at the root of most political disputes and would occupy the center of attention for most of the officials of government. Texas is no exception. Most observers of Texas politics agree that economic groups are the most powerful and best organized in the state.[2] In a state where many citizens champion the pursuit of financial gain, economic interest groups proliferate and come to wield considerable influence over the political system. *Economic interest groups* are concerned with promoting public policies that directly or indirectly lead to the group's members gaining a larger share of the state's financial and economic resources. Ultimately, specific economic interest groups are concerned with gaining an advantage over rival economic forces in the state by manipulating rules in a manner beneficial to the group.

Economic interest groups are numerous and powerful because government has the power and responsibility to regulate the individual and corporate pursuit of profit in a manner consistent with the public interest. Everyone in a capitalist society has an economic interest in the actions of government that bear on our economic security. Conditions of employment, the ability to earn profit and income, access to markets and resources are affected by government policies. Thus, the *potential* for forming economic interest groups is as vast as the complexity of the modern economy. It is safe to conclude that all sectors of modern economic life are politically organized to protect their interests. Businesses and corporations support politicians and policies they believe promote a "good business climate." Most business groups are opposed to a state income tax. They want fewer regulations on businesses, are opposed to generous welfare benefits for the needy, and support reforms that limit business liability *(tort reform)* in areas such as consumer safety, worker compensation, and illnesses linked to environmental hazards.

There are literally hundreds of economic interest groups trying to influence public policy in Texas. Table 4.1 is a list of only a few of the more prominent groups.

Table 4-1. Texas Economic Interest Groups

Automotive Service Professional of Texas	http://www.adwizards.com/asp-texas/
Texas Association of Business and Commerce	http://www.tabcc.org/index.html
Texas Retailers Association	http://www.io.com/txretailer/index.htm
Independent Bankers Association	http://www.ibat.org/
Texas Independent Producers	http://www.tipro.org/
Texas Association of Life Underwriters	http://www.talu.org/
Texas Bankers Association	http://www.txbanc.com/
Texas Chemical Council	http://www.txchemcouncil.org/
Texas Association of Builders	http://tx.bin.net/
Texas Hot Mix Asphalt Association	http://www.txhotmix.org/
Texas Hotel and Motel Association	http://www.texaslodging.com/
Texas Good Roads and Transportation Association	(512) 478-9351
Texas Association of Broadcasters	http://tab.org/history.html
Texas Farm Bureau	http://www.fb.com/txfb/index.html
Small Business United of Texas	http://www.sbutx.org/
Texas Association of Realtors	http://www.tar.org/
Texas Apartment Association	http://www.taa.org/

Labor Groups. The labor unions have been faced with considerable resistance in Texas. As a result, labor unions do not have the visibility or the power in Texas that they do in other industrialized states. Labor unions have historically promoted the adoption of laws which favor the ability of workers to organize for collective bargaining, support the legal right to strike, uphold unemployment compensation, encourage higher wage structures, and promote fair labor practices and occupational safety. Two of the large labor groups in Texas are the state chapters of the AFL-CIO and the Texas Oil and Chemical Workers Union.

Public Employee Groups. The largest employer in Texas is state government. In addition, many local government workers, such as teachers, receive salaries from the state that are channeled through local school districts. (In fact, the greatest portion of the salary of the instructor in this class is likely to have been provided by the State of Texas.) Because the state budget affects salaries, fringe benefits, retirement benefits, working conditions, health care, and leave-policies, public employees have organized to promote their concerns (See Figure 4.2). The largest such group is the Texas Public Employee Association. The Texas State Teachers Association (TSTA) represents local teachers and the Texas Community College Teacher's Association (TCCTA) represents community college teachers. Law enforcement officials in many of the larger metropolitan areas of the state have groups to represent their views and interests before city government. The Houston Police Officers Association (HPOA), for example, is an active force in representing Houston police before the Houston City Council.

Table 4.2. Labor and Public Employee Groups

Labor

American Federation of Labor/ Congress of Industrial Organizations	http://www.texasaflcio.org/
Oil, Chemical, and Atomic Workers Union	http://www.webshells.com/ocaw/
Texas Federation of Teachers (TFT)	http://www.tft.org/
United Food and Commercial Workers Union	http://www.ufcw.org/
Continental Teamsters	http://www.cal-teamsters.org/

Public Employee

Texas Classroom Teachers Association (TCTA)	http://www.tcta.org/
Texas State Teachers Association (TSTA)	http://www.tsta.org/
American Federation of State, County and Municipal Employees	http://www.afscme.org/
Texas Municipal League	http://www.tml.org/
Texas Association of Community Colleges	http://www.tacc.org/index.html

---

Professional Groups. These are the fastest growing kind of interest group in the United States and Texas. This growth is associated with the transformation from an industrial to a service-based economy. A professional group is typically concerned with the state policies for the licensing and regulating of a particular professional occupation. In addition, these groups represent the economic interests of the profession. The practice of law, accounting, and numerous medical-related fields (hospitals, physicians, nursing, dentistry, and nursing homes) are affected by public policy. Table 4.3 lists some of the significant professional organizations in Texas.

Table 4-3. Professional Groups

Society of Petroleum Engineers	http://www.spe.org/
Texas Society of Architects	http://www.tsaonline.org/
Texas Medical Association	http://www.texmed.org/
Texas Hospital Association	http://www.thaonline.org/
Texas Trial Lawyers Association	http://www.ttla.com/default.htm
Texas District and County Attorneys Assoc.	http://www.tdcaa.com/
Texas Bar Association	http://www.hnba.org/
Texas Society of Certified Public Accountants	http://www.tscpa.org/

Public Interest Groups. Some interest groups do not have as their primary focus the advancement of an economic or professional concern. *Public-interest* groups attempt to promote conditions of civic life the members feel are necessary to create and sustain a good society. "Public interest" groups do not seek to advance directly the financial conditions of their membership. Rather, public interest groups seek to advance "public" causes that the membership will be beneficial to the society as a whole. The National Rifle Association promotes the freedom of individuals to own and bear arms. Winning support of this freedom in public policy would benefit both the group's members and all other citizens who have an interest in personal liberty. Of course, not everyone will agree with the cause that is being championed or that the goals would be necessarily good for society. Texans for Gun Control is an interest group working to limit the ability of citizens to bear arms. This group believes they are serving the public interest in trying to reduce instances gun related violence. The League of Women Voters is a well-known group dedicated to promoting civic education and increasing voter participation. The name, public interest group, then, is more of a description of a kind of interest group than it is a moral observation about intentions of the group's members. Merely because a group labels itself as a "public interest group" is no guarantee that in fact the group's action will lead to a more secure public interest. Disagreements about the meaning of the "public interest" are one of the key aspects of political life.

Public interest groups are affiliated with numerous "good causes." The American Civil Liberties Union promotes the defense of civil rights in Texas and the nation. The National Association for the Advancement of Colored People was created to defend the legal rights of black Americans when legal segregation was permitted. The Sierra Club and the Gulf Coast Conservation Association are dedicated to protecting the environment. The Consumers Union is a strong advocate for the American consumer. Common Cause is dedicated to reforming the system of campaign financing. The presence of these and other groups allow citizens enjoy numerous opportunities to become involved in the democratic political process. Table 4.4 lists some of the more prominent and visible public interest groups in Texas.

Table 4-4. Public Interest Groups

Common Cause of Texas	http://infinity.ccsi.com/~comcause/
National Rifle Association	http://www.nra.org/
Mothers Against Drunk Driving	http://www.madd.org/
Texas League of Women Voters	http://www.main.org/leaguewv/home.html
Texans Against Gambling	P. O. Box 710217 Dallas, TX 75371
Texas Right to Life Committee	http://www.gartl.org/
National Organization of Women	http://www.now.org/
Texas Against Gun Violence	http://www.insync.net/~tagvhou/index.htm
American Civil Liberties Union	http://www.aclu.org/
National Association for the Advancement of Colored People	http://www.naacp.org/
Planned Parenthood of Texas	http://www.ppnet.org/
League of United Latin American Citizens	
Communities Organized for Public Service (COPS)	http://www.lulac.org/ http://iisd1.iisd.ca/50comm/commdb/desc/d19.htm
Justice For All	http://www2.jfa.net/jfa/
Texas Taxpayers and Research Association	http://www.ttara.org/toc.htm

One of the most effective and powerful public interest groups is the Texas Taxpayers and Research Association. (Because of its close association with corporate and business interests, it might also be classified as a business interest group.) Individuals and corporations with business interests in Texas support the TTARA. It specializes in conducting research on state policies affecting the cost of doing business in Texas—inheritance laws, property tax conditions, worker's compensation, welfare rules, and corporate liability laws. The TTARA reports are widely distributed among the state's top policymakers. These reports often serve as the beginning point for major efforts to reform existing policies. One of the key areas of interest to the TTARA is the biennial budget process. The organization prepares a biennial budget report that is made available to all of the state's leading newspapers. Thus, the TTARA's views on the budget (and related taxing/spending items) frequently find their way into print. No interest group in Texas can match the TTARA for its ability to influence the budgetary process of state government.

The Continuing Dominance of Business Groups in Texas

Individuals and business groups are guaranteed the same constitutional rights to participate in the political process. Most individual citizens do not exercise their right to make campaign contributions and petition their government. Thus, the majority of citizens in Texas are passive observers in the political process of gaining access to power. In addition, widespread political apathy gives business groups a competitive advantage over individuals when influencing policy. Many Texans simply don't care about politics. The success of business in wielding influence in Texas politics, however, is not due solely to the apathy of the general public. Business groups simply have more of the important political resources needed for success in politics: organization, leadership, information, money, an effective communication's strategy, and access to decision-makers. So long as these resources are unequally distributed, business groups will have a competitive advantage over other groups in Texas.

Most observers of Texas politics rate the business lobby as being the state's most established, well-run, and powerful of the state's organized interest groups. The reasons for this dominance can be found in the political resources available to business groups. First, business interest groups are cohesive. *Group cohesion* means that a group can easily unite and support the agenda of the group and its leaders. Having the backing of a tightly knit, cohesive group is a tremendous advantage when business leaders lobby government. Second, business interests command tremendous financial, intellectual, and organizational resources that can be committed to political action. Campaign contributions can be solicited from the group's members, lobbyists can be hired, paid professional staff can be hired or given release time to conduct research, and all the organizational infrastructure of business (computers, telephones, data banks, etc.) can be thrown into the political arena. Third, economic interests generally have the ability to stay focused on their political goals. Whereas a large political party must address a variety of issues and concerns to attract voters, economic interest groups have the advantage of pursuing a very narrow range of goals. The more focused a group remains, the less likely it is to be splintered by extraneous concerns. A simple example can serve to explain this group dynamic. Business leaders find it easy to unite behind a pro-business agenda *so long as the agenda remains strictly business-related*. If the Texas Chamber of Commerce were to introduce a proviso that members of the group should only support politicians who are "good Christians" the potential for internal conflict would make it difficult for the group to achieve its goals. Fourth, business groups generally want something very specific and "doable" from government decision-makers. A change in a regulation, a modification of special business taxes, relaxing an environmental regulation are goals that are specific and often do not require the cooperation of large numbers of officials. Fifth, business interests often succeed in their political action because there is no effective *organized* opposition.

In a democracy, the power of public opinion is not directly organized or focused. Although elected officials, in particular, must appeal to the majority of the voting public, the attention of the public is far removed from the halls of power in the legislature or a regulatory agency. The public is often not an informed watchdog of its own business and the media is too entertainment driven to provide effective coverage of the activities of interest groups. In a practical sense, the only counterbalance to interest group pressure *is more group pressure.* Lastly, business groups are often successful because the benefits the members receive greatly exceed the costs of their participation. Small groups can offer large benefits to each member if the membership is willing to invest in the group's operation.

This last aspect advantage is what the political scientist, Anthony Downs, described as the "law of small groups.[8] It works like this. A small group such as the Texas Trial Lawyers Association stands to profit by preventing reforms that would limit the liability settlements in legal suits brought against negligent employers (*tort reform*). A reasonable case can be made that the general public ultimately pays the costs of large liability settlements in the form of higher insurance rates for employers. These costs are simply "passed along" to the public in the form of higher prices for products and services. In this instance, those in opposition to change have a *greater potential reward* than each member of the public has in seeking the reform. The economic incentives of the opponents are stronger than the economic incentives of the supporters even though the supporters are in the majority. Small interest groups can thus defeat the public's interest in spite of their limited numbers. A simple, but proven, fact of democratic politics is that majorities do not always win. Majorities sometimes become victims of the "law of small groups."

How Interest Groups Influence Politics and Government

Politics and government are multi-faceted and the activities of interest groups are as diverse as the system in which they operate. Goals determine tactics. Some groups will focus on changing public opinion about specific issues. Other groups attempt to shape the foundations of civic culture by molding fundamental moral and political beliefs and attitudes. The much-covered media "sit-ins" at family practice centers by Operation Rescue are part of an overall strategy to change public law by first altering moral attitudes about abortion. Most interest groups concentrate their efforts on achieving very specific objectives such as winning a tax break for its members or postponing the implementation of an environmental regulation. As a general rule, the more specific a goal is, the greater the likelihood is that a group can achieve it through political action.

It is also helpful to recognize the impact that the separation of powers has on interest groups. Some groups will focus their actions exclusively on the legislative process. Many economic interest groups attempt to influence the budget writing process by lobbying key legislators. Other groups will concentrate on the state bureaucracy and the regulatory process. Utility companies will lobby the Public Utilities Commission in order to gain the regulatory approval to charge higher utility rates. Still other groups will focus on the legal system by attempting to elect judges who will "get tough" with criminals.

Methods.

The methods available for interest groups to influence governmental action fall into six broad categories.

- Electioneering—assisting candidates campaigning for public office.
- Campaign Financing—providing financial support for candidates seeking elected offices.
- Lobbying—influencing decision-makers by providing them with background reports, position statements, and "perks."
- Influencing the Regulatory Process—recruiting individuals to serve on key regulatory agencies and lobbying regulators.
- Litigation—engaging in legal actions on behalf of individuals and groups seeking legal redress.
- Opinion Cultivation—molding the public's perception of an issue or interest.

Electioneering.

Many interest groups distribute information about candidates to the group's members. The purpose is to help the members cast informed votes and thus to back public officials who are supportive of the group's political goals. The voting decision is influenced by many factors and there is no guarantee that interest group recommendations are powerful enough to influence the voter's decision. Some groups attempt to educate the membership by distributing the *voting records* of candidates. The Christian Coalition claims to have distributed over 80 million voter guides during the 1994-1996 election cycle. The National Rifle Association regularly distributes information regarding candidates who fail to support the NRA's legislative goals. In recent years so-called *single-issue-voters* have emerged as a factor in some elections. The legal status of abortion is one issue where large numbers of voters will cast votes based on how the candidates stand on this issue. The presence these single-issue voters provides an opportunity for interest groups to distribute information about candidates.

A subtle but equally effective technique for winning influence with elected officials is *candidate recruitment*. Although this is a traditional function of political parties, interest groups have become active in encouraging individuals who are sympathetic with group's goals to seek office. This entails recruiting candidates and providing them with a source of campaign revenue. The purpose, of course, is to have officials in positions of power that share the basic values of the group. Especially in races requiring substantial amounts of spending to wage a campaign, potential candidates want to line-up support and to "test the waters" *before* they actually run. Guaranteeing financial support of groups is a critical step in campaigning for elected office. The purpose of this recruitment is, of course, to place "friends" in position of influence.

Groups can also make membership lists available to potential candidates. These lists are used to obtain contributions, volunteers, and votes. Because labor unions, in particular, typically cannot match the financial resources of business groups, they will provide candidates with volunteers to help in campaigns. In recent election cycles in Texas, religious groups have played an important role for many Republican candidates. These groups provide candidates with an ample supply of volunteers. Religious leaders in Houston's minority communities have long provided political assistance to candidates sympathetic to their interests. The Texas Right to Life Committee acts as an umbrella-like organization where individuals recruited from churches of various denominations may volunteer their services in opposition to abortion. As religious groups continue to grow and prosper, one can only expect their influence on elections will expand.

It is important to note that only the best-financed, professionally staffed, and efficiently organized groups can effectively compete in the election process. Poorly financed and poorly organized groups simply do not have the resources needed to shape the outcome of elections. Of course, there is no absolute guarantee that an elected official will always decide to support the position of the interest group. Officials sometimes solicit support from groups with different views on specific issues of policy. Because groups do not always agree, officials cannot please all of their supporters all of the time. Ultimately, individual voters must decide for whom they will vote. The views of interest groups are but one factor in this complex decision. Interest groups in Texas almost certainly will continue to compete for influence in the election arena in the years to come.

Campaign Financing. *Political Action Committees* (PACs) raise and distribute money to candidates for elected office. The purpose of making a campaign contribution is to have "friendly" officials in positions of power and influence who will support the group's political goals. Texas law places *no limits* on the amount of money PACs may contribute to candidates. Because running for public office is increasingly expensive, the significance of PACs has grown accordingly. PAC spending is dominated by economic, business, and professional interest groups.[4] Interestingly, Texas law *prohibits* the proceeds of corporations and labor unions from being *directly* contributed to individual candidates. This limitation, however, proves to be a mere *technicality* as corporations and unions form Political Action Committees and charge them with the task of raising and distributing money to candidates.

There are over 1300 PACs organized and operating in Texas. Table 4.5 is a categorized list of some of the more visible and well-financed PACs.

Table 4-5. Political Action Committees in Texas

Phone Numbers and Mailing Addresses May Be
Obtained from the Texas Ethics Commission.

http://www.ethics.state.tx.us/

Real Estate and Construction
Texas Association of Realtors
Texas Association of Builders
Contractors PAC

Banking, Finance, and Insurance
Texas Bankers Association
Concerned Texas Insurance Agents
Bank of America
American Insurance Association

Business
Texas Association of Business
Electronic Data Systems PAC
American Airlines
Contractors

Agriculture
Beef PAC
Texas Southwest Cattle Raisers
Texas Diary Association

Public Interest
Texas Abortion Rights League
Texas United for Life

Medical
TEXPAC (Medical Association)
Texas Health Maintenance Organization

Energy
Mid-Continental Oil and Gas
Exxon Employees PAC
Chevron Employees PAC

Legal
Texas Trial Lawyers Association
Texas for Lawsuit Reform
Citizens for Qualified Judges
Committee for Judicial Reform

Transportation
Texas Good Roads Association
Texas Auto Dealers Association
Association of General

Beverage
Texas Association of Distributors
Coca-Cola Enterprises
Texas Soft Drink PAC

Political Party
Texas Democratic Party
Texas Republican Party

Teachers
Texas Federation of Teachers

Typically, a committee of the directors of the PAC will review the service and voting records (where established) of candidates and, when feasible, have an interview with the individual before making a contribution. PACs are ideally suited to the needs of the modern campaign. The rising expense of waging an effective campaign requires candidates to spend more time raising money. Candidates may raise more PAC money in an afternoon of fundraising than in entire weeks or even months of soliciting funds from individuals.

PAC contributions to candidates follow a consistent pattern. Most importantly, the contributions favor incumbents (those holding the office) over challengers. Incumbents get more support because lobbyists for the group want to gain access with the candidates most likely to win. Incumbents in both Texas and U.S. elections are reelected in overwhelming proportions. PACs also focus their financial support on the Lt. Governor, the House Speaker, and committee chairs with oversight responsibilities important to the group. According to one account, thirty of the state's top lawmakers received 62% of their campaign funds from PACs, lobbyists, and special interests in 1990.[5]

Beginning students of politics and government often believe that campaign contributions "buy votes." Tit-for-tat (*quid pro quo*) deals between lobbyists and PACs are in fact illegal. The influence of campaign contributions on policy rarely takes so crass a form, although it does happen from time to time. (Two recent Speakers of the Texas House resigned when allegations of ethical misconduct were raised. Eventually both were tried in court and found innocent of violating state conflict of interest and campaign finance laws.) The impact of PAC money is more sublime. Without access to political power an interest group is severely limited in its ability to accomplish its political goals. Campaign contributions from interest groups "buy" access to decision-makers. Campaign contributions typically make it possible for lobbyists to meet with legislators in order to present the group's views on policy decisions officials must make.

Does money "buy" influence? Did Bo Pilgrim buy himself some politicians and thus buy himself a change in the law? Political scientists and careful observers of the Texas (and national) political system have debated this kind of question for many years. As the example of Bo Pilgrim illustrates, anecdotal evidence seems to suggest that money buys influence. During each legislative session the major state newspapers are filled with reports of how key elected leaders perform numerous "favors" for one or more of their "powerful" backers. These examples are so commonplace that most students reading this textbook (in addition to the general public) readily believe that money buys power. The academic community, however, is more divided over this question.[6] Most academics are skeptical about reducing the complexity of political power to the simple equation: money = power. It is important to put the role of money in its political context. Interest groups seek out politicians who are predisposed to favor their interests. Agricultural interests in the state will, therefore, seek out legislators with large farming interests (and many farm votes) in their districts. Money buys other important resources such as organization, professional staff, communications, and public relations. Thus, money buys all the necessary resources needed to participate in the process of influencing the public agenda.

But it is important to remember that raising money for politicians is part of a larger political process. Many elected leaders perform special favors for lobbyists because they do not want to risk alienating themselves from the potential votes the group represents. For candidates, votes can "speak" as loud as money. It is also important to know that lobbying *can be an extremely competitive process*. Interest groups do not always "line-up" on one side of a political issue. Lobbyists from the insurance industry, for example, typically oppose lobbyists for the Texas Trial Lawyers Association when *tort* reform is considered in the Legislature. Money does not "always wins" because one group's money will loose when interest groups oppose one another. Money is necessary to participate in the practice of trying to influence public officials, but money alone does not guarantee success.

Interest group money exerts a *systemic* influence on Texas politics. In order to participate fully in the process of influence peddling, individuals must be organized. The public perception is that the public at large cannot compete with the well-oiled campaign fund-raising/lobbying machine of special interests. The agenda of the legislature often appears to the public to be captured by the special interests. Indeed, increasingly special interests are "buying" influence with legislators that they helped recruit, finance, and elect to public office. Little "arm twisting" has to take place in an environment permeated by close relations between elected leaders and special interests. It is this perception of close ties between lobbyists and legislators that promotes public cynicism and undermines confidence in our public institutions.

Lobbying. Lobbying is one of the most effective tactics interest groups use to achieve their political goals. The primary goal of all lobbying is to persuade decision-makers to support the political agenda of the group. Information is the primary resource lobbyists in their efforts to persuade officials. Because the legislative session is brief (140 days) a premium is placed on having timely access to critical information. The Texas Legislature is a part-time institution and legislators simply do not have sufficient time or the necessary staff resources to become adequately informed regarding the issues that they will be asked to vote on. Lobbyists recognize this limitation and provide legislators with background reports and position papers. Lobbyists may also provide legislators with legal research, assistance in drafting legislation, and speech writing services.

Most groups hire independent lobbyists for a fee. Most of these lobbyists are lawyers (or law firms specializing in lobbying), are themselves former legislators, or are former aids for key legislative committees. All successful lobbyists must know how the informal legislative process works. Most successful lobbyists carefully nurture their contacts with government officials and private interests[7] Because many legislators themselves go on to a second careers as lobbyists, the special interest groups often find a receptive environment in which to work. Many lobbyists are former colleagues of the very people they now seek to persuade.

The first task of any lobbyist is to *gain access* to officials who have the power to make policy in the area affecting the group's interest. This critical task is made easier by campaign contributions as described above. Another way to gain access to legislators is to provide them with perks. *Perks* (from perquisites) are "favors" that lobbyists provide to officials. Such favors might include free meals, free entertainment at sporting and cultural events, and *honoraria*. *Honoraria* are stipends and awards given to (typically) legislators in recognition of their accomplishments. Both perks and honoraria were significantly limited by the 1991 legislation creating The Texas Ethics Commission. (See Table 4.6).

All legislative bodies are subject to political pressure from lobbies, but part-time, under-staffed, and lowly paid legislatures are especially open to political influence. Part-time legislators have fewer staff and less time and money for issue-research. In addition, part-time legislators are poorly paid, especially when compared to the salaries of the lobbyists. It is one of the grand ironies of Texas politics that the general public often expects public servants to serve the greater good of the community when they have so few resources available to help them. In this environment, lobbyists are used to draft proposals for legislation. The most effective lobbies will actually employ an individual (typically an attorney) whose skill is simply composing legislation. In Texas (and most legislative bodies) it is common for individual legislators to introduce and orchestrate support for bills that have largely been crafted by special interests (a practice known as "carrying a bill").

The rush of legislation that must be passed in the 140-day legislative session in Texas places great demands on individual legislators and lobbyists. During a typical legislative session lobbyists will outnumber legislators in Austin. Austin hotel rooms, restaurants, and bars bristle with the political activity of lobbyists. Typically, bills are crowded onto the calendar in the session's remaining days and legislators have precious little time to study carefully all of the details of the bill. If amendments to bills are made from the floor they must be voted on with little time for review. All of these factors combine to place individual legislators at a severe disadvantage. They are asked to digest complex, often obscurely worded information with little opportunity for reflection. In this atmosphere some legislators are reduced to looking for voting-signals from lobbyists who are assembled in public galleries above the floors of the House and Senate. (State law prohibits lobbyists from being physically present on the floor of the House and Senate while voting on legislative proposals takes place. Lobbyists retire to "lobby row" in the galleries above as they monitor the action below.)

Lobby Reform. In response to growing criticism about the influence of special interests in the Texas Legislature, a new effort aimed at "ethical" reform was launched during the 1991 legislative session. This law (1) created new registration rules for lobbyists, (2) imposed restrictions on the use of gifts, *honoraria*, and other perks, (3) established new rules for disclosing the sources of campaign contributions, and (4) created and empowered the Texas Ethics Commission to investigate allegations of rules violations. Table 4.6 is a brief summary of some of the key elements of the statutes.

The general intention of these reforms follows the "light of day" strategy. Rather than trying to limit access to public officials the reforms attempt to expose lobbying efforts to the general public. The assumption is that full and open disclosure of influence peddling will act as a deterrent to the most egregious efforts of special interests to "buy favors" with lawmakers.

Table 4-6. Selected Features of Texas Ethics Code

Texas Ethics Commission

http://www.ethics.state.tx.us/

Two-year ban on retired officers of state government from lobbying their former associates.

Ban on paid honoraria and expense-paid trips by lobbyists.

Cap of $500 per legislator for food and beverage spending by lobbyists.

Mandatory registration of lobbyists.

Lobbyists must file detailed reports of their activities, including all contacts with public officials for the purpose of influencing public affairs. (These reports can be accessed at URL

Disclosure of campaign contributions by PACs.

Disclosure of campaign contributions received by candidates.

There are at least two weaknesses with this strategy. First, the statute itself is complex. Consequently, the ethics reports are not easy for the lay person to understand. The second weakness in the ethics code is the relative freedom that legislators have on the use of their campaign contributions. Prior to 1991 it was possible for legislators to use campaign contributions directly for personal use! This is no longer directly permitted, but the legislation prohibiting it is full of loopholes and gaps. Legislators can use campaign contributions for living expenses they incur while in Austin during the legislative session. Thus, they can use contributions for housing, meals, and entertainment. Furthermore, state law imposes *no limits* on what legislators can do with campaign contributions once they retire from active public office. Legislators can, in short, accumulate a nest-egg for retirement. These and other loopholes severely weaken the legal restrictions on the use of campaign money.

A system that allows, even encourages, private interests to influence public officials will inevitably generate some controversy. In order to be elected, public officials must raise large sums of money to wage effective campaigns. In order to represent the interests of their clients lobbyists must gain access to legislators. This is an opportunity for mutual benefit waiting to happen. PACs need politicians as much as politicians need PACs. The problem this poses for democratic government is simple—it weakens the ability of average citizens to have their voices heard, to participate in the process of having ones views represented at the seat of power. Unless one has the financial means to make substantial campaign contributions and to follow this with an intensive lobbying effort, one is increasingly disenfranchised from the "system." This is not to suggest that politicians are "for sale," as is commonly believed. It is to suggest that only a few of the state's most powerful and well-financed groups have the financial ability to gain access to officials on a consistent basis. This access gives these interests a competitive advantage over other groups *and* the public regarding matters of public policy in Texas. The system, in short, is biased in favor of those who are possess the knowledge, the financial resources, and the organizational abilities required to make the system work for them.

Grass-Roots Lobbying. Grass-roots lobbying encompasses the efforts of interest groups to mobilize members to support or oppose government actions and policies. These efforts typically encourage members to phone or write letters to officials regarding a particular issue or vote. Personal visits to the offices of officials may be arranged. Group members may also be encouraged to call to radio talk-shows to promote an issue. Groups may also plan marches and demonstrations in order to "stage" an event for television. The goal of these efforts is to create greater public awareness about the group's cause and to promote among officials the sense that the group represents a vast number of active citizens who are knowledgeable and willing to act in defense of their values. In short, the groups seek to impress officials with a rising groundswell of public opinion. Elected officials must take seriously the views of citizens because they are potential voters and donors.

Because elected officials are sensitive to voter pressure, the more active and committed the members of a group are, the greater the chance the group will have in influencing public policy. For grass-roots lobbying to be effective, three ingredients are necessary. First, the group itself must have a clear sense of purpose and agreement on its priorities. Having an able leadership strongly supported by the rank and file members is an essential component to any successful political group. Second, groups must have invested in the infrastructure necessary to communicate with the membership. Having the technical resources to produce phone calls, mass mailings, and newsletters is essential. Third, the membership itself must zealously support the group's agenda and be willing to mobilize when asked by the leaders of the group. Members of successful grass-roots lobbying groups must be willing to sacrifice time, energy, and money to achieve the group's goals. Passionate followers are the life-blood of any grass-roots lobbying effort. Groups that possess these ingredients are able to create the impression that the officials are confronting a rising tide of popular sentiment. When legislators are showered with letters, telegrams, personal visits, and letters to the editor in the local newspapers back home they take notice of the group's interest. Two groups that effectively use the grass-roots approach are the National Rifle Association and Communities Organized for Public Service (COPS).

Opinion Cultivation. Some pressure groups concentrate their actions on the difficult and elusive task of molding public attitudes and opinions about particular issues and causes. Having public opinion on ones side can be a tremendous advantage in creating an agenda for democratic governments. Many of the policies of state government rest on broadly and deeply held opinions about personal and public values. Thus, lobbyists for the Texas Good Roads and Transportation Association do not single-handedly create pressure for funding highway construction and maintenance. The lobby operates within a context in which public opinion generally supports the policy of maintaining a first-rate road system in Texas. The lobby can maintain support for this policy by encouraging motorists to drive the back roads of Texas, by asking the Highway Commission to designate "scenic" roads, or by lending support to the "adopt a highway" program that makes driving the roads of Texas a more pleasurable experience.

When public opinion is divided or confused, groups will sometimes undertake campaigns to reshape public attitudes. This kind of opinion cultivation is part of a comprehensive strategy to change public law by changing public attitudes. Once public opinion has been molded, public officials can more easily adjust public policy to coincide with the majority opinion. This type of strategy requires long-range strategic thinking and can only be conducted by groups with financial staying-power or whose views rest on some fundamental issue broadly held by the public. Mothers Against Drunk Driving has staying-power because the public feels increasingly threatened by unsafe drivers on the highways. Often this type of opinion cultivation addresses the broad moral issues of civic life, such as racial and sexual equality, rights to abortion, alternative lifestyles, substance abuse, and other matters of personal responsibility. The pro-life movement spearheaded by the National Right to Life Committee, for example, has distributed graphic visual materials of abortions, organized marches, and staged demonstrations near family practice centers in order to gain more exposure for the pro-life cause. MADD, Citizens for Victims Rights, and other local groups typically will "stage" events for the media to highlight their cause. Who has not seen a MADD crucifix or Star of David along a state road? The point of these activities is to slowly but inexorably move public opinion and its glacial-like power to alter the political landscape.

Influencing Appointments and Regulations. Both the regulatory authority and the number of boards, commissions, and agencies in Texas have expanded in recent decades. Of these numerous boards and commissions, only the Texas Railroad Commission and the State Board of Education are elected by the voters. Gubernatorial appointments fill all of the other positions. (See Chapter 8 for an overview of these agencies.) Governors typically consider the advice and suggestions of campaign contributors, personal friends, senior party leaders, and lobbyists for special interest groups when these appointments are made.

State regulatory agencies shape virtually every major economic activity in the state. The health, legal, medical, and accounting professions are regulated and licensed by state agencies. Educational policy for the public schools, colleges, and universities, all public utilities, the criminal justice system, social services, water development, gambling, alcohol consumption and distribution, and environmental and outdoor practices are regulated by the state bureaucracy. In short, there is hardly an economic or recreational activity in the state that is not affected by some regulatory power of state government. Consequently, virtually every sector of the Texas economy works to have "friendly" regulators appointed to the regulatory posts. The vast network of regulatory power and authority means interest groups will inevitably try to influence both the selection of the leaders and the content of the regulations.

Interest groups seek to influence regulations by controlling the appointment of those who have immediate decision-making responsibility over the area most important to the group. Thus, college teachers are concerned with the policies of the Coordinating Board of Higher Education, utility companies are concerned with the policies of Public Utilities Commission, and so on. Because the governor has the authority to make appointments to these positions, the gubernatorial campaign serves as a lightning rod for group campaign contributions and electoral support. Inevitably, it seems, many of the state regulatory bodies thus come to be headed by individuals with close ties to the industry they are legally bound to regulate. *Regulatory capture* occurs when an interest group is successful in placing a number of its allies in regulatory offices and thereby is able to shape regulations in a manner favorable for the group. When the regulated succeed in controlling the regulator, then regulatory capture is complete. Not all groups are successful in "capturing" a regulatory agency. Interest groups frequently compete with each other in this process. Governors have political debts to pay-off that may override a group's effort to influence an appointment (although this debt may be to another group). Typically, groups with more political resources prevail over those with fewer resources in regulatory politics. Organization, money, lobbying skills, and commitment are the critical variables. Thus, utility companies (and their PACs) have far more interest in influencing the appointments to the Public Utilities Commission than the average citizen does (or another interest group, for that matter). The complexity of most regulatory issues means that regulated groups often control the critical information that regulatory agencies need in order to make decisions. Given this dependency of the regulators on the regulated, the seasoned observer of state politics has reason to wonder if the state regulatory agencies are truly "independent" of politics at all.

Litigation.   Given the growing complexity of state and national laws and a increased willingness of state and federal courts to hear legal challenges to existing policies, more interest groups are turning to the legal system to pursue their interests. Environmental groups have been effective at using lengthy (and expensive) legal maneuvers to delay construction projects they oppose. In the early 1990s the Gulf Coast Conservation Association successfully blocked the construction of a large Japanese-owned copper smelting plant along Galveston Bay by threatening legal actions that would delay construction. Faced with vocal opposition and the potential for costly delays, the firm decided on another location. School funding is another area frequently litigated by interest groups. A consortium of Hispanic interests represented by the Mexican American Legal Defense and Education Fund successfully challenged the state in the now famous case *Edgewood v. Kirby*. State and local chapters of the National Association for the Advancement of Colored People (NAACP) and the American Civil Liberties Union (ACLU) have provided individual Texans with the legal resources needed to challenge state policies. Numerous other groups have established *legal defense funds* to assist their members in pursuing court actions. The Texas Trial Lawyers Association has been successful in preventing legal reforms that would make it more difficult to bring personal injury lawsuits against employers. Because of these efforts, the Texas legal system remains open to interest groups seeking to advance their interests via the courts.

Interest Groups, Political Power, and Public Policy in Texas

From the previous discussion a few general propositions regarding political power can now be advanced. First, political power is primarily the result of organized action taken by groups. Groups provide individuals with an effective means for setting goals, communicating values and interests, plotting strategies for action, and concentrating political resources on those areas of government most relevant to the group. Second, not all groups have equal power. Some groups have larger constituencies with greater political resources and are more zealously committed to achieving their objectives. Many legislators and seasoned observers of Texas politics rank the business, economic, and professional lobbies as the most powerful and influential. Third, interest groups primarily address the concerns of the propertied class. Clashes over property, as James Madison predicted, dominate the arena of interest group politics. Members of interest groups in Texas are most likely to be better-educated, own property, have higher incomes, work in some white-collar profession or business, and engage in other forms of political action. Fourth, interest groups are effective in a highly decentralized and fragmented political system. The sheer number of government agencies, the division of constitutional powers, and the number of elected offices contribute to the formation and success of interest groups.

Assessing the ability of interest groups to achieve their political goals has never been an easy undertaking. Despite the many pitfalls, seasoned observers of politics in Texas generally agree that interest groups wield considerable influence in the making of regulatory and legislative policies. Interest groups play a crucial role in recruiting candidates for public office (both elected and appointed). They are instrumental in financing the campaigns of elected officials. Because of limited research abilities and staff, many Texas legislators must rely on information provided to them by interest groups. The appointed heads of many state agencies and regulatory commissions often have close ties to the interests they monitor. Interest groups also influence the public's perception of controversial issues. All of these factors contribute to an environment in Texas politics that enhances the ability of groups to influence policy.

Interest Groups and the Prospect of Representative Government

The Rise of Functional Representation. Interest groups pose an interesting dilemma to serious students of Texas politics and government. Groups are at once a vehicle for citizens to express and mobilize their concerns and they are also one of the chief causes for declining support in our public institutions. The ability to organize and represent *specific* concerns is called *functional representation*. Every citizen has transportation, education, and economic interests. In a free society it is inevitable that interest groups will form around each of our functional needs and interests. Interest groups are the practical necessities, the "necessary evils," for mobilizing the functional concerns of the public. Indeed, as the above analysis indicated, groups have proven to be one of the most effective and efficient means for representing the functional needs of certain individuals.

But it is also important to ask what effect special interests have on the laws and character of public life. By definition, interest groups do not speak for the whole public. At best, they represent only their members. Do the voters and the people lose their voice in government as lobbies seek to influence legislation and regulatory rules? Do special interests, in short, have too much power and influence in the halls of government and does this influence lead to policies harmful to the public? Have we become a state (and country) of separate interests and voices with little or no common law for the community? Or do the people gain their voices only *through* their interest group actions? Rather than subvert the public will, do interest groups help to vocalize it and bring it to political life? These questions strike at the very heart of representative government and deserve our consideration.

The Diminishment of Civic Representation. The ideal of self-government consists in the belief that through free and open participation, citizens with diverse interests can ultimately achieve policies that embody the basic values and interests of the citizens. Interest groups are one means available to citizen to exercise their political liberties. Clearly Texans amply avail themselves of this opportunity. Yet, it is commonplace today for citizens to express distaste for government and disfavor of special interests. Civic alienation from both the process (politics) and the product of government (law) is on the rise everywhere. What once was an attribute of people on the fringes of political life now infests the majority. Public opinion polls routinely show that the public is distrustful of a government that "does not care for people like me." Many citizens and seasoned observers attribute this alienation to the ever-expanding power of special interest groups.

A political system organized around strong interest groups fails its citizens on at least three accounts. First, participation in democratic politics via interest groups tends to be passive in nature and fails to reward any sense of general citizenship. Sending an annual check for dues is no substitute for good citizenship and active participation in self-government. Modern citizens thus lack psychological depth to their participation. Civic alienation abounds and collective impulses such as patriotism and a sense of community are weakened.

Second, participation is fragmented. In order to be "fully represented" every citizen would have to belong to and participate in a whole plethora of interest groups. Most citizens have neither the energy nor the resources to belong to more than two or three groups. The poor and the less educated have even fewer realistic opportunities to influence government. Fragmentation of interests generates stasis on the large issues of public life while encouraging activism on the small ones. The result is a government torn between contradictory impulses. The public wants "less government," for example, while the special interests want favors (often leading to more government).

Third, and most serious of all, excessive special interest influence on the public's business can and will produce policies that are genuinely harmful to the public interest. One needs to look no further than the debilitating impact special interests had on the state's and nation's Savings and Loan industry during the past fifteen years to find evidence of what can happen when special interests come to dominate the economic powers of government. By their very nature, special interests are designed to advance the values and interests of their members. Unfortunately, the interests of the few do not always coincide with good of the many.

A genuine dilemma thus looms. A free people cannot live without interest groups, but a democratic public cannot live with them. The challenge facing self-government in Texas in the next generation is to develop organizations that strengthen democratic institutions and forge genuine civic bonds between individuals.

On-Line: Interest Groups

The Internet is an excellent resource to use when analyzing the influence of money on the political system.

The Center for Public Integrity

http://www.publicintegrity.org/main.html

The Center for Responsive Politics

http://www.crp.org/

Common Cause

http://www.commoncause.org/index.html

Campaign Finance Reform: A Sourcebook

http://www.brook.edu/gs/campaign/sourcebook.htm

ENDNOTES

1.   The academic literature on interest groups is generally divided between those who view groups as essential for democratic representation and those who see interest groups as mechanisms for elite domination of the masses. The defenders of interest groups are usually called pluralists. The critics of interest groups usually defend some idea of majoritarian democracy. The critics see argue that groups weaken democracy because groups tend to advance the interests of the well-connected over the interests of the majority of citizens. They are sometimes called "elite theorists." Both sides agree with the proposition that organized interests are now the backbone of modern-day politics. For a classic exposition of the pluralist position, see Robert Dahl, *Democracy and Its Critics* (New Haven: Yale University Press, 1989). For an excellent summary of the elitist position, see Thomas Dye, *Who's Running America* (New York: Prentice Hall, 1976).

2.   There are numerous studies that underscore the influence of business and economic interests on Texas government. One of the most comprehensive studies of the power of economic interests is to be found in James Lamare, *Texas Politics: Economics, Power, and Policy,* 5th Edition, (Los Angeles: West Publishing Company, 1994). An excellent historical view can be found in George Norris Green, *The Establishment in Texas Politics: 1938-1957* (Westport, Connecticut: Greenwood Press, 1979). Perhaps the most vitriolic account is to be found in Harvey Katz, *Shadow on the Alamo City* (Garden City, NY: Doubleday, 1972).

3.   Anthony Downs, *An Economic Theory of Democracy* (New York: Harper & Row Publishers, 1957).

4.   Wayne Slater and George Kuempel, "Texas' 'Third House,' *Dallas Morning News,* March 29, 1987.

5.   Wayne Slater, "Big Donors Hedge Bets in Elections," *Dallas Morning News,* March 5, 1990.

6.   The academic research on money and politics is voluminous. Two of the more important studies of the impact of money on elections are, Frank Sorauf, *Money in American Elections* (Glenview Press, 1988) and Herbert Alexander, *Financing Politics: Money, Elections, and Political Reform,* 4th ed. (Washington, Congressional Quarterly Press, 1992). A critical study of the impact of interest groups can be found in Darrell West and Burdett Loomis, *The Sound of Money* (W.W. Norton & Company, 1998).

7.   For an "insider's view," see H.C. Pittman, *Inside the Third House: A Veteran Lobbyist Takes a 50-Year Frolic Through Texas Politics* (Austin: Texas, Eakin Press, 1992).

Chapter 5

Political Parties

Learning Objectives

After reading this chapter, the student should be able to:

- ✪ Define a political party and the functions and benefits of political parties.
- ✪ Trace the development of political parties in Texas
- ✪ Understand the temporary organization and permanent organization of political parties in Texas
- ✪ Compare and contrast the significant differences and platforms of the Texas Democratic and Texas Republican parties
- ✪ Discuss typical characteristics of Democrats and Republicans in Texas
- ✪ Analyze the partisan characteristics currently seen in Texas and consider dealignment possibilities

Political Parties

In a democracy, the people select their government and influence its policies through their votes. Those same people differ greatly however, when deciding the direction that government should take on any given issue. When like-minded people join together to achieve common political goals, a political party results.

There are three elements that must be present in a political party. These are the following:

1. **Shared Beliefs.** The members should believe in the same general political philosophy and be willing to work for the same goals.
2. **Program.** The members should agree on a general program for translating their beliefs into law and policy once their candidates have been elected.
3. **Chance of Success.** The members should have a realistic chance of winning an election or gaining support for their programs, either now or in the future.

Functions of Political Parties

The most important function of a political party is to win elections in order to influence government decisions, laws, and public policy. However, political parties have other important functions.

1. **The Power Broker Function.** Political parties bring conflicting groups together. The modify and compromise the views of different interests and groups and help to unify the people. They soften the stance of extremists at both ends of the political spectrum.
2. **The Recruiter and Nominator Function.** Political parties recruit party leaders and choose candidates. Parties are the best device found thus far to do these jobs. The nominating function is almost exclusively a party function.
3. **The Stimulator-Information Function.** Political parties help inform people on the nature of political conflict. Parties stimulate the interest of voters and encourage participation in the political process and in public affairs. It is important to remember that the parties will inform the voter in a way that will be advantageous to their specific party. Parties use pamphlets, buttons, signs, newspaper ads, television ads, speeches, and conventions to inform and stimulate the voter.

Why The Donkey?

Why The Elephant?

Two unlikely animals-the donkey and the elephant have become the universally recognized symbols of the Democrat and Republican Parties. The great American political cartoonist of the nineteenth century, Thomas Nast, (1840-1902) is credited with these endearing and politically rallying "foes" representing America's two great parties.

The donkey made its debut as a politically symbol in the Presidential election of 1828 when Andrew Jackson's opponents labeled him a "jackass" for his populist views and slogans. Jackson turned this name calling to his advantage by adopting the donkey as his campaign motif. During his presidency, the donkey was often used to depict his stubbornness.

But it was not until 1870 that Nast showed a donkey in Harper's Weekly, kicking a dead lion-Edwin M. Stanton, a controversial Republican who had recently died. Nast did not intend the donkey to represent the Democratic Party, but a fraction of the party with which he disagreed. Nonetheless, the symbol captured the public's fancy and stuck.

The Republican elephant was "born" in another Nast cartoon. In 1874, the year after President Grant began his second term, the old New York Herald came out with an editorial raising the false cry of "Caesarism" against Grant for supposedly aspiring to be a dictator by seeking a third term.

In that same year, in yet another attempt to boost newspaper sales with sensational headlines, the New York Herald ran a story that was to become known as the Central Park Menagerie Scare of 1874. The story, though a hoax, was effective in its dramatic description of zoo animals escaping and searching for prey.

Nast exploited the coincidence of these two hoaxes to lampoon the Herald's editor, demagogic Democrats crying "Caesarism," and Republicans who were bending under the Democratic-inspired bad press surrounding Grant.

The cartoon shows an ass (Democrats), having put on a lion's skin (the Old New York Herald), roaming about in the forest, and amazing himself by frightening all the foolish animals (other newspapers, the public, etc.) he meets within his wanderings. One of the "foolish" animals was an elephant-intended as a criticism of the Republicans-grown weak and unwieldy.

Today, the donkey and the elephant have become the accepted symbols of America's Democrats and Republicans. As former United States Representative, Wright Patman observed, "Democrats consider the donkey a symbol of homely, down-to-earth appeal. Republicans look upon the elephant as standing for intelligence and impressive strength."

Source: Reprinted with permission of Taft Institute for Two Party Government, New York, New York.

4. **The Governmental Function.** Government in the United States and in Texas may be quite correctly described as government by party. Public officeholders, those who govern, are regularly chosen on the basis of party. Congress and the Texas Legislature are organized and conduct much of their business on a partisan basis. Most appointments to executive offices, both federal and

Texas, are made on a partisan basis as well. Committee chairs and presiding officers are typically decided with partisan considerations.

5. **The Watchdog Function.** Political parties act as a 'watchdog' over the conduct of the public's business. This is particularly the function of the party out of power. It plays this role as it criticizes the policies and behavior of the party in power. In effect, the out-of-power party attempts to convince the voters that they should "throw the bums out" and elect their candidates instead.

Benefits from Political Parties

The benefits that political parties provide include the following:

1. **Providing Labels.** Political parties provide assistance by giving the voter labels. Labels help the voter decide and give the voter information. Otherwise, most candidates are just names on a ballot.
2. **Simplifying Alternatives.** Political parties simplify the voter's alternatives which keeps the races from being confusing with great numbers of unidentified candidates running for each office.
3. **Assisting Candidates.** Political parties provide assistance to people who run for office. Otherwise, this would be limited to very wealthy candidates. Parties also provide training sessions for candidates and their campaign staffs, and sometimes even send candidates to organized classes to help them look and act the part of a candidate.
4. **Organizing Opposition.** Political parties help keep those in power honest and question the agenda of the other party by playing the role of organized opposition.

Development of Political Parties

Political parties are a relatively new invention. Parties did not exist in England before the American Revolution in a form that is recognizable today, even though politicians divided themselves into Whigs and Tories. George Washington warned against the development of political parties in his Farewell Address:

"Let me now . . . warn you in the most solemn manner against the baneful effects of the spirit of party generally. . . It serves to distract public councils and enfeebles the public administration. It agitates the community with ill-founded jealousies and false alarms. It kindles the animosity of one part against another."

The advice went unheeded. By the end of Washington's term of office in 1797, the United States had already established the pattern for a two party system. When Texas became a state in 1845, the two party system was well established nationally.

Figure 5-1. POLITICAL PARTY DEVELOPMENT IN TEXAS

1845	Texas joins Union: no strong parties in Texas.
1857	Democratic party gains control of Texas politics.
1861-1865 Civil War	Democratic party firmly established in Texas.
1865-1876 Reconstruction	Parties re-organizing; Republican governor elected.
1876-1961	Democratic one-party state. Occasional minor party challenge.
1961-1980	Republican party emerges and begins to challenge Democrats; Republicans experience some successes; Democrats still dominant party in Texas. Modified one party state.
1980-Present	Republicans becoming more and more successful. Two-party competition developing throughout the state.

Before Texas entered the Union, it had no organized political parties. Texas entered as a slave state. Nationally, the Republican party began to develop and was opposed to slavery. Democrats approved of slavery, so Texans had an inclination to lean toward the Democratic party.

By the Civil War (1861-1865), the Democratic Party had established itself and controlled Texas. After the Civil War, during Reconstruction (1865-1876), the Republican Party organized in Texas. The Reconstruction era saw the Republican Party control Texas government. The Reconstruction government was very unpopular with most Texans: taxes increased, the state police were very strict, and carpetbaggers had the opportunity to establish themselves.

Following Reconstruction, the Democratic Party strongly established itself as the one and only viable party in Texas. For example, from 1876 to 1978, all Texas governors were democrats. William P. Clements, a Republican elected in 1978, was the first Republican elected governor in 102 years. The last Republican governor had been Edmund J. Davis who was governor during Reconstruction. The Texas Legislature was overwhelmingly Democratic as well.

From Post-Reconstruction (1876) to the 1960's, Texas could be characterized as a one-party, Democratic state. The term 'yellow dog Democrat' fit the average Texan voter during this period. A 'yellow dog Democrat' is a person who is totally loyal to the Democratic Party; the saying goes that if the Democratic Party ran a yellow dog for elected office, this voter would still vote Democratic.

During that period, there were other minor parties that successfully ran candidates for office such as the Populist Party. While this party never captured the governor's position, it did impact Texas politics. In 1896 the Texas Populist Party joined the Texas Democratic Party, and the one-party status existed again.

One party systems are less competitive. Texas elections were typically decided in the Democratic primary because Democratic candidates were usually unopposed in the general election. The decision was made in the Democratic primary, where there may have been three or four candidates for the Democratic nomination, and the November general election was simply a required confirmation for the Democrat.

Without two-party competition, the Democratic party in Texas became less responsive to the needs of the people of Texas. By the 1960's Americans were split ticket voting (voting for candidates from different parties in an election) in general elections more than ever and this created an opening for the Republican Party in Texas.

In 1961, John Tower, a Republican, was elected to the U.S. Senate. He was the first Republican elected statewide in Texas since Reconstruction. Tower won election through a special nonpartisan election. The Texas Election Code specifies that in a special election all candidates from both parties run in one election. This election was held because Lyndon Johnson gave up his Senate seat to assume the vice-presidency in 1961. Tower won with the assistance from many Democrats in Texas. He served in the U.S. Senate until 1984. Current Senior Senator from Texas Phil Gramm, another Republican, was elected to succeed Tower.

The Republican Party continued to make very small gains in Texas politics over the next fifteen years.

Figure 5-2. CHART ON GROWTH OF REPUBLICAN OFFICE HOLDERS

The number of Republicans holding elective office in Texas has grown steadily.

	U.S. Senate	Other Statewide	U.S. Congress	Texas Senate	Texas House	County Offices	District Offices	State Board of Education	Total
1974	1	0	2	3	16	53	?		75+
1976	1	0	2	3	19	67	?		92+
1978	1	1	4	4	22	87	?		119+
1980	1	1	5	7	35	166	?		215+
1982	1	0	5	5	36	191	79		317
1984	1	0	10	6	52	377	90		446
1986	1	1	10	6	56	504	94		578
1988	1	5	8	8	57	608	123	5	692
1990	1	6	8	8	57	717	170	5	802
1992	1	8	9	13	58	814	183	5	911
1994	2	13	11	14	61	734	216	8	1059
1996	2	20	13	15	68	938	278	9	1343
1998	2	29	13	16	72	1098	280*	9	1372+

Source: Republican Party of Texas

Texas Political Parties Today

With the 1996 election, both Democrats concede and Republicans scream that Texas is now a two party state that either party can win. It is clear that any open seat in Texas can be won by either a Democrat or a Republican. This is a drastic change from Texas politics 20 years ago when the Democrat had the automatic advantage.

For the first time since Reconstruction, Texas has a Republican governor (George W. Bush), Lt. Governor (Rick Perry) and two Republican senators (Phil Gramm and Kay Bailey Hutchison). Every statewide office in Texas is now held by a Republican. There are a total of 29 statewide positions. Kay Bailey Hutchison's landslide defeats of the Democratic handpicked candidate Bob Krueger in 1993 and Richard Fisher in 1994 were two large blows to the Democratic dominance previously seen in Texas. Democrat John Sharp's 1998 loss to Rick Perry in the Lt. Governor's race was yet another blow to the Democratic Party in Texas. The Republican party is now a consistent major player, and most recently, the dominant player, in Texas politics. Texas is a naturally conservative state that does not like a great deal of change and the Republicans have done a better job of delivering the conservative line.

In 1998, a non-presidential election year (called an off-year election), 662,194 voters participated in the Democratic primary; 599,011 people voted in the Republican primary. While the pattern established in the 1996 primaries, when Republican voters outnumbered Democratic voters in the primary for the first time, Republicans continue to be competitive. While in the past, Texas was overwhelming Democratic, the primary voter numbers reflect the changing patterns of political parties in Texas.

Figure 5-3. Texas Primary Votes

Year	Race	Republican Primary Vote	Democrat Primary Vote	Republican as % of Democrats
1972	Governor	114,007	2,192,903	5.2
1974	Governor	69,101	1,521,306	4.5
1976	President	456,822	Caucus	n/a
1978	Governor	158,403	1,812,896	8.7
1980	President	526,769	1,377,354	38.2
1982	U.S. Senate	262,865	1,264,438	20.8
1984	U.S. Senate	336,814	1,463,449	23.0
1986	Governor	545,745	1,093,887	49.9
1988	President	1,018,147	1,759,958	57.9
1990	Governor	855,231	1,489,267	57.4
1992	President	792,444	1,480,415	53.5
1994	Governor	557,340	1,036,944	53.7
1996	President	1,019,797	923,244	110.5
1998	Governor	599,011	622,194	90

Source: Republican Party of Texas

In the near future, Texas Republicans will focus upon keeping their numbers up and continue to mobilize their voters. They would like to be the new majority party in Texas. Officials with the Republican Party see the 1998 elections as another sign that the Republican Party is becoming the dominant party in Texas. While the Democrats may have once taken for granted Texas voters, it is obvious they no longer can do that. Past Democratic strategies are not working and the Democratic Party finds itself in the position of playing "catch-up" to the Republicans in Texas. The Democratic Party in Texas is less organized than the well organized state Republican Party.

In the 1996 presidential election, Bob Dole carried the state of Texas, further reflecting the statewide strength of the Republican party seen in Texas today. The Democrats/Clinton carried most of far East Texas, Austin (Travis County), San Antonio (Bexar County), El Paso, and most of the Rio Grande/South Texas area. The Republicans/Dole however carried the heavily populated Dallas-Ft. Worth and Houston regions.

County-by-county vote, 1996 Presidential Race.

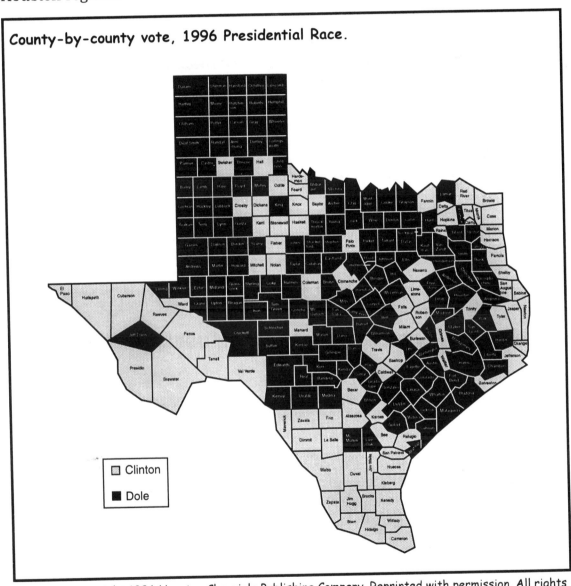

Party Structure

Both the Democratic and Republican parties in Texas are similar in structure. The Texas Election Code requires each party to have a temporary organization and a permanent organization.

Temporary Party Structure

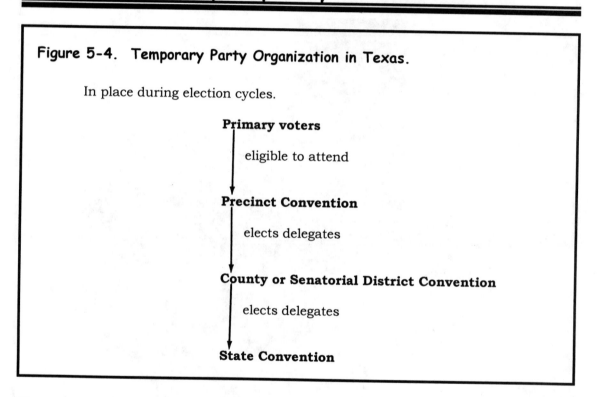

Figure 5-4. Temporary Party Organization in Texas.

In place during election cycles.

Primary voters

eligible to attend

Precinct Convention

elects delegates

County or Senatorial District Convention

elects delegates

State Convention

The temporary organization in Texas political parties consists of the conventions. The Democrats have a separate set of party conventions from the Republicans. The temporary party structure is only active during the election cycle (every two years).

Precinct Convention

The first level of the temporary organization is the precinct convention. Counties in Texas are divided into election precincts for conducting elections. The more people in a county, the more precincts it will have. The precinct convention is held the date of the primary, March of even numbered years. The polls are open and citizens vote from 7 a.m. to 7 p.m. At 7:30 p.m. the day of the primary, each party holds precinct conventions in the same locations as the precinct members vote.

Figure 5-5.

Precinct 515 Convention Agenda

March 12, 1996 - 7:30 p.m. - Brill Elementary School

The agenda which we are required to follow under rule #21 of the Republican Party of Texas is as follows:

a. Call to Order.
b. Preparation of List of Qualified Participants.
c. Announcement of agenda and basic rules of procedure.
d. Election of Permanent officers of the Convention (Chairman & Secretary) by Majority Vote.
e. Announcement of Senatorial District 7 Convention - Saturday, March 30, 1996 8:00 a.m. George R. Brown Convention Center.
f. Election of Delegates and Alternates to Senatorial District Convention by Majority Vote; Certification of Eligibility of each Delegate and Alternate by the Secretary.
g. Resolutions.
h. Other Business.
i. Adjourn.

This convention will be conducted in compliance with governing provisions of the Texas Election Code, the Rules of the Republican Party of Texas, and Robert's Rules of Order Newly Revised. Questions regarding optional procedures will be decided by General Consent or by Majority Vote of those present. (A "General Consent" is defined as informal agreement of those assembled; silence gives consent.)

NOTICE: Republican State Convention to be held June 20-22, 1995 1:00 p.m.; Alamodome, San Antonio, Texas.

Republican Party of Texas
211 East 7th Street, Suite 620
Austin, Texas 78701 (512)477-9821

Source: Sharry DeVore, Harris County Republican Precinct Official #515, Houston, Texas.

Any person who voted in the primary is eligible to participate in the precinct convention. The precinct convention is used to choose delegates to the next level party convention, the county/senatorial district convention. At the precinct convention, resolutions can also be considered. Typically, the precinct conventions are sparsely attended, however recently in the Republican Party, ideological battles between the moderates and the evangelical Christian members of the party have resulted in over 100 people attending some precinct conventions. By having their supporters elected delegates to the next level convention, a group can accumulate power and influence the direction of the political party at the subsequent party conventions.

The following two articles describe what happened at a Republican Precinct Meeting and a Democratic Precinct Meeting. These meetings were held March 12, 1996.

Political Parties

Figure 5-6. Republican Precinct Meeting Article

Precinct 436:
A battlefield in miniature

Andrew Maller is a civil engineer with good intentions. After voting Tuesday in the Republican primary, he decided to go to his precinct convention, part of his resolution to get more involved in civic affairs.

When it was all over, Maller looked like he'd spent two hours in a sausage factory.

"This is the first time I've been to a convention, and I was shocked by the division I've seen," he said.

As it has been for the last dozen years, Precinct 436 was a battlefield in miniature. Its convention, held in the cafeteria of Grady Elementary School in the heart of Republican west Houston, reflected the schisms within the party and the culture beyond it.

This time the conflict started early, with election judge Senya Lemus and Christian activist Doug Elliott engaging in a shoving match as soon as the polls closed. Lemus wanted time to get the voting business finished and the convention organized. Elliott, convinced his longtime foe was rigging the convention rules against him in his absence, tried to force his way into the cafeteria.

"You're acting like a child," Lemus said as she tried to push Elliott out the door.

"You are excluding me from the process," Elliott snapped back.

Lemus called police. By the time they arrived, however, Lemus was going about her chores and Elliott was quietly marshaling his forces in the hallway. The cops, perplexed and slightly peeved, left quickly.

Welcome the Grass Roots 101, where social issues and power politics become entangled with a vague understanding of Robert's Rules of Order and a momentary sense of importance. The result on this night was a clumsy, tedious, predictable and altogether American display of democracy in action.

"Our point of view has been excluded," said Elliott, 34, a patent lawyer who was spearheading the Nehemiah Project in Precinct 436. "Their goal, and they have expressed this in the past, is to change the Republican Party platform."

The idea behind the Nehemiah Project is to get Christians more active in government. Second Baptist Church is behind the project, and Elliott had plenty of company on the right side of the aisle.

The battle was for 23 delegates to the senatorial district convention. If Elliott and his allies could get a majority, they could send the delegates they want to the convention, and a far more conservative batch it would be than usual.

Sondra Epstein had seen the challenge before. In the Republican Party, she counts as a liberal, and though she holds little sway over the party in general, she's steered her precinct convention away from the grasp of people who she claims see no separation between church and state.

"It's going to be close tonight," Epstein said as the convention started.

For two hours they haggled over motions and substitute motions, but the issue really was decided early, with a telling vote for convention chair. Each side proposed a candidate. Elliott lost 28-20.

That assured selecting Epstein's proposed slate of candidates. But it did not stop a lengthy debate over alternates or prevent the inevitable discussion of abortion. A resolution offered by Epstein's side asked that the anti-abortion plank in the party platform be removed.

In short order the rhetoric took a predictable course. There was talk of the founding fathers' religious attitudes and the proper role of government. An anti-abortion speaker asked his opponents to look into their hearts and be saved. Jews on the other side squirmed. Each faction accused the other of ruining the party.

The resolution passed, a small victory for Epstein, given it has no chance of making an impact at the larger convention. For that matter, neither does her slate of delegates.

"I am tired of trying to save this party," Epstein sighed. "We're going to lose big time at the senatorial convention. But I think it does make a difference."

So does Elliott, who will be back in two years to try to claim his precinct.

As for Maller, who wanted to be a delegate but found himself shut out before the voting even started, he vows to return, sadder but wiser.

"Hardball is sure what they were playing tonight," he said.

Figure 5-7. Democratic Precinct Meeting Article

Democratic caucus action light, lively

Ronni Greenwood took one look at Bruce Johnson's University of Oklahoma cap and joked, "You're a Democrat even though you went to OU?"

It was mostly fun and games Tuesday night for the 35 Democrats of Precinct 60 who gathered at their polling place at Lanier Junior High School to begin the process of selecting delegates to the Democratic National Convention.

With President Clinton assured of renomination, the gathering lacked the drama of four years ago, when his supporters fought it out with backers of Jerry Brown and Paul Tsongas for the right to go to the state and national conventions.

But for "first-timers" like Greenwood, a crisis counselor for the Mental Health and Mental Retardation Association, and Johnson, an attorney, attending the caucus was an opportunity to see democracy in action.

"We're trying to figure out what it is all about," said Johnson, who attended with his wife, McNair Johnson, after they learned about the caucus from a poll worker earlier in the day. "We came in late, so what we've figured out so far is things move very quickly."

Indeed, within 20 minutes of the polls' closing, caucus voters met and selected delegates to attend the Senatorial District Convention, to be held at the Jury Assembly Center in downtown Houston on March 30, and adjourned.

They also unanimously passed four resolutions, seeking the repeal of the Texas concealed weapons law and

calling for reduced military spending, restricting international trafficking of weapons, and encouraging entrepreneurship.

The resolutions will be considered at the district convention and could be part of a state and national platform.

All across Houston, the action was much the same as Democrats gathered to select their delegates.

In the library at Pleasantville Elementary School, residents were getting down to business quickly.

By 7:26 p.m., the Democrats of Precinct 259 in Pleasantville had elected their chair-woman—Brenda Phillips—and were selecting names for their 64 delegates to take to the district conference.

"The ultimate goal is getting to the national convention. You get people you want to vote for who will be willing to bring your issues forward," said Deborah Gardner, on the voters at the precinct convention.

The residents in this room ranged from 36 years old to well into their 60's. They were retirees, professionals and blue-collar workers.

They also considered resolutions to be forwarded to the senatorial district level.

The main resolution for these residents related to the storage of hazardous chemicals in residential areas. After their scare last year they wanted to give neighborhoods some assurances that residents wouldn't continue to be put in danger.

Houston City Councilman Michael Yarbrough was among

the voters in this precinct convention.

"Generally they (residents) are kept in the dark and generally it's in the minority communities. We would like to be part of a national agenda. We want to be heard," he said.

Meanwhile, at Lanier Junior High, Lee and Hardy Loe, who have been coming to the precinct meetings since 1967, have seen the Montrose precinct shift over the years from conservative to liberal.

"The conservatives used to snicker behind our backs," says Lee Loe, editor of Houston Peace News. "But it was a way for anti-war people to get to know each other."

Everyone who attended the caucus will have the opportunity to attend the Senatorial District Convention, since the precinct may send 33 delegates and 33 alternates to the convention.

While turnout was low, Sue Lovell, who was elected the party precinct chairman, believes it is a good way to start the selection process.

"If nothing else, you get to visit with your neighbors," she says.

For, "first timer," Greenwood who provided the caucus as an opportunity to get involved at the Montrose precinct.

"I (complain) all the time about politics," says Greenwood. "So I want to come and see if I can do something about it.

County Convention/Senatorial District Convention

The next level convention is the county convention or senatorial district convention. Some counties make up only a portion of a state senator's district; those counties hold county conventions. The more populous counties, such as Harris, Dallas, Tarrant, and Bexar have more than one state senator representing different parts of the county. In the populous counties, the next level meeting is based on state senatorial district lines.

The county or senatorial district convention is held toward the end of March. Delegates elected at the precinct convention participate in choosing delegates to the next level convention, the state convention. Resolutions are also considered.

State Convention

Each political party holds its state convention in June of even-numbered years. The state convention is used by each party to do these things:

1. Certify to the secretary of state the names of party members nominated in the party's primary to run in the general election.

This is normally a formality with little controversy.

2. Adopt the party's platform outlining goals and ideas the party wishes to pursue if their candidates are elected. The writing of the platform has frequently been the place where major internal ideological battles are waged. These platforms are the documents reflecting future party stances on issues, however certain candidates may try to avoid the platform if it takes an extreme position on an issue. Republicans have struggled in recent years over whether the party should continue to address the issue of abortion.
3. Selecting members of the party's state executive committee, which is part of the permanent organization to be discussed later.

Executive committee members have influence on the state party organization and focus of the state party.

In a presidential election year, 1996 for example, the state convention is used to complete these tasks as well:

1. Elect some members from the state convention delegation to serve as national delegates at the party's national convention. The national conventions are held later that year. The total number of national delegates a state has is determined by the national party organization. For example in 1996, Texas had 229 national delegates to the Democratic National Convention. There were a total of 4320 national delegates to that convention. Texas had 123

national delegates to the Republican National Convention. There were a total of 1990 Republican National delegates.(Source: Republican Party of Texas and Democratic Party of Texas)

2. Elect national committee members to serve in the national party's organization.

3. Elect a slate of electors to cast the state's electoral votes, if their party's presidential nominee wins a plurality (largest number) of the vote.

Permanent Party Organization

Between election cycles, the permanent party organization keeps the party focused on its goals, promotes the party, and plans for future elections. Each party has its own permanent organization. In Texas, the precinct chairs, county, district, and state executive committees make up the permanent party organization of each party. Some precincts do not have chairs; this is common in areas that traditionally vote strongly in favor of one party.

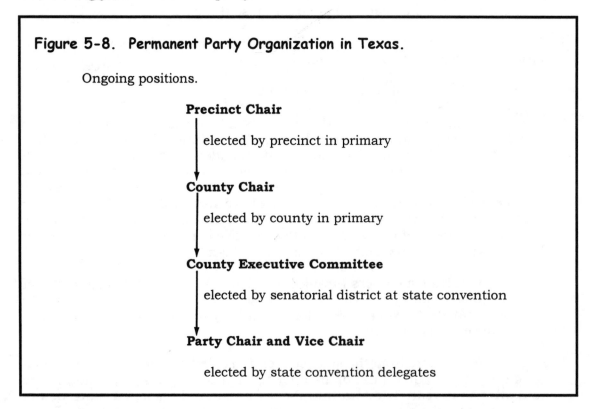

Figure 5-8. Permanent Party Organization in Texas.

Ongoing positions.

Precinct Chair

elected by precinct in primary

County Chair

elected by county in primary

County Executive Committee

elected by senatorial district at state convention

Party Chair and Vice Chair

elected by state convention delegates

Precinct Chair

The precinct chair is the permanent officer of the committee. The precinct chair is elected from each party in the primary for a two year term. The precinct chair administers the primary election and organizes precinct conventions. Additionally, the chair will try to increase voter turnout, raises funds, recruits candidates, and serves on the county executive committee. There are over 1200 precincts in Harris County (Houston).

County Executive Committee and County Chair

The county executive committee is made up of all precinct chairs and the county chair. This committee works to promote the party, increase voter turnout, and raise funds for the party. The committee receives filing petitions and fees from primary election candidate's in county elections. The county chair serves as one of the leading spokespersons for the party. The county chair also reviews candidates for office, chairs the Executive Committee, and raises money to support local party operations.

The county chair for each party is elected every two years in the party primary. The county chair is the key party official of the county and is well informed on party affairs.

State Executive Committee

The state executive committees (SREC-State Republican Executive Committee and SDEC-State Democratic Executive Committee) is made up of one man and one woman from each of Texas' thirty-one state senatorial districts, a chair of the state party, and a vice-chair of the state party. The party chair and vice chair must be of the opposite sex. The executive committee is the highest permanent party organization of the state. The committees develop state party strategies, arrange state party conventions, raise funds for the party, work with the national party organization, unify the state party, and generally promote the party.

The state chairs and vice chairs preside over executive committee meetings and serve as chief spokespersons for the parties. The sixty-two committee members, the chairs, and vice chairs are elected at the state conventions.

Party Platforms

A platform is the written declaration of the principles and policy positions of a political party and its candidates for office, drafted at that party's convention.

Democrats	Republicans

School Curriculum

Favor bilingual education equal access to quality library materials and to computer networks, smaller class sizes and an emphasis on science and math.

Oppose bilingual education. Believe "the educational system should return to the basic standards. . . a curriculum of reading with an emphasis on phonics, mathematics, geography, history, science, English, citizenship and constitutional government and should provide a return to traditional moral values in a disciplined environment."

Civil Rights and Homosexuality

Oppose discrimination on the basis of "race, sex, sexual orientation, ethic or national origin, disability, economic status, color, creed, age, or other difference."

The practice of sodomy leads to the breakdown of the family unit. . . Homosexuality should not be presented as an acceptable alternative lifestyle in public schools. No person should receive special legal entitlements or privileges based on sexual preference. We oppose marriages between persons of the same sex and homosexuals obtaining the right to adopt or obtaining child custody."

Workers

Support collective bargaining and oppose employer attempts to hire replacement workers for striking employees. Favor extending the minimum wage and unemployment compensation to farm workers.

Favor abolishing the minimum wage, support Texas' right-to-work laws and oppose mandating Worker's Compensation coverage for all employers.

Guns

Support a "ban on assault weapons that have no legitimate hunting purpose" and support a penalty for anyone who sells or gives a gun to a minor.

Support "legislation permitting law abiding, mentally competent adult citizens to carry firearms for their protection." Want prosecutions of persons who illegally supply minors with weapons.

Crime

Favor a comprehensive approach to crime, including prevention programs, adequate police staffing, "tough but fair justice and meaningful punishment," rehabilitation and remedial education of offenders.

Favor a prison system of protecting society first, punishment second, and rehabilitation third. Favor the death penalty for persons who sell illegal drugs to minors.

Democrats	Republicans
Family	
Support full reproductive rights and full access to choice (abortion) and family planning services and information for all citizens. Backs programs aimed at reducing unwanted pregnancies, especially by teenagers, and endorses age-appropriate self-responsibility education in health and responsible family life, including prevention of AIDS and sexually transmitted diseases. Supports universal healthcare. Safe, adequate, and affordable child care should be available, and workers should be allowed family leave. Domestic violence should be recognized as a threat to the value of the family unit.	Support a constitutional amendment to prohibit abortion in all cases except to save the mother's life. No-fault divorces should be restricted. Parental rights should not be restricted in rearing, disciplining, or educating children or in their medical or surgical treatment. Opposes euthanasia, assisted suicide, and withholding food or water to the terminally ill or handicapped.

The political parties platforms address a variety of issue including school finance, workers' rights, hunger, immigration, abortion, parental responsibilities, and condoms. The Republican platform is much more conservative than the Democratic platform.

Complete copies of the state platform can be obtained from the county party headquarters throughout the state.

Membership in Political Parties in Texas

Membership in either party is purely voluntary. A person is a Republican or a Democrat — or belongs to a minor party or is an independent — simply because that is what he or she chooses to be. In some states a person must declare a preference for a particular party in order to vote in that party's primary election. That declaration is usually made as a part of the voter registration process, and it is often said to make one "a registered Republican (or Democrat)." Texas does not require a person to declare a preference before participating in a primary election. In Texas, there is no such thing as a "registered Republican" or "registered Democrat," even though people in Texas may incorrectly label themselves as such.

The two major parties are very broadly based. That is, they are multi-class in nature. The parties try to attract as much support from as many individuals and as many groups as they possibly can. Remember, the main goal of a party is to have its members elected and the parties attempt to please the largest number of people.

Each party has always been composed of a variety of types of people. There are both Democrats and Republicans that are Protestant, Catholic, Jew; white, black, Hispanic; professional, farmers, union members; old persons young persons; urban, suburban, and rural dwellers.

Members of certain segments of the voters may tend to align themselves more with one or the other of the major parties. Currently blacks, labor union members, and females tend to associate with the Democratic Party in larger numbers. White males, evangelical Protestants, and business owners tend to associate with the Republican Party.

Recently, the gender gap has been an issue closely watched by both parties. Women appear to be aligning in larger numbers with the Democratic Party than in the past. This can be partially attributed to many women's concerns about their families, their pocketbooks, and the nation's social safety net. This translated in the 1996 presidential election into the largest gender gap ever. The gap totaled 17 points nationally. Even in Texas, where President Clinton was not overwhelmingly favored, there appeared a 17 point gender gap.

Gender Vote in Texas in 1996 Presidential Election

	Clinton	Dole	Difference
Men	39%	53%	14% advantage to Dole
Women	48%	45%	3% advantage to Clinton

(**Source**: Houston Chronicle)

Leslie Wolfe, president of the Center for Women Policy Studies said this gender gap was ". . . dramatic, and it was less Clinton versus Dole than it was the Democratic Party versus the Republican Party." (source: Houston Chronicle) Even in states with Republican strongholds, the gender gap was measurable. This is an issue that the Republican Party will be examining in the future. Women continue to vote in larger numbers than men and this is not a voting faction that the Republican Party can afford to alienate if it intends to continue to grow in strength in Texas and in other parts of the United States.

The Republican Party has historically vastly underestimated Hispanics in Texas. Governor Bush's 1998 reelection slogan and focus on "Juntos Podemos" (Together We Can) reflects his knowledge and understanding that Hispanics are potentially a very important voting group. Certainly, he and the Republican Party plan to do what they can to appeal to Hispanics. Historically, Hispanics have not participated in politics in large numbers and when they have, they have identified more with the Democratic Party, both in Texas and nationally.

Figure 5-9. The Scripps Howard Texas Poll

Total Adults Questioned	1,001 Number	% of total	N=331 % Republican	N=326 % Democrat
Sex:				
Male	480	48	50	42
Female	521	52	50	58
Registered to Vote:				
Yes	847	85	91	87
No	150	15	9	12
Intention to vote in Spring Election:				
Very Likely	635	63	69	65
Somewhat Likely	127	13	11	15
Not very likely	73	7	7	5
Not at all likely	144	14	11	12
Not sure	22	2	2	3
Political affiliation:				
Republican	331	33	100	
Democrat	326	33		100
Independent	234	23		
Other	75	8		
Not Sure	34	3		
Length of residence in Texas:				
One year or less	25	3	4	2
2-10 years	112	9	10	3
11-less than "all my life"	337	35	35	34
All my life	527	53	51	61

Methodology: The Winter 1999 Texas Poll©, was conducted January 21-February 5, 1999 by the Scripps Howard Texas Poll. 1,001 adult Texans were surveyed by telephone in a systematic random sample of active telephone exchanges statewide. Margin of error for whole sample, ± 3 percentage points; slightly larger for subgroups. Responses are given in percentages, rounded to the nearest whole number.

Reprinted with permission.

Party Identification and Dealignment

The party that an individual identifies with is called his party identification. A person may psychologically feel attached to the Republican Party, the Democratic Party, a minor party, or be an independent (not psychologically attached to any party).

People identify with certain parties for a variety of reasons. Family is a very important determiner. A person is likely to politically identify with the party affiliation of the parents. Education, socio-economic status, religion, race, age, work environment, and gender can also be factors that influence one's party identification. Since there are exceptions to any generalization, it can be risky any time they are used to predict voter allegiance.

The term realignment is used to describe a situation when voters abandon their current psychological attachment to a political party and develop a new psychological attachment to another party. A realignment is a durable, sustained change, and not simply a one-time shift to the other party. A temporary shift is called a deviation.

What appears to be occurring now is a dealignment. A dealignment is when voters abandon the psychological attachments they have with a particular political party but fail to develop new psychological attachments to other parties. This can be seen in the United States and in Texas with the increase of split-ticket voting. The number of people who identify themselves as independent is large and growing. This can especially be seen with younger voters.

In Texas, the Republican Party has gotten stronger and as party competition in Texas continues, both parties will likely encounter voters who are unwilling to make a strong, long-term commitment to any political party.

Over time, most Texans have had mixed feelings about political parties. Most people see political parties as necessary institutions, but there has been decline since the late 1960's in the attachment voters have with specific political parties.

Independent, split-ticket voters have increased. People in Texas identifying with the Republican Party have increased. Those psychologically attached to the Democratic Party have decreased. Reforms that were designed throughout this century to end party corruption have resulted in more open parties. Television has become a forum for candidate-oriented campaigns rather than political party driven campaigns.

It is clear however that political parties remain entrenched in American society and government. The present day party system has existed longer than other parties anywhere in the world. While political parties may be in a bit of turmoil and appear to be going through changes, they still perform a number of necessary functions.

The Democrats have their work cut out for them in a state they once took for granted. Republicans will try to focus on sustaining gains they have made, increasing their numbers, and mobilizing their supporters to attempt to attain true majority-party status in Texas.

On-line: Political Parties

Note: There are hundreds of Web sites dedicated to political parties. The following are several of the better all-purpose sites for state party organizations.

Political Parties List

http://www.lib.umich.edu/libhome/Documents.center/psusp.html#party

Master List of Political Parties

http://dir.yahoo.com/Government/Politics/Parties/By_Country_or_Region/

Texas Democratic Party (Links to County Chapters)

http://www.txdemocrats.org/

Republican Party of Texas

http://www.texasgop.org/

Texas Reform Party

http://www.realtime.net/~jmonaco/

Libertarian Party of Texas

http://www.tx.lp.org/

Chapter 6

Campaigns and Elections

Learning Objectives:

After reading this chapter, the student should be able to:

- ✪ Review the 1996 and 1998 election returns and how they relate to Texas
- ✪ Describe the problems of judicial elections
- ✪ Describe the historical evolution of Texas election law
- ✪ Describe the conflict between majority rule and minority rights
- ✪ Describe the special interest election law using the LBJ law as an example
- ✪ Explain the major problems associated with running a campaign in Texas
- ✪ Explain the failure of third parties in Texas

1996 Election Review

Nationwide, the general election returns of 1996 were such a mixed bag that almost any explanation sounds reasonable. The Republicans, while losing seats in the House retained a House majority and actually increased their numbers in the Senate. The Democrats maintained the Presidency, increased their numbers in the House, and lost ground in the Senate. The most rational explanation seems to be that the voting public was buying into a new form of checks and balances and aiming towards a centrist position rather than going for extremist positions.

The 1998 election returns were similar to the 1996 ones; except that the Republican "anti-Clinton" message seemed to back fire more than it helped. The Democrats held their own in the national Senate and picked up House seats.

It is quite clear that the 1996 and 1998 elections indicate a voter dissatisfaction with the Democrats in Texas. However, in one sense in Texas, the more things change the more things remain the same. The majority of Texas voters (not necessarily the majority of Texans!) have traditionally been more conservative than in many other states. From Reconstruction until the 1980's the Texas political scene (with a few notable exceptions) had been dominated by conservative Democrats, with governors, senators, national House members, the state legislature, and local officials all having claimed this allegiance.

Once the Republican party regained respectability in Texas more and more Texans switched allegiance. The process has been gradual because of the vested interest in Democratic seniority. In a few parts of the state the switch has yet to take place. For example, the 1999 session of the Texas legislature has 78 Democrats and 72 Republicans in the House and the Republicans have actually taken a majority of the seats in the Senate. There is considerable debate over if or when the Texas legislature will organize along partisan lines as is done at the national level. A large number of the rural members are conservative Democrats.. When they join forces with the Republicans, conservatives are clearly in a majority. Party alignment would probably benefit the Republicans but it might not be as well for conservatism. The 1999 legislation session was organized primarily in a non-partisan manner, so the questioned change hasn't taken place.

Not too surprising is that there is a significant gender gap even in Texas. Where the Democrats have lost ground in Texas is among male (especially white) voters. At the national level women voted for Clinton over Dole by a 54% to 38% margin. Men voted for Dole over Clinton by a 44% to 43% margin (this is considered a 17 point gender gap). In Texas women voted for Clinton over Dole by a 48% to 45% margin. Texas men voted for Dole over Clinton by a 53% to 39% margin (also a 17 point gender gap). According to Irene Navidad, Chairwoman of the Women's Vote Project '96, "Even in this Republican stronghold [Texas], the gender gap was measurable".[1]

With the easy 1998 re-election of Governor Bush and the Republican sweep of all statewide elections in Texas, it is clear that the Republican party dominates statewide elections in Texas. The two national Senators and a majority of the state Senate are Republicans. At the same time a majority of the Texas Congressional delegation and a majority of the Texas House members are Democrats. Seniority seems to have saved a number of conservative Democrats.

Obviously a majority of Texas voters tend to vote conservative. While this is good news to Republicans there are several factors that tend to complicate matters: 1) A majority of non-voting Texans seem likely to favor the Democrats. Any scenario that would activate this group would benefit the Democrats. 2) All demographics point to Hispanics as being the fastest growing ethnic group in the state. This group traditionally favors Democrats. Many Republicans, led by their aggressive efforts of Governor Bush, are making direct appeals to the Hispanic voter.

The recent election returns appear to indicate that Texas has reached a political point of no return. In Texas, as in the rest of the country, major philosophical differences will tend to be fought out in the general elections rather than in the primaries. If a majority of Texans who vote continue to vote conservative, then we have witnessed the change from a predominately Democratic to a predominately Republican State.

Judicial Elections

About once every decade, in recent years, the judicial election returns yield surprising winners. There are several reasons for this phenomena. First, the average voter knows very little about judicial candidates, and second, all judicial candidates run as partisans, i.e. you must have either the Republican or Democratic nomination to win in November. In a Democratic year, such as 1982, good incumbent Republican judges are defeated by some very questionable Democratic candidates. In a Republican year, such as 1994, good incumbent Democratic judges are defeated by some questionable Republican candidates.

Of course this happens in many other races when you have a party sweep; however we like to think that the judiciary, to some extent, is above partisan politics. There seems to be some philosophical differences between Democratic and Republican platforms; nevertheless most knowledgeable observers think that this difference should not be reflected in judicial matters. Although there is some sentiment to emulate the federal system of lifetime appointments, most Texans oppose such a system. A bipartisan study group prepared a list of options to Lieutenant Governor Bob Bullock for the 1995 legislative session. One of the reform proposals passed the Senate but died in the House.

The Texas Commission on Judicial Efficiency went back to the drawing board and finalized in December of 1996 their recommendations for the 1997 session of the Legislature. Although several alternatives were presented, all the proposals had at least one thing in common: nonpartisan elections.

"Together these proposals offer solutions to the problems of a politicized judiciary and concerns about qualifications and diversity among the judiciary" said Tom Luce, chairman of the Judicial Selection Task Force, a panel of 42 judges and legislators that presented the proposals to the Commission. Among the problems with the current election system, the commission said, is a lack of racial diversity and the perception of partisanship. Again, as in 1995, the 1997 session saw all proposals die in the Legislature. While the issue has been addressed in the 1999 session, as of the writing of this chapter, chances of any substantive change seem minimal.[2]

Both the Governor and political parties have a vested interest in the current system; therefore it will be difficult (as we have seen in the past) to legislate any real change.

Voting under Texas Election Law

The existence of election laws is to insure an orderly method for citizens to vote. Such laws should also protect against fraud and be structured so that all citizens have equal opportunity and access to a secret ballot. The laws should also provide protection against any form of intimidation during the entire process. 1999 Texas election law probably does a pretty good job of meeting such criteria. However, that certainly has not been the case in the past.

From the early 1900's until the 1970's, Texas election law was clearly structured to discriminate against the poor, African-Americans, and Hispanics. These so called "Jim Crow" type laws included the poll tax, early and limited voter registration, literacy tests, the white primary, the grandfather clause, and other restrictions designed to exclude, or at the very least minimize, minority participation in the selection of public officials.

From an historical perspective the white primary has been of particular interest to Texans. The laws in most southern states allowed "whites only" to participate in Democratic primaries (the Republican party in the South at this time was moribund). When the United States Supreme Court finally decided that such state laws were unconstitutional, the Democratic party simply adopted the previous state restrictions as part of their party rule.

A series of legal challenges going all the way to the Supreme Court resulted in a piecemeal dismantling of the white primary. The majority of these cases originated in Texas, starting with *Nixon v Herndon* in 1927. The major case was *Smith v Allwright* in 1944; although it took one more case, *Terry v Adams* in 1952, to nail the coffin shut on the white primary.[3]

Over the years a combination of federal legislation and federal court decisions have knocked down these Jim Crow restrictions one by one.

Initially the previously disenfranchised turned out and voted in substantial numbers that resulted in some rather dramatic changes in the public sector. However, the more recent elections have resulted in a lower percentage of voter turnout among minorities. There is considerable debate as to the reason or meaning to this lack of participation. In any event, it is clear that the so called "angry white male" has been a dominant voting factor in the elections of the 1990's.

The national system calls for elections for national office (Senate, House, and Presidency) to be held on a two year cycle, the election being held in even numbered years (1998, 2000, etc.). In Texas state and county office elections are handled in the same manner at the same time.

The mechanics in all of these elections include partisan primaries with the various party winners facing each other in the November general elections. Texas law also requires a majority vote to win the party primary. As a result the party holds a number of run off elections among the top two candidates when no one candidate in the primary gets a majority.

On the other hand, elections for most local offices are held in the odd numbered years. Voting for school board, city council, etc. at a different time make it less confusing to the voter. However, it makes for overlapping terms for elected officials. This is of particular interest to ambitious officials. Even though the law has been tightened up, in many cases a candidate can run for another office while retaining the office they already hold. If they lose the race they still maintain the current office.

As you saw in chapter 2, the Texas Constitution, in reflecting the desires of post-Reconstruction Texas voters, is quite restrictive. As a result local government in attempting to deal with new or recurring problems often does not have appropriate authority. In order to be certain of their authority they go to the legislature. A law is passed giving the local government authority to deal with that specific problem. This is frequently done by the creation of a special district. As a result there are a number of special districts throughout the state. Many of the districts call for a separate set of office holders and usually call for periodic elections. Often the home owner finds that this special district (utility district, for example) has more impact on their life style than any other level of government.

In regard to voting in the future it will be interesting to see what happens. The technology now exists whereby the citizen could cast a vote at home and have it electronically submitted to election central. There is no push at the present time to move to such a system (possible fraud is one problem cited); however there is the possibility of a real dollar savings and it may be only a matter of time.

Election Districts

James Madison, although a strong proponent of the American constitutional system, was quite outspoken in his warnings. Many of our so called checks and balances try to guard us against what he refers to as factions. One faction would be what we refer to as special interest groups, i.e. a small faction pushing their own program that might not be good for the citizenry at large. He also warns us against the emotional excesses of the mob, i.e. majority tyranny. There is a fine line between majority rule and discrimination against minorities. In the context of this discussion minority simply means whichever group has less votes than the majority. That means that all of us at some time find ourselves in the minority.

Democracy must have more guidelines than just majority rule. The concept of majority rule is very important and must be a significant ingredient in our system. However, if the majority always prevailed it would be unacceptable. A lynch mob is an example of a society based solely on majority rule. You have a small and insignificant minority of one and everyone else is saying "String him up!". What could be more majoritarian?

Much of the history of election laws has seen this conflict between majority rule and minority rights played out on the floor of the legislature and in the court rooms of the judiciary. Gerrymandering (that is the drawing of political boundaries to benefit partisan groups) is probably present in every redistricting effort. However, for the first hundred years or so it was not a major problem in the United States. We had a fairly stable, rural population. Growth was accommodated by people moving west and/or increasing the number of elected officials.

As immigration increased, we filled out the continent. Industrialization quickened and urbanization began to take hold. The wards in the cities became noted for their graft and corruption. As ward bosses learned to abuse the system, the reformers of the early 20th century Progressive movement looked to multi-member (at large) districts to break the power hold of the ward bosses. As frequently happens, the reforms brought a new set of problems. Minorities within these larger districts were effectively cut out of significant input or representation. If the new larger districts contained 20% of such minorities (Irish, Asian, Hispanic, Black, etc.) and 80% majority then it was virtually impossible to elect a minority who was a real spokesperson rather than just a token allowed by the majority.

In addition, the rural domination in the state legislatures ensured that any state drawn redistricting would minimize urban gains and maintain rural domination. This dual discrimination exercised against urban minorities continued in Texas until a series of United States Supreme Court cases in the 1960's and 1970's.

At the same time that the rural legislatures were squeezing the urban areas on numbers they were also drawing up single member districts for rural areas and multi member districts for urban areas. This had the effect of maximizing the

Campaigns and Elections

urban "establishment" and minimizing minorities in the urban areas. The courts forced the Texas legislature to base districts on population thus giving the urban areas more representation. At the same time the courts have classified multi member districts as a "suspect" classification. This means that they are not outlawed but there must be proof that they do not discriminate. As a result of the court actions minorities now have a much greater impact in the electoral process than previously.

A current controversy concerns the legality of redistricting to actually create districts in which a minority group is dominant. In several judicial cases (notably *Bush v Vera*, 1996) the United States Supreme Court has made it clear that redistricting to "...segregate the races for purposes of voting, without regard for traditional districting principles...is unconstitutional". They go on to point out that redistricting that involves consideration of race is constitutional as long as other factors are also considered.[4]

This case lead to the reconfiguration of a number of Texas congressional districts after the 1996 party primaries and run offs. As a result we had "open" races during the November general elections with any necessary run offs being held in December. In most instances Democrats and Republicans filed. In some cases primary winners faced their defeated opponents and opposition party candidates. Altogether some thirteen Texas congressional races were impacted by this ruling. In three congressional districts there was a December 10th run off.

When the November voting was over there were a number of criticisms as to the results of this court ruling. For example, in Harris county (where there were the largest number of court ordered changes) 18% of those who cast votes had no valid vote in the congressional elections. That would be an average drop off from the top of the ballot to the bottom of the ballot. However, the congressional races were at the top of the ballot. That is the voter had to go past the congressional race to get to the presidential race! In the three run off districts there were over 29, 000 ballots voided because a vote was cast for more than one congressional candidate and almost 132, 000 more ballots registered no vote for any congressional candidate. Fortunately the 1998 election cycle was conducted within the normal electoral process.[5]

In any event, it is quite clear that since the 1960's the federal and state courts have been quite willing to hear challenges to redistricting and in many instances have voided such proposals.

The LBJ Law

Texas has had more than its share of attempts to tailor election law for specific purposes. One example has been the notorious "Jim Crow" laws prominent in the early 1900's, that we discussed earlier. Probably one of the most successful special interest election laws is the so called LBJ law. Although subject to considerable criticism it clearly has achieved its intended purpose.

In the late 1950's Lyndon Johnson was the Senate Majority Leader and he had designs on the presidency. It was recognized that he would be a major contender for the 1960 Democratic nomination. Unfortunately his senate term expired at the same time. Under existing Texas law he could not be on the ballot for re-election to the senate and at the same time be on the ballot for the presidency. Using the argument that it would be good for Texas to have a Texan for President but bad for Texas if they lost the majority leader and failed to get the presidency, the law was changed. Johnson supporters convinced the 1959 session of the Texas legislature to amend the state election code. The amendment adopted allowed a candidate for president or vice president to also be on the ballot for another office. Although Johnson had to settle for the vice presidential nomination, the new law enabled him, at the same time, to be reelected to the Senate.

As an aside: the odds of Johnson receiving the presidential nomination or failing that to accept the vice presidential nomination and having to give up his senate seat were quite long. As a result the only Republican to file against Johnson for the senate seat was a little known Midwestern University professor named John Tower. Tower subsequently won the special election to secede Johnson and had a rather distinguished career of his own.

Except for the fact that the Democrats lost the seat, the bill worked the way it was designed. Johnson went to the White House; if he had lost he still would have been the Senate Majority Leader. In 1988 Lloyd Bentsen was able to use the same provision of the law to run for reelection to the senate and as the vice presidential candidate under Dukakis. They lost the presidential race but Bentsen was reelected to the Senate.

Phil Gramm made it clear that he planned to follow the same path. He intended to run for President in 1996 and that was the same year that his senate term expired. He did not know whether he would be on the Republican national ticket until long after the filing deadline for Texas office. Therefore he filed for reelection to the Senate while at the same time pursuing the Republican presidential nomination. His presidential hopes cratered early enough for him to concentrate on his successful senate reelection campaign.

A similar attempt at legislation designed to aid the presidential ambitions of John Connally resulted in a bizarre series of events known generally as the "Killer Bees". In 1979 Texas conservatives attempted to amend the Texas election code to separate the presidential primary from the regular primary (the so called Spilt Primary bill). The strategy was to allow conservatives, Democrats and Republicans, to vote for Connally in the presidential primary and return to the regular party primaries for all other races.

The Texas Senate, for reasons beyond the scope of this chapter, does not follow a regular calendar in conducting business. Bills are considered in the Senate by a motion to suspend the rules (the Intent calendar). Thus it always takes two-thirds of the Senators present to approve the consideration—not passage!—of a bill. It became obvious that 12 Senators (out of 31) would continue to oppose the consideration of the Connally proposal. Finally Lieutenant Governor Bill Hobby let it be known that the proposal would come up on the regular calendar, which requires only a simple majority of Senators present. The opposition considered this to be changing the rules in the middle of the game and were furious.

Their strategy: absent themselves from the Senate chambers. Since it takes two-thirds to constitute a quorum, the Senate was unable to conduct business. For five days the dozen Senators remained hidden from all, including law enforcement officials. Ultimately Bill Hobby bowed to reality and the Senate returned to its usual method of conducting business. The Bees returned in triumph and the spilt primary bill died.

Name Identification

"What is the single most important problem facing a candidate for public office?"

Although this question draws many answers in my classes, I can always count on some student coming out with "Money!" Whereupon a majority of the class concurs. At this point a satisfied feeling settles upon the class. The satisfaction of having successfully met the challenge of the question thrown out by the professor.

Then, after a short pause for emphasis, "Wrong! Money is not the single most important problem!" —pause— "Now, do not misunderstand me, money is important. But why is it important? It's certainly not going to be used for a trip to Hawaii! So, why is it important? What is the money going to be used for?" Maybe once upon a rural past, elections were won or lost because of family connections (or lack thereof). However, in modern urban United States this is seldom the case. In addition, most elections do not have high profile, well known candidates. Most elections are quite localized with candidates that are relatively unknown to the general electorate. So—the major problem facing most candidates is name identification!

Most voters know next to nothing about most of the names they see on the ballot. Therefore, the number one priority for the candidate is to get enough people to recognize their name. The most impressive credentials mean nothing if the voters draw a blank when it comes to your name. Although money is referred to as "the mother's milk of politics!", it is just one of the tools used to get a candidate known to the public. There have been a surprising number of races when a well financed candidate lost to a candidate with less money but a better campaign. In my own political career I ran eight winning campaigns out of nine tries. In all four of my hotly contested races I was considerably outspent, but managed to win three of them. In the 1994 elections that resulted in numerous Republican victories, there were a number of interesting Democratic victories. Diane Feinstein in California, Charles Robb in Virginia, and Ken Bensten in Texas are examples of victories against the Republican tide in spite of being outspent by considerable amounts. Also in the special congressional run off election of December 1996, Republican Kevin Brady was elected although he was easily outspent by his opponent. In just about every election cycle, one can find similar results.

In short, a candidate must have enough money to run a creditable race but the candidate with the most money does not automatically win.

Raising Money

In the judgment of many the most difficult and distasteful job facing any candidate is raising money for the campaign. Texas election law dealing with money is really quite simple compared to federal law and the laws of many other states. Texas law concentrates on public disclosure. If a candidate is not seeking federal office, that candidate must file a number of periodic reports that specify where the money comes from and where it goes. Contribution limitations that you hear about are a result of federal regulations dealing with federal elections. Since Texas has thirty congressional districts and two national Senators, candidates for any other office in Texas need only comply with Texas election laws. This means that unless a candidate is extremely careless or trying to hide something they can concentrate on raising money with a minimum concern about reports.

Texas is like the rest of the country in that the bulk of the campaign money comes from Political Action Committees (PACs), either directly or under the guise of "soft money". PACs provide the legal avenue for special interest groups to consolidate, coordinate, and channel (CCC) their campaign financial aid into races that appear to be the best investment for their group.

There are literally thousand of PACs in existence. However, they usually fall into one of several categories: business interests, labor, professional associations, and public interest groups. A circular relationship develops. Money is hard to come by unless you are considered a probable winner and you are not considered a probable winner unless you have money. This dilemma is recognized and dealt with by some PACs. For example, EMILY (Early Money Is Like Yeast! it causes the dough to rise!). EMILY is a PAC that primarily aids Democratic women candidates. EMILY gives early money, but even so, they do not give to everyone that seeks their help.

A candidate must use every contact they can to gain access to PAC decision makers. Dealing with PACs underscores a continuing problem that faces every candidate. To what extent does campaign help, particularly as it relates to money, carry with it a "quid pro quo" obligation? Public officials take an oath that states: "...I furthermore solemnly swear/affirm, that I have not directly nor indirectly paid, offered, or promised to pay, contributed, not promised to contribute any money or valuable thing, or promised any public office or employment, as a reward for the giving or withholding a vote at the election at which I was elected..." Many experts and some courts have interpreted "valuable things" to include votes while in office.[6]

It is difficult to over emphasize the influence and importance of PACs; nevertheless individual effort on the part of the candidate frequently makes the ultimate difference in a winning campaign.

It is a sad, but true, fact that most people have very little interest or experience with the nitty gritty of campaigns. This means that the candidates have at their disposal a vast reservoir of untapped talent. Friends, relatives, and acquaintances must be energized by the realization that your election can make a difference. Then taking this new found energy and directing and channeling it into a winning effort becomes the avenue to successful campaigning. There is a legitimate debate over whether or not a professional campaign manager should be hired to run the entire campaign. There is no debate concerning the need for someone knowledgeable to coordinate the campaign activities.

Third Parties and Future Election Evolution

There is considerable discussion and concern about the two party system and the way it operates, or fails to operate. Ironically, the founding fathers did not even envision a party system for the United States. However, ever since the disagreements between John Adams and Thomas Jefferson we have seen all major state and national election revolve around the two party system.

With some voters dissatisfaction with the major parties has led to the desire for another alternative. Most of the time when desire for change becomes strong enough, one or both of the major parties pick up on the hot issue and thus satisfy the demand (for example the Democrats in 1896 on the silver issue or the 1994 Republicans on big government). Of course just about every election has evidence of minor dissatisfaction as witness the presence of the Natural Law party, the US Taxpayers party, the Libertarian party, and the Independent party on the Texas general election ballot of November 1996. The 1998 election saw an unexpected third party governor, Jesse Ventura, win in Minnesota.

Periodically, however, dissatisfaction reaches the point where a large number of voters actively seek a viable alternative. The presidential elections of Jefferson in 1800, Jackson in 1824, and Lincoln in 1860 signified major changes in the role of the presidency.

Within Texas, in this century, we have seen substantial dissatisfaction among a number of more conservative Texans as the Democratic party became more "New Deal". Because the Republicans were moribund in Texas until the last few decades, revolts occurred within the Democratic party. In the early 1940's we had the Texas Regulars (conservatives with limited success). By the 1948 election the Dixiecrats (Strom Thurmond) tried unsuccessfully to deny Harry Truman's retention of the presidency. In 1968, George Wallace garnered almost 600,000 votes in Texas and most likely cost Nixon the Texas vote. At the other end of the political spectrum, in 1972 Ramsey Muniz, running as a third party candidate received 213,000 votes and almost cost Dolph Briscoe the governorship.

The more recent attempts by Ross Perot provide almost a textbook example of the fate of "serious" third party efforts. His effort to tap the dissatisfaction earned him about 19% of the popular vote in 1992 (zero electoral votes) and quite possibly cost George Bush reelection. By 1996 his efforts resulted in approximately half the percentage he received in the previous election. It is not likely that he will be a serious contender in the future.

What we have witnessed is that whenever there was enough dissatisfaction with both of the major parties one of two things occur: 1) A new party came into existence replacing one of the major parties (Republicans replacing the Whigs in the 1850's) or 2) One of the major parties adopted the attractive features of the budding opposition and the potential new major party fades away (Democrats in 1932). The net result has been the continuation of a two party system after a short period of turmoil and change. Recent third party attempts such as George Wallace, Ross Perot, and others have suffered the same fate.

As long as we have elections based on a "winner take all" format it is difficult for any new party to mount an effective challenge to the established parties. Many other democratic nations have proportional representation, cumulative voting, or other systems that encourage multi-party competition rather than a two party system.

Some observers think that a type of party restructuring may come about through a relatively new approach being utilized in a number of urban communities throughout the nation. Community based organizations energizing the lower middle class have been quite successful in focusing on specific needs. COPS (Communities Organized for Public Services) in San Antonio, TMO (The Metropolitan Organization) in Houston, and others of a like nature have been able to persuade local officials to deal with issues that have been ignored in the past.[7]

It has not been demonstrated that these type of groups can have influence beyond the local level. At the same time there are some experts that feel that it is only a matter of time before such an attempt is made. This seems more probably than having the state legislature passing laws to encourage the dismantling of the two party system.

It is difficult today to hold the parties responsible for the actions of individual party members. In the past political success had been tied directly to party support and discipline. With the advent of massive media coverage and the increase in political consultants, candidates now run campaigns based on individual images rather than party affiliations.

Although, in Texas and most states, it is still necessary to win in a party primary, it is no longer necessary to have the blessing of party officials. Party attempts to discipline maverick members more often than not result in favorable media coverage for the maverick. This is turn usually means that the individual becomes even more popular and thus even less beholden to the party. A prime example is Phil Gramm. He took Democratic party discipline and used it as a springboard to Republican success.

One thing we should never forget is that democracy as structured under the Constitution will never be an efficient form of government. Checks and balances and the Bill of Rights traded in governmental efficiency for citizens protection against governmental abuses. When the restrictions of the Texas constitution, with its distrust in government bias, are imposed on top of the US Constitution it is impossible to have anything except inefficient government. Better than we have at present? Possibly. Efficient? Not possible!

On-Line: Campaigns and Elections

Elections Division of the Texas Secretary of State Contains official results for Texas elections, voter registration procedures, election forms, a list of all elected officials, information about upcoming elections, and much more.

http://www.sos.state.tx.us/function/elec1/index.html

Project Vote Smart Vote Smart is "the major program of the Center for National Independence in Politics, a national non-partisan organization focused on providing citizen/voters with factual information about the political system, issues, candidates and elected officials." Vote Smart is one of the best political sites on the Web.

http://www.vote-smart.org/

The League of Women Voters of Texas The League is a non-partisan resource for information regarding Texas elections, candidates, and issues.

http://www.main.org/leaguewv/home.html

Texas Ethics Commission houses records on campaign financing, lobbying activities and rules, and legal opinions. See who is giving how much to whom!

http://www.ethics.state.tx.us/

Endnotes

1. Lori Rodriguez. *Houston Chronicle*. 13 November 1996. p 9A

2. Associated Press. *Dallas Morning News*. 14 December. p 39A

3. Darlene Clark Hine. *Black Victory*. (KTO Press, 1979)

4. Bush v Vera. 116 Sct. 1996

5. Alan Berstein. *Houston Chronicle*. 15 November 1996. p1

6. Article 16, Section 1. *The Texas Constitution*

7. Peter Skerry. *Mexican Americans*. (New York: The Free Press, 1993)

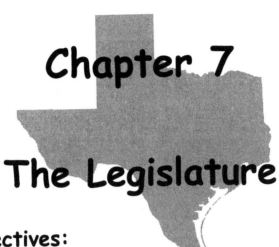

Chapter 7

The Legislature

Learning Objectives:

After reading this chapter, the student should be able to:

- ✪ Explain how the state legislature has changed over time
- ✪ Understand how unique the Texas Legislature is compared to legislatures of most large states
- ✪ Recognize the limitations of the state legislature
- ✪ Be aware of how important leadership and interest groups are in the legislature
- ✪ Identify at least 10 important facts about the legislature
- ✪ Access sources of additional information on the legislature
- ✪ Relate humorous anecdotes about various legislators

The Reagan Revolution of the 1980s began a recent and significant trend towards reducing the role of the federal government in formulating domestic policy, and turning that responsibility over to the state governments. Reagan's hypothesis was that the state governments are closer to the people and are more capable, flexible, and innovative than the federal government in helping to address domestic public policy problems.

Ronald Reagan was not from Texas

Reagan's state government experience came from his having been governor of California. The California Legislature, which whom he worked, is and was a highly professionalized legislature. California also has a very liberal initiative and referendum law, which makes it relatively easy for citizens to propose legislation and vote on it without having to go through the legislative process.

Texas, on the other hand, has a relatively unprofessional legislature, and its citizens have not been given the right of initiative and referendum at the state level. The historic inability of the legislature to redraw legislative and congressional districts, or to adequately fund and supervise the Texas public school system, state prison system, mental health facilities, etc. has been legendary. The Texas legislature frequently finds itself under court order to change the way it conducts business, and even ignores court orders whenever possible.[1]

It is doubtful that, had Mr. Reagan been governor of Texas, he would have been so enthusiastic about turning things back over to the states. None the less, with the enactment of the Welfare Reform Act of 1996, and other laws, Congress can be expected to continue to shift domestic policy burdens to the states. This burden may impact Texas more dramatically than other states since Texas is the largest, most urban state in the union to be equipped with a part-time legislature. Large and urban states tend to place greater demands on government services, such as education, roads, social services and law enforcement. It is doubtful that the Texas legislature will be able to handle this additional burden without some major constitutional and statutory reforms being put in place.

So What's Wrong with the Texas Legislature?

If Texas today was a relatively under-populated, rural state, as it was in the 1870s, there would be nothing structurally "wrong" with the legislature. Non-professional or part-time legislatures, per se, are not bad things when they are found in small, rural states. When describing any legislature as part-time, political scientists are generally referring to legislatures which...

- Pay their members low wages (and sometimes no wages)
- Meet in biennial sessions (every other year rather than annually)
- Have a relatively low or limited access to full-time staff
- Exhibit a tendency for members to quit or leave at relatively high rates
- Are relatively limited by constitutional and statutory law over their policy options.
- Find they must conduct their business over a relatively short time span

Some of these states compensate for having a part-time legislature by giving their Executive Branch more power. However, this is not the case in Texas. Like most other southern states, the Texas executive branch is relatively weak compared to most non-southern states. The radically different histories of states like Texas and California has resulted in radically different government structures, despite current similarities in size, urbanization and general demographics. The $50,000 question, so to speak, is whether a more intense policy environment in the future will cause Texas government to become structurally more akin to California.

Since the 1960s, state governments in general have seen a dramatic increase on demands for adequately funded and supervised governmental services. In the area of higher education, for example, many more high school graduates are attending college now, and that number is expected to only increase in the future. As a result, the states have built more colleges and universities, which have to be funded through state and local taxes. To its credit, the Texas legislature has responded to the increased policy demands of the last 30 years by:

- Increasing the size of its legislative staff
- Dedicating more resources to legislative functions
- Building a huge new office complex to house legislators and their staff
- Relying more frequently on interim committees to handle legislative business between its biennial sessions.
- Allowing legislators to "pre-file" bills before the regular legislative session begins
- Often making use of special sessions to tackle difficult issues.

And yet, although its institutional capacity has increased, it has struggled to keep pace. In the 1999 session alone, there were over 6,000 bills and resolutions introduced.[2] The Texas Constitution only allows the legislature 140 days to consider which of these 6000 bills deserve to become law. The number of bills introduced in the legislature has tripled over the last 30 years. The number of bills passed has doubled. And yet, the time that the legislature has to carefully consider this legislation has remained unchanged. Special sessions have become more commonly used than in the past, but data indicates they are not nearly as productive as a regular legislative session.[3]

Should demands for state services continue to increase, which is especially likely as the federal government sheds many of its programs, the gap between demand and output is only likely to increase. Any change to the length or frequency of Texas legislative sessions to bring demand and supply, (as it were), into line will require a constitutional amendment. Every state which even approaches Texas in terms of size and/or urbanization allows their legislatures to meet in annual sessions. It is likely only a matter of time before Texas joins the crowd.

One key argument against longer or more frequent legislative sessions was brought up in an early 1980s documentary on the Texas Legislature, entitled "The Best Little Statehouse in Texas". In the video, then representative Craig Washington made the point that the short, biennial legislative sessions limits the damage that the legislature causes to the state.

This rather pessimistic view of the legislature to function adequately by one of its own was recently echoed at a recent invocation, when a visiting minister offered up this prayer for the Texas Senate.

"Father, I pray for these men and women. You know how much they need it. They are facing problems that are much too immense for them to handle alone. They are not smart enough nor do they have the capacity. I ask that you would do miracles for them"[4]

The image of the average state legislator in Texas is not a good one. To put it mildly, the legislature has had more than its fair share of, shall we say, personnel problems. Some say it's the nature of Texas' diverse culture. Others hypothesize that southern politics in general tend to be a bit more colorful than in other places. Still others point to the $7200 annual salary legislators receive.

If you in any way subscribe to the idea that you get what you pay for, then this fact alone should give you a good idea of how the legislature operates. Just meditate for a while on the fact that the people who determine how much money schools should get, how many prisons to build, the type of taxes we will pay, which industries will be regulated and how, are paid $7200 a year to make those decisions.

A grocery store clerk, working 20 hours a week at $7.00 an hour makes more money than a state legislator does in Texas. And the only important decision they face is paper vs. plastic, and they let YOU make that call.

What does Texas get for its $7200 annual investment in legislative personnel? A lot of entertainment value for the dollar. It gets representatives like Warren Chisum of Pampa. Chism has voted against expanding foster care for babies born with AIDs; opposed a hate-crimes bill because, "gays bring violence upon themselves"[5]; and has opposed sex education on the basis that most sex education promotes homosexuality.[6] However, this has not stopped him from profiting from AIDs deaths. Chism buys the life insurance policies of AIDs victims for about half their actual value or so, gives them the cash, and collects the full face value of the policy when they die.[7]

Here's the scary part. Chism is considered one of the best legislators in Texas.[8]

For $7200 a year Texas gets representatives like Sergio Munos of Mission, who was arrested for possession of marijuana a while back. Six hundred twenty six POUNDS of marijuana.[9]

He probably needed the money for snack food.

Texas gets laws passed which makes it a felony to possess more than six "phallic sex toys"[10], or to say anything disparaging about Texas agricultural products (which got Oprah in trouble)[11]. Heated debate breaks out over whether the Armadillo or the Longhorn should be the official state mammal. State reptiles, fossils and soups are selected with due consideration. Resolutions are passed praising Edward De Salvo for his work in population control, etc. etc.[12]

Every man who has served as the Speaker of the Texas House over the last 20 years has left office under indictment and/or conviction for wrongdoing. The current Speaker reimbursed himself over $600,000 for state-related business use of his Cessna for a six-month period alone in 1996. At the legally permitted rate of about $1.50 per mile for airplane expenses, the plane would have had to have been in the air 16 hours a day, 7 days a week for a solid six months.

The question of whether there are more competent legislators than incompetent ones is akin to the glass half-full vs. half-empty dilemma. On average, it stands to reason that the average level of competence in the Texas legislature is probably well below that of most other large state legislatures. How else do you explain the fact that state and federal courts have been forced to order the legislature to change the way they fund and/or run schools, prisons, mental health facilities. Contrary to popular belief, judges can't just step in and demand the legislature do something unless a suit has been filed and a writ has been issued. And in order to initiate that suit, there needs to be a substantially organized and well-funded effort to even bring the suit to court in the first place. And in order to have a substantially organized and well-funded effort; you need an awful lot of very unhappy and very committed people who wish to see this thing through.

So why don't legislators make more money? The answer, in part, is that's the way Texans want it. Legislative pay was set in the 1876 Texas Constitution. Consequently, any raise in pay requires a constitutional amendment to make it so. An amendment to raise pay to around $11K a year passed the legislature but was defeated by the voters in the early 1990s.

Texas legislators, in all fairness, are not the lowest paid legislators in the US. Texas is, however, the largest state to pay their legislators so little. The historically low pay has had serious policy implications in addition to the more comical ones mentioned above. Until 1991, legislators could spend excess campaign donations any way they pleased, even to pay off personal debts, or to enhance their lifestyles. More often than not, these campaign contributions came from Political Action Committees representing special interest groups. In one particularly disturbing, but not uncommon example, a former chairman of the House calendars committee raised (and presumably spent) over $130,000 in an election year where he had no opponent.

Since 1991, the problem has abated a bit. Legislators may only use extra campaign money to reimburse themselves for "legitimate" job-related expenses. However, the previous airplane reimbursement story should serve as a reminder that there can be a rather loose interpretation of what constitutes a "legitimate" expense.

Of course, nothing prevents a legislator from using his position to line up a higher-paying job for him/herself either between sessions or once their legislative career has ended. Quite frequently, legislators and staffers end up taking much higher paying jobs working for lobbying firms once the tax-payers have effectively paid for their legislative training. Other legislators are able to take advantage of their increased visibility in the legislature to enhance their business or law firm's "traffic". This of course, raises the question of whether the legislators are there to look out for their own financial interests, or ours. At $7200 per year, unless they are independently wealthy, or willing to live well below the poverty level, they really don't have a choice.

Any change in state legislative pay will require a constitutional amendment, which means a 2/3rds vote of the legislature and approval from a majority of citizens, neither of which seems likely any time soon. The average Texans' reluctance to pay their legislators a living wage in all likelihood costs the average Texan a lot more money in a lot more ways than they could possibly imagine, given the almost legendary tendency of state legislators to protect special interests at the expense of everyone else.

As of 1996, the Texas legislature employed a total of 2,420 staffers, ranking it 4th out of the 50 states.[13] This is the only area where the Texas legislature resembles that of other large states. The lack of constitutional restrictions on legislative staff has allowed the legislature to nearly double its staff since 1979. In

1997, an $85 million four-story underground office complex was completed in Austin to house the legislators and their staff. Staff is important to a legislature because it allows legislators to conduct independent research on proposed bills and resolutions, to determine their impact on the state. Non-profit, out of state institutions, such as the National Conference of State Legislatures holds workshops, seminars and other events to bring legislators and staffers of the 50 states together to share policy ideas (what works, what doesn't), and provides information to the legislatures and scholars thereof on current trends and movements within state government.

Without the ability to conduct independent research, legislators and staffers would have to rely exclusively on interest groups to provide them with fair and accurate information on policies, which directly affects those particular interest groups. Although the total number of Texas staffers is quite high, it is difficult to determine how many of those staffers are full vs. part-time. A legislature with 2000 part-time staffers is no better staffed than one with 1000 full-timers.

The allocation of staff resources is of paramount importance in any legislative setting. In Texas, the Speaker of the House and the Lieutenant Governor exert quite a bit of direct and indirect influence on how staff is to be allocated. The Legislative Research Council, upon which they both sit and appoint all members to, allocates research staff to legislators requesting assistance. The committee chair in each chamber largely controls committee staff allocation. As it happens, the Speaker in the House, and the Lt. Governor in the Senate make all committee chairmanship decisions, giving them indirect control of committee staff. And perhaps it goes without saying that the secretary who answers the phone for the legislator is paid more money than the legislator him/herself.

With the exception of staff resources, what's wrong with the Texas legislature is that its institutional capabilities are not up to par when comparing it to other large states. Changes to the legislature's basic design (pay, session length, etc.) require constitutional amendments, which so far have been difficult at best to get passed. Despite a general consensus amongst legislative observers, scholars and the like that major reform of the legislative system is desirable; no major reform is likely any time soon. It will probably take a state crisis of monumental proportions to occur before Texas changes the way its legislature is run.

So, what else do I need to know about the Texas Legislature?

It may seem a bit odd to start with the basics in the middle of the chapter, but so be it. These are, after all, the kinds of things professors love to put on exams. Given the fact that this book is designed more as a Texas reader than a full-blown textbook, and given that the book is almost exclusively used in US Government courses and not Texas Government courses, then best way to approach this may be to simply mimic David Letterman and finish the chapter in the form of a Top 10 list.

Top 10 Things You Should Know about the Texas Legislature (In No Particular Order)

10. The Texas legislature is similar to the US Congress in a number of ways. Its bicameral, meaning it has a House of Representatives and a Senate. Each chamber has its own set of rules, leaders, customs, committees, constitutionally delegated powers, etc. Tax legislation must start in the House. The Senate confirms Gubernatorial nominees.[14] The impeachment process is identical, as is a 2/3rds vote to pass a constitutional amendment. The Senate has filibusters,[15] and the legislative process is very similar and equally complex.

9. The Texas House of Representatives has 150 members who are all elected to 2-year terms of office. They are all up for re-election again in 2000. House

members are elected from districts, which are approximately equal in population. The leader of the House is called the Speaker. The Speaker is elected at the beginning of every new legislative session by a majority vote, and has always been a member of the majority party. The current Speaker is Pete Laney, a conservative Democrat from west Texas. The Speaker makes all committee chairmanship decisions, decides who will sit on what committees, and exerts a great deal of influence over his chamber. He sits on and appoints members to every interim committee the legislature uses when it's out of session. House members of either party, if they wish to get anything done, must generally be willing to work with the Speaker (be a member of his team, so to speak).

8. The Texas Senate has 31 members who are elected to 4-year terms of office. One half of the Senate is elected in Presidential election years, like 2000; the other 1/2 will be up for re-election in 2002. Unlike US Senators, Texas Senators are elected by district, with each state senate district being approximately equal in size to each other. Because state senate districts are larger than state house districts, it generally takes more money to get elected to the Texas Senate rather than the Texas House. However, it is generally believed that Senators have more power than do most House members. The leader of the Texas Senate is the Lt. Governor, and the current Lt. Governor is Rick Perry. Senators do not elect the Lt. Governor; rather, he is elected by the citizens in a statewide vote, so he is not necessarily going to always be a member of the majority party in his chamber. The Lt. Governor makes $7200 per year like the other legislators. He also makes all committee appointments, all chairmanship decisions, and has vast influence and power over how the Senate is run. With the Speaker, he sits on and appoints members to every interim committee the Legislature has. It is a generally accepted belief that the Lt. Governor actually exerts more influence and power over public policy in Texas than the Governor. Don't ask if he's more powerful than the Speaker is. It's too close to call, and nobody really cares.[16]

7. Historically, the Democratic party has dominated the Texas legislature. From the 1870s through the mid 1990s, the Democrats held a majority of seats in each chamber. For most of those years, up to 1960 or so, they typically held 99% to 100% of the seats. Through the 1960s and most of the 70s, they typically held over 90% of the seats, and even by 1989, still held about 2/3rds to 3/4ths of the seats. The Republicans won a majority of Senate seats in 1997, and the Democrats still hold a narrow majority in the Texas House following the elections of 1998. Which party actually controls the legislature is probably irrelevant. Texas has always been a conservative state, and has always had a conservative majority in the legislature regardless of party affiliation. Unlike Congress, a change in majority party status in Texas does not signal a change in ideology.[17] It has not been uncommon for Democratic Lt. Governors and Speakers to place Republican majorities on certain

committees, and even award some chairmanship positions to Republican legislators. This would be unheard of in Congress.

6. Interest groups tend to exert a great deal of influence on legislative leaders and followers. As previously mentioned, for a long time the lack of restrictions on converting campaign dollars to personal dollars allowed much undue influence. A more enduring source of influence has been the fact that most legislators, like most Texans, are generally conservative (pro-business and anti-government), while at the same time the largest and best funded interest groups are those which represent businesses and other conservative causes. With the vast majority of legislators and interest groups sharing common values it should not be surprising to find the legislature enacting pro-business legislation on a regular basis. Groups representing union, environmental, civil rights and educational concerns usually exert little influence in Texas. Consequently, Texans fall below the national average when it comes to income, life expectancy, and scholastic test scores and per-capita taxation and above the national average when it comes to poverty, crime, dropout rates, pollution and cancer death rates.

5. Texas makes extensive use of interim committees. By definition, these are committees, which meet and conduct business when the legislature is not in session. As previously mentioned, the Lt. Governor and the Speaker sit on and appoint all the members of these committees. The Legislative Budget Board (LBB) and the Legislative Research Council (LRC) are probably the two most important interim committees. The LRC assigns staff to assist legislators wishing to conduct research on proposed legislation. The LBB is THE major player in the budget process. Final budget numbers are usually much closer to those figures proposed by the LBB rather than the Governor. The Governor's role in the budget process is primarily limited to the line-item veto once the budget has been passed by the legislature.

4. The legislature is not very representative of the state, in terms of demographics. Legislators tend to have more education and enjoy higher incomes than the average Texan. Women and minorities are underrepresented in the legislature. Until 1966, when Barbara Jordan was elected, about the only time women served in the legislature was to finish the term of their husbands, who had expired before their term of office did. Racial minorities did not exist in the legislature until a series of US Supreme Court decisions and the Voting Rights Act of 1965 outlawed the suppression of minority voters. Data on Congress and state legislatures indicates women and minorities vote differently than white upper-class men, come from a more varied background, and posses a different perspective on what constitutes good public policy. The relative lack of female and minority representation generally results in the legislature ignoring or downplaying issues which do not directly affect the interests of upper-class white men. In all fairness, no US legislature is demographically representative, and Texas is more

representative demographically than some, although it is below average nationally. While there is no one region, which does a better job of electing women and minorities, these groups tend to be most under-represented in the South.

3. Most of the work done in the Texas legislature is done in committees. Legislators spend more time in committee meetings reviewing proposed legislation, taking testimony from interest groups, and voting on which bills to send to the full chamber for their approval, than anything else.[18] This is generally true of all US legislatures. Consequently, deciding who will or will not be allowed to sit on certain committees can have a significant impact on which bills will pass and which bills will die. Whether committees are relatively more powerful in the House or Senate, or in Texas vs. other states would be difficult to assess without a very large grant from the National Science Foundation.[19]

2. During the last couple of weeks of a regular session of the Texas legislature, members vote on a logjam of legislation, unparalleled in the world. Bills are sometimes voted on as frequently as twice a minute. It is not uncommon for popularly backed legislation to die simply because it did not get voted on in time. It is also not uncommon for legislators to find themselves voting for bills which they are not at all familiar with. Quite often they will vote for or against a bill on the basis of the reputation of the sponsor. It is not unheard of for legislators to occasionally claim to be undecided on an issue in order to attract campaign contributions from interest groups on both sides of the issue. Texas legislators have a distinctive advantage over their Congressional counter-parts in that regard since there are no limits on campaign contributions in Texas. Consequently, PAC contributions tend to make up a higher percentage of the re-election funds of Texas legislators than US Congressmen, enhancing the ability of these groups to gain access to, and get a favorable hearing from state reps.

1. Maybe this is the most important thing you should know. If these "Ten" items leave you yearning for more information on the Texas Legislature, then you can probably find the information you need at the state legislature's web site. If you wish to find out more about state legislatures in general, check out the National Conference of State Legislature's web site. If you have never heard of the internet, the Book of the States is a good written source, as are previous editions of this text. Texas Monthly's ten best and ten worst legislator articles are available by back-order at a cost of $2.50 per article. These articles are typically printed in July of odd-numbered years, with the exception of 1991. The Texas Observer often features satirist Molly Ivins and Jim Hightower who are also rich sources of humorous and/or agitating stories regarding the antics of the legislature and its members, which are too numerous to list here. And finally, y'all have 2 members of the legislature, a rep and a senator, who are SUPPOSED to be looking out for your interests, and frequently complain of a lack of input from their constituents. If you try, you might be surprised to find out these folks are relatively easy to get a hold of and talk to. After all, you are their boss. Or at least, you should be.

On-Line: The Legislature

Texas Legislature Online is where you can research bills by number, title, subject, and keyword.

http://www.capitol.state.tx.us/

Texas House of Representatives

http://www.house.state.tx.us/

Texas Senate

http://www.senate.state.tx.us/

The Legislative Budget Board is the nerve center for preparing the state's budget.

http://www.lbb.state.tx.us/

National Conference of State Legislatures keeps you up to date on events affecting the states.

http://www.ncsl.org/

The *Austin American-Statesman* provides daily coverage of legislative activities and maintains a good archive for each legislative session.

http://austin360.com/news/features/legislature/legemain.html

Endnotes

1. In 1991 George Green was awarded a $13.7 million judgement against the state, which the legislature refused to pay, until the Legislative Budget Board unilaterally agreed to dole out $8.9 million.
2. *Houston Chronicle*, March 13th, 1999
3. Since 1987 24% of bills introduced in regular sessions has passed vs. 14% in special sessions.
4. Ivins, Molly: "*You Got to Dance With Them What Brung You*", p. 199
5. IBID, p. 186
6. IBID
7. IBID
8. *Texas Monthly*, July 1997
9. Ivins, Molly: "Nuthin' but Good times ahead"
10. IBID
11. IBID
12. De Salvo is better known as "The Boston Strangler"
13. National Conference of State Legislatures, March 1999
14. by a 2/3rds margin rather than a majority vote as in the US Senate
15. Leaders of a filibuster in Texas cannot "give the floor" to another Senator. A Texas state senator holds the world record for the longest filibuster.
16. The Texas Senate has a "bill of the day" rule which is unique to any legislative chamber in the world. It effectively allows the Lt. Gov. to decide which bill will need a majority vote to pass, and which ones will need a 2/3rds vote to pass.
17. By most accounts, the KKK actually held a majority of seats in the Texas legislature through most of the 1920s when the Democrats held most, if not all of the seats.
18. Whew! What a long sentence!
19. Fortunately for legislative researchers, the NSF does not require that the knowledge obtained by observing legislatures in any way improves the human condition. Only the tenure position of those researchers need be at stake.

Chapter 8

The Executive

Learning Objectives:

After reading this chapter, the student should be able to:

- ✪ Describe the legal aspects of the governorship including qualifications, salary, and benefits, terms of office, tenure, and succession
- ✪ Describe the executive powers of the governor, including the power of appointment
- ✪ Describe the legislative posers of the governor and provide examples of how they may be used in order for the governor to influence the content of public policy
- ✪ Describe the limited judicial and other powers of the governor
- ✪ Describe the executive branch of Texas, outline the types of agencies, describe their functions, and explain their relationship to the people

Introduction

In all fifty states the chief executive officer is called the governor. The governor is to the state what the President is to the nation—the highest elected official.

In Texas, as in the other forty-nine states, the governor is elected by a direct popular vote. In Texas a plurality is needed to be elected, that is, more votes than any other single candidate. In 1972, for example, Dolph Briscoe, Democrat from Uvalde, was elected with 46% of the vote. His Republican opponent, Henry Grover, from Houston, received 43% and a third party candidate, Ramsey Muniz, an attorney from San Antonio, running on the La Raza Unida party ticket, received the remaining 11%. In 1978, when only the second Republican in the history of Texas was elected, William Clements, Jr., from Dallas, received 12,000 votes more than his democratic opponent, Attorney General John Hill, from Houston, with yet another third party candidate, Deborah Leonard, also from Houston and running on the Socialist Worker's Party ticket, receiving 37,000 votes. So, in each case the simple majority won.

The qualifications to be Texas governor are simple—be at least thirty years of age, be a citizen of the United States and have lived in Texas for at least five consecutive years before taking office. While governor you may not hold any other elected public office or be on active military duty or hold any corporate office. You do not have to be a registered voter and when W. Lee O'Daniel was first elected in 1938, he was not able to vote since he had not paid his poll tax and registered for that year. It is also required that while the legislature is in session the governor must live where they are meeting unless authorized to live somewhere else. Governor Bush, for example, has sold his home in Dallas and moved his family to the governor's mansion in Austin.

Notice that there are no qualifications concerning education, gender, race, or religion. Most of our governors have been college educated and many have had law degrees. We have had two female governors (with Texas being the only state that has had more than one) but all forty-four people who have served have been caucasian and Protestant. Also since 1890 only two governors have not been native-born Texans - W. Lee O'Daniel born in Ohio and coming to Texas at an early age, and current Governor George W. Bush born in Connecticut and coming to Texas at age two when his parents, George and Barbara Bush, moved to Midland.

Texas has no limit on the number of terms or years that the governor may serve but as you can see from Figure 8-1, the governor who served the most number of years was William Clements, Jr., who served eight years (two non-consecutive terms) with Governor Allan Shivers serving the most consecutive years with seven-and-a half. Assuming that Governor Bush serves out his full second term then he will tie Governor Clements with eight years and beat Governor Shivers with eight consecutive years. Since the four-year term went into effect in 1974 Governor Bush has been the only governor to be re-elected to a consecutive second term.

Figure 8-1. Governors of Texas since Statehood, December 29, 1845

Governor	Years Served
J. Pickney Henderson	1846 - 1847
A. C. Horton	1846 - 1846 (1)
George T. Wood	1847 - 1849
P. Hansborough Bell	1849 - 1853 (2)
J. W. Henderson	1853 - 1853
Elisha M. Pease	1853 - 1857
Hardin R. Runnels	1857 - 1859
Sam Houston	1859 - 1861
Edward Clark	1861 - 1861
Francis R. Lubbock	1861 - 1863
Pendleton Murrah	1863 - 1865
Andrew J. Hamilton	1865 - 1866
James W. Throckmorton	1866 - 1867
Elisha M. Pease	1867 - 1869
Edmund J. Davis	1869 - 1874 (3)
Richard Coke	1874 - 1876 (4)
Richard B. Hubbard	1876 - 1879
Oran M. Roberts	1879 - 1883
John Ireland	1883 - 1887
Lawrence Sullivan Ross	1887 - 1891
James S. Hogg	1891 - 1895 (5)
Charles A. Culberson	1895 - 1899
Joseph D. Sayers	1899 - 1903
S. W. T. Lanham	1903 - 1907
Thomas M. Campbell	1907 - 1911
Oscar B. Colquitt	1911 - 1915
James E. Ferguson ("Pa")	1915 - 1917 (6)
William P. Hobby	1917 - 1921
Pat M. Neff	1921 - 1925
Miriam A. Ferguson ("Ma")	1925 - 1927 (7)
Dan Moody	1927 - 1931
Ross Sterling	1931 - 1933
Miriam A. Ferguson	1933 - 1935
James V. Allred	1935 - 1939
W. Lee O'Daniel ("Pappy")	1939 - 1941 (8)
Coke R. Stevenson	1941 - 1947
Beauford T. Jester	1947 - 1949 (9)
Allan Shivers	1949 - 1957
Price Daniel, Sr.	1957 - 1963
John B. Connally	1963 - 1969
Preston Smith	1969 - 1973

Figure 8-1. Continued

Dolph Briscoe	1973 - 1979 (10)
William Clements, Jr.	1979 - 1983 (11)
Mark White	1983 - 1987
William Clements, Jr.	1987 - 1991
Ann Richards	1991 - 1995
George W. Bush	1995 - (12)

(1) Lt. Gov. Horton served as temporary governor while Governor Henderson was serving in the Mexican War.
(2) Resigned to serve in the United States Congress.
(3) First Republican governor. Served during "Radical Reconstruction" period.
(4) Resigned to serve in the United States Senate.
(5) First native-born Texan to serve as Governor.
(6) Only Texas governor to be impeached and convicted.
(7) First woman to serve as governor. Elected because of popularity with the voters of her husband, ex-Governor James E. Ferguson. Campaigned with the slogan, "Two for the price of one!"
(8) Resigned to serve in the United States Senate.
(9) Only Texas governor to die while serving.
(10) Last governor to serve a two-year term and first to serve a four-year term.
(11) Only the second Republican to serve as governor.
(12) Third Republican to serve as governor and the son of ex-President George H. W. Bush.

Texas has had, therefore, forty-four people to serve as governor forty-seven times since Governors Pease, M.A. Ferguson and Clements served two non-consecutive terms.

Of the forty-four people who have served as governor forty-one have been Democrats and three, Davis, Clements and Bush, have been Republicans.

Until 1974 governors served two-year terms and starting that year, as a result of the passage of an amendment to the state constitution in 1973, the term was extended to four years. Governor Briscoe, therefore, was the last of the two-year term governors, elected in 1972, and the first of the four-year term governors, elected in 1974.

Salary and Benefits

The current salary of the governor is $115,345 with the state legislature determining the salary. Until a constitutional amendment changed it in 1955, the salary could only be changed by the legislature proposing an amendment to the state constitution and the voters approving it. But since 1955 the salary is set by the legislature and voter approval is not needed.

The governor also has the use of the mansion as home and office plus office space in the capitol building. A limousine with a combination driver/body guard is provided but most recent governors have used their own personal automobile if traveling around Austin. A state-owned airplane is also at the governor's disposal for official business use. The governor receives no entertainment expenses so that they either pay these out of their own pockets or use money from political contributions.

Succession in Case of a Vacancy in the Office

There are three ways in which a vacancy can occur in the office of governor - (1) death, (2) resignation or (3) conviction of impeachment by the Texas House of Representatives and Senate. Texas does not have a provision, as we do at the national level, to declare the governor unable to carry out the duties and responsibilities of office. If a vacancy occurs, then, next in line is the lieutenant governor. If for some reason the lieutenant governor is unable to serve then the president-pro-tempore of the State Senate would take over. If this person was also unable to serve next in line is the speaker of the Texas House of Representatives. Next would be the attorney general followed by the chief judges of the fourteen Texas courts of appeals in numerical order - each of the fourteen (with the first court of appeals located in Houston and its surrounding area) has a chief judge and several associate judges all of whom are elected by the voters in the areas served by each court for six-year terms. Realize, of course, that except for the senate president pro-tempore serving as "Governor for a Day" once every two years Texas has never had to go beyond the lieutenant governor to fill a vacancy in the governor's office.

Powers of the Governor

Executive Powers include many things. The governor has the power to appoint more than two thousand positions. However, there are many limitations on the appointment power. Although the governor serves a four-year term many appointments are made for six year periods which means that, for instance, many of Governor Richards appointments are held over into the administration of Governor Bush and some even into his second term. Since he was reelected he, then, will end up having all appointed positions his selections. It is true that upon Governor Bush's elections some of Richard's appointments resigned but there is nothing to force them to do so.

Another limitation is that a number of state-wide executive officers, independent of the governor, are elected directly by the voters. The Attorney-General, John Cornyn, is one of these. Another is David Dewhurst, Commissioner of the General Land Office. Still another is Commissioner of the Texas Department of Agriculture Susan Combs. Yet another is Comptroller of Public Accounts Carole Keeton Rylander. The voters also elect the three members of the Texas Railroad Commission and the fifteen members of the State Board of Education. The governor, as chief executive officer of Texas, therefore, has the responsibility to see that these elected officials do their jobs properly yet the governor cannot control who they are since they are all elected officials. The main reason for so many elected officers is the reaction the people of Texas has to the administration of Governor Edmund J. Davis during the "Radical Reconstruction" period in Texas following the Civil War which was replete with much favoritism, graft, corruption and most of the other evils associated with poor governance. This situation was addressed in chapter two of the text. But is should be noted that as a result of the 1998 elections all of these elected officials, with the exception of six members of the State Board of Education, are Republicans and since the governor is usually recognized as the leader of his state political party organization this should make the job somewhat easier for Governor Bush.

Still another limitation is the requirement of two-thirds of the State Senate to confirm appointments made by the governor. On the national level it takes only a majority of the United States Senate to confirm an appointment made by the President but in Texas we still remember Governor Davis and what happened under his administration so we want to make sure that not just a majority but two-thirds of the members of the state senate approve.

Another restriction, but one which is probably good, is that some of the appointments must actually be qualified for the job. For instance the head of the state Department of Health must be a medical doctor and the head of the Department of Transportation must be a graduate civil engineer. Also at least two members of the State Commission for the Blind must be legally blind themselves.

It is also understood that, since the senate must confirm an appointment, "senatorial courtesy" will prevail." that is, the governor will first check with the state senator in whose district the prospective appointee lives to get the senator's approval since if the particular senator disapproves the chance of senate confirmation is almost impossible.

The removal power of the governor is limited. Basically the only way the governor can remove most appointed officials is with a two-thirds approval of the state senate and this is most unlikely. The governor can, of course, remove a member of his or her immediate staff and certain other people but basically once appointed the person stays on for the whole term. Of course, the governor can ask a particular person to resign and this request would, in all probability, be honored by the person in question.

Financial powers are also limited. The governor recommends the budget to the legislature during each regular session and the governor has, of course, a lot of assistance in establishing the proposed budget. It must be realized that about 84% of the state budget is already earmarked either by statute or federal law which also places limits on the governor in this area. The fiscal area will be fully discussed in Chapter 10.

The governor is the chief planning officer of Texas. The governor works with regional planning groups, called Councils of Government, and with state agencies to make sure that Texas will be able to cope with whatever might happen during future years. An adequate water supply, for instance, is a potential problem in years to come so this is one area in which the governor is active. Besides working with local and state groups, the governor also cooperates with the national government in its overall plans for the future of the whole country.

As head of state, the governor is responsible for official communications between Texas and other states plus between Texas and the federal government. The governor regularly meets with governors of other states, particularly those of Texas' neighboring states, individually or at regularly scheduled conference of all fifty governors. In dealing with the federal government the governor has an official liaison person in Washington to represent the State of Texas. Actually, this person has the title of Director of the Office of State-Federal Relations and reports directly to the governor who, in turn, keeps the legislature and other areas of Texas informed about what is happening.

The governor also has law enforcement powers since the governor is basically responsible for seeing to it that all laws passed by the legislature are properly carried out. Of course, these responsibilities are delegated to appropriate state agencies but it is the governor's ultimate responsibility to see that this is done.

And finally, under executive powers, is the limited military power the governor has. The governor can, under emergency situations, activate the National Guard and the Texas State Guard to assist local authorities when needed. For example, in 1983, when Hurricane Alicia did significant damage on West Galveston Island, Governor White called units of the National Guard into active service to help local officials. For about ten days the Guard helped to keep law and order effective on West Galveston Island until the local officials were satisfied that they could once again handle things. The Governor can also use the Highway Patrol and the Texas Rangers, in times of emergency, to assist local authorities to maintain law and order.

Legislative powers are in three categories. The governor may veto bills passed by the legislature; may call special sessions of the legislature; and may make recommendations or send messages to the legislature.

The veto is probably the most effective of the three since it is difficult to override—it take a two-thirds vote of each house of the legislature, acting separately, to accomplish this and, as a matter of fact, only once in the last fifty years has the legislature been able to do this—in 1979 a veto by Governor Clements exempting Comal County from the state's game laws was overridden. And part of this was due to the fact that Governor Clements was a Republican with an overwhelmingly Democratic majority in both the State House of Representatives and State Senate. In the 76th Legislature in 1999 the Senate had, for the second time, a Republican majority with the Democrats still controlling the House which made it even more unlikely that a veto could be overridden. Also, most of the time simply a threat by the Governor that a bill will be vetoed is enough to stop the legislature from passing it realizing the difficulty in overriding a veto.

The governor also had the "line" or "item" veto on appropriation or spending bills only. That is, the governor may veto specific things in this type of bill without having to veto the whole piece of legislation.

The second legislative power the governor has is to call special sessions of the legislature. As has been seen in chapter 7 the legislature meets in regular session for only 140 days during odd-numbered years and with the growth Texas has experienced especially in the last thirty years these 140 days usually are not enough to accomplish what needs doing. Special sessions can be called only by the governor, nobody else. Special sessions are limited to thirty days. The governor will also specify what the legislature will deal with when such a session is called and the legislature is limited to that. If the legislature does not finish by the end of thirty days the governor can call a second special session on the very same topic. If they do not finish during the second thirty days a third special session can be called on still the same topic. Between the 1991 and 1993 regular sessions, for instance, there were six special sessions called by Governor Richards and four of these dealt with public school financing - the first three went the full thirty days and finally before the end of the fourth appropriate legislation was passed. We did not have a special session called between the 1993, 1995, and 1997 regular sessions and this was the first time this had happened in about twenty years. And it might be added that if the legislature, during a special session, want to discuss something that was not called for by the governor they may only do so with the permission of the governor.

The final legislative power of the governor is that of sending messages or recommending legislation to the legislature. This can be done by a number of ways such as the "State of the State" address that the governor makes to the legislature shortly after the beginning of each regular session. Or recommendations can be made through conferences with legislative leaders such as the speaker of the house and the lieutenant governor or meetings with other members of the house and senate. The governor also has legislative liaison people through whom messages or recommendations can be sent to the Legislature. Informally this can also be done at the myriad social functions that take place attended by the governor and members of the legislature.

While it is certainly not one of the formal legislative powers, Governor Bush, having first been elected in 1994 and facing his first legislative session (the 74th Legislature in 1995,) which had a Democratic majority in both houses, appointed as one of his top aides ex-State Senator Dan Shelley who had, in previous years, been a Republican member of the Senate from one of the districts in Harris County. At Shelley's urging Governor Bush would, when he was able during the session, and accompanied by Shelley, go across the street to the Capitol and Annex during the late afternoon hours when things had quieted down some and if an office door was open the Governor would go in and simply introduce himself to the member and the member's staff. This, of course, was done informally but it was very effective and helped Governor Bush in his legislative program with the legislature.

The third category, and the least important, are **judicial powers**. The governor can grant a pardon or a reprieve. These powers are somewhat limited since many recommendations for either must be made by the Board of Pardons and Paroles, a division of the Texas Department of Criminal Justice. Perhaps the most common form of pardon is that given to a person convicted of a felony who has served most or all of their time and does not have a second offense. In Texas, once a person is convicted of a felony their right to a vote is permanently taken away unless they have received a pardon from the governor and this frequently happens under these circumstances. Fortunately pardons given due to a mistaken conviction of an innocent person are very rare in Texas since convictions of innocent people are few and far between.

Reprieves are usually either a reduction of the sentence or a postponement of carrying out the sentence. A convicted felon, say, has been sentenced to twenty years for a certain crime and the governor reduces the sentence to ten or fifteen years. Or perhaps a death penalty is reduced to life imprisonment but in these situations the above mentioned Board of Pardons and Paroles would make the recommendation. Another example of a reprieve is the tradition in Texas of delaying the date of execution thirty days. This means that once the judge actually sets the execution date in a capital punishment case the governor delays the date by thirty days to give the condemned person this extra time to appeal the decision. Under current circumstances this seems unnecessary since it now takes eight or more years for an execution to take place after conviction but historically the time was much shorter so the thirty days was most appropriate.

The governor has the authority to appoint an appellate or district judge to replace those who die, retire, or resign during a term. Nearly half the state's judges are appointed rather than elected.

The final category of the governor's powers are the **other powers** that cannot be classified under executive, legislative, or judicial. The main power here is that the governor, as the state's highest elected official, is considered the leader of the political party that the governor is a member of. Most Republicans in Texas, would now agree that Governor Bush is the leader of the state Republican organization. Former Governor Richards was recognized as the leader of the state Democratic party during her four years. Until the 1960's, when the Republican party in Texas came into existence, Texas basically was a one-party state and that was the Democratic party. Therefore governors until that time were quite powerful since they were recognized as the leader of the only organized political party Texas had at the time. Governors such as Allan Shivers, Price Daniel and the early years of John Connally's administration, had much more power and influence than recent governors have had. But Governor Bush has the loyalty of Texas Republicans since he is the governor and his party members will listen to him and respect what he says. Of course, so will many democrats and independents since, after all, George W. Bush in Texas's chief executive officer and was elected to do the job.

Governors also are listened to when they are able to get certain things done. Governor John Connally, for example, is highly respected because of his efforts in the establishment of the Texas Higher Education Coordinating Board in the area of higher education in Texas along with his efforts in the area of developing adequate supplies of water.

The Governor and State Administration

The governor is aided by more than two hundred state agencies, departments, bureaus, boards, etc. Some of these were established by the current state constitution but most have been set up by legislative action since the present constitution was established in 1876.

There are three main reasons why the number of state-level agencies has increased - (1) the state has taken over functions that had belonged to local governments, (2) the state has expanded in areas in which it has always been involved, and (3) the state has gotten involved in wholly new functions.

Two examples of where the state has gotten involved in **local functions** are public education (grades Kindergarten through 12) and roads and highways.

Prior to the early years of the 20th century public education was basically a county responsibility with each county in Texas handling its own schools, deciding at what grade level a certain subject should be taught, determining how many days would make up the school year, hiring its own teachers and deciding what qualifications they would have, and so forth. This made it quite difficult for families with school age children to move from one county to another since the school curriculums were different - where one county might, for instance, teach reading at one grade level another county might teach it at another. So appropriate state agencies were established to standardize curriculum so that reading would be taught at a particular grade level in all schools in Texas, arithmetic at a particular grade level and so on. Also a standard number of credits (currently a minimum of twenty-one) would be required for graduation from high school and certain subjects, such as a minimum of four years of english, two years of math, two years of history, etc. would be needed. Even though at this time most control of public education is still in the hands of a locally elected school boards, there are these state standards in place throughout Texas.

The second example is the development of our system of roads and highways. Until the advent of the automobile, and even for many years afterwards, each county was responsible for its own system of roads and highways and it built and maintained its system to suit itself. When the automobile came to Texas and especially after the assembly-line method of making automobiles was perfected making automobiles affordable to most people, the demand rose for roads to allow people to drive across county lines and travel throughout Texas so that the state took over the construction and maintenance of roads designated by numbers - interstate highways, state highways and farm-to-market roads. Counties still build and maintain their own county system of roads and bridges but now with more than two hundred thousand miles of paved roadways built and maintained by the state every corner of Texas is now accessible to motor vehicles.

The main example of **expanding existing state activities** is in the area of higher education, something Texas has been actively involved in since 1876. True, in 1840, while the Republic of Texas was in existence, President Mirabeau B. Lamar recommended to the Congress of the Republic that they set up a system of higher education which they did. But due to statehood in 1845 followed by the pre-Civil War period, then the Civil War itself, then Reconstruction, a state higher education system did not come into actual effect until 1876. At that time the first state-supported institution of higher education, now Texas A & M University, was established with a first class of twenty-one young men. This was followed by Prairie View A & M, then Sam Houston State University, then the University of Texas at Austin and now we have thirty-five state supported colleges and universities (not including medical or dental schools) with an enrollment of just over four-hundred thousand students. Plus there are fifty community college districts in Texas with an additional four hundred thousand plus students. So to accommodate this growth the necessary state-level agencies have been established.

Examples of the state getting involved in completely **new functions** can be seen in the areas of aid to senior citizens and public health. In a very small way Texas was involved in these two areas before the federal government became involved during the mid 1930's. Texas still does things in cooperation with the national and local levels of government so that the necessary agencies have been established to deal with these areas.

Major State Agencies

We have already seen the elected state-wide officials but now need to deal somewhat with what their departments do. All of these, from the Attorney-General through the Railroad Commissioners earn an annual salary of $92,217.

The **Attorney General** is the chief law officer of Texas and his office would represent the state in legal matters. There is a staff of more than two hundred assistant attorneys-general plus many other employees. This office is also the legal advisor to the governor and all other state officials, agencies, departments, educational institutions, etc. The attorney general's office also assists members of the state legislature in drafting bills. The office is responsible for securing the necessary land (rights-of-way) for the building of new state highways. The office also investigates and prosecutes election frauds involving two or more counties. The attorney general is also responsible for a consumer protection division with offices scattered all over Texas which will handle legitimate consumer complaints. The office is also responsible for procuring back child support payments from "deadbeat dads." In other words, the attorney general is the state's "family lawyer."

The **General Land Office** is responsible for all state-owned lands not including state parks or roads and highways which are under different agencies. Texas, today, owns about twenty-two million acres of land which includes the "tidelands" in the Gulf of Mexico. Texas is unique in the way it entered the United States in 1845. Before the United States Constitution was adopted, in 1788 there were thirteen states. The other thirty-seven all entered the union after this time. Thirty-six of those were either broken off other states (as Maine was from Massachusetts in 1820) or were territories under the jurisdiction of the federal government and when the territories became states there was no change in the ownership of these public lands. Texas, of course, was the thirty-seventh and entered the Union directly from being an independent country, the Republic of Texas. In the Republic, public lands were owned by the Republic and when Texas became a state these lands came under state control and were placed under the General Land Office. Since 1845 much state-owned land has been sold or given away such as the area that is now Big Bend National Park in Southwest Texas, the Padre Island National Seashore area along the Gulf of Mexico and military bases such as Fort Hood whose three million acres make it the largest military base in the world.

The **Texas Department of Agriculture** was established in 1907. Most Texans think that this department deals only with people involved in agriculture such as farmers and ranchers and it is true that the department does these things and also works very closely with the United States Department of Agriculture and county agricultural officials. This department is responsible for the Texas Agricultural Products campaign that promotes products grown in Texas. Market information bulletins are regularly published and the department is also actively involved in the control of pests and fungus that might infect crops, such as the vitally important citrus industry in the Rio Grande Valley, grown in Texas. But the department is also very much involved with people who live in urban areas. For instance, the department closely inspects commercial egg farms, which is a major agricultural activity in Texas since most of the eggs sold in stores are produced in the state probably fairly close to where they are bought. They inspect all electrically operated fuel pumps so that when you buy any type of fuel for your motor vehicle you will see a blue inspection stamp displayed on the pump. No, they do not regulate the price we pay for our motor fuel, but they do tell us that the pump is accurate and we are getting the right amount of fuel for our money. They also inspect public scales all the way from the scales at truck stops to the scales at check-out areas in grocery stores - in other words, if someone is charged according to the weight that appears on the scale it is considered a public scale. Again, the department does not regulate prices, just the accuracy of the scale.

The **Comptroller of Public Accounts** is the person in charge of the state's money. All state taxes are collected by the Comptroller's office such as sales tax, motor fuel tax, alcoholic beverage tax and the myriad of other state taxes that we have in Texas. When the taxes are collected they are immediately deposited with most of the money going into interest -bearing accounts until it is needed. When a state warrant (another name for check) is issued it, too, is done by the Comptroller's office. The largest source of state income comes from federal government grants. The three biggest sources of in-state income, per year, are the sales tax at $11,000,000,000, the motor fuel tax at $2,500,000,000, and the tax on car sales, rentals and trailers at $2,200,000,000. It should be noted that neither the tobacco or alcoholic beverage taxes are major sources of income with the tobacco tax bringing in about $610,000,000 and the alcoholic beverage tax bringing in about $442,000,000.

Another point to make about the Comptroller's office is that is we, as consumers, think we are being cheated in paying the sales tax, for instance, a complaint can be filed with the Comptroller's office, of which there are many scattered around the state. For instance, if you are being charged 8¼ percent in an area where 7¼ percent is in effect you have a legitimate complaint. Or if you are being charged the sales tax on each individual item as it is being rung up you have a legitimate complaint since the sales tax is supposed to be added to the total, not each individual item.

The **Railroad Commission** was set up under the administration of Governor James S. Hogg in the 1890's to regulate railroads in Texas since railroads were the main form of travel within the state at that time. As the oil industry grew in Texas the Commission moved into regulating that industry. Today, Texas still produces about 30% of all domestically produced crude oil in the United States and the commission has the authority to set an "allowable" which means that the Commission can, in may cases, regulate crude oil in the United States and Commission has the authority to set an "allowable" which means that the Commission can, in many cases, regulate crude oil production. The Railroad commission also regulates natural gas rates in Texas along with the regulation of intrastate trucking companies and taxicab and bus companies operating within Texas that carry people for payment of a fare and that are not already regulated (such as is Metro in Houston) by another level of government. Because of its involvement in the oil industry, the Texas Railroad Commission has been called the most powerful state-level regulatory agency in the United States and realize that the petrochemical industry is the largest economic activity in Texas with agriculture being second.

The **State Board of Education**, made up of fifteen members elected from fifteen separate districts, basically sets the state standards for public education in Texas, including the selection of textbooks that are used in public schools, establishing the minimum number of credits that a high school students needs for graduation along with the required courses that high school students must take and even getting involved in what courses prospective teachers take to get their teaching certification in order to teach in public schools in Texas. Their decisions are then carried out by the **Texas Education Agency**.

Among the larger agencies headed by appointed officials is the office of the **Secretary of State**, who is considered the highest appointed official in Texas and is currently Elton Bomer from Anderson county. The responsibilities of the Secretary of State almost defy description. He is the state official in charge of voter registration and you will notice in the upper right corner of the front of your voter registration certificate an 800 telephone number for any questions. This number will connect you with the election division of the Secretary of State. This office also is responsible for determining the official election results of people running for state office and also makes sure they have the qualifications to run for the office in the first place. His office keeps the official seal of the State of Texas which must be affixed to all official documents signed by the governor. He is custodian of all official state records and keeps the original copy of each law passed by the legislature. His office is responsible for the registration of lobbyists and their financial statements along with records of campaign expenditures of candidates. With the exception of banks and insurance companies, the Secretary of State is responsible for chartering Texas corporations and if an out-of-state company wants to do business in Texas they must get a permit from this office. The Secretary of State is also responsible for the publication of the *Texas Register*, the official newspaper of Texas which is available to the public. One can say with some accuracy that if something comes up that you do not know to whom it should be given or you do not want to create a new agency to handle it, give it to the Secretary of Sate.

The **Texas Higher Education Coordinating Board**, made up of eighteen members, is responsible for higher education in Texas. In Texas we have thirty-five state-supported Universities, fifty community college districts, thirty-nine independent universities and two independent community colleges. THECB approves or disapproves requests for new degree programs and courses that a college or university might want. It deals with transfer of credits between colleges and universities and is responsible for administering state student financial aid programs. The board is involved in the authorization of new community college district, and it deals with legislative appropriations for colleges and universities in Texas. It is, in other words, the state agency that deals with all higher education institutions in Texas whether they be community colleges, senior colleges and universities, and other related institutions.

Texas Department of Public Safety deals with state law enforcement. Included in the DPS is the Highway Patrol which has the authority to patrol all state and federal highways in Texas along with the usual duties of a police agency. Also included is the issuance of driver's license's and inspection of motor vehicles. In Texas it is relatively easy to get and keep a driver's license—a person is actually tested on their driving ability when they first apply for a license (usually at age sixteen) and from then on, provided there are no serious driving law violations, renewal can be done by mail with renewal, following age eighteen, being every four years with the only "examination" being your eyesight since many Texans do need "corrective lens" when driving a motor vehicle. The DPS is also responsible for the annual motor vehicle inspection and while they do not do the actual inspection they certify those garages, mechanics, car dealers, etc. who do the actual inspection on your vehicle and make sure that the inspections are being done according to law. The DPS also has one of the most extensive criminal laboratories of any state located at their Austin headquarters. The fabled Texas Rangers are also part of the DPS, as is the Texas Ranger Museum located in Waco.

The Texas Department of Transportation is responsible for the building and maintaining of federal and state highways in Texas and with 77,145 miles of paved highways designated with a number (interstate, federal, state and farm-to-market) this is a major responsibility. Much of the construction and maintenance is done by private contractors but the DOT has overall supervision.

The **Texas Department of Human Services** is responsible, on the state level, for social programs such as assistance to those who fall under the federal poverty guidelines, aid to senior citizens, assistance to those who are permanently disabled and aid to the needy blind. This is the second biggest expenditure only following money for education. About three-quarters of the money spent by the TDHS comes from federal funds.

Texas Department of Criminal Justice. The primary division of the TDCJ that we hear about is its Institutional Division which used to be called the Texas Department of Corrections. The Institutional Division runs the State's prison systems. Texas State Senator John Whitmire, as Chairman of the Senate Criminal Justice Committee, has said that the Texas prison system has approximately 165,000 inmates with seventy to eighty percent of them being involved in drugs prior to being incarcerated. It costs something over 2.2 billion dollars annually to house them. It is also estimated that about 79% of Institutional Division inmates did not finish high school. The Institutional Division does have provisions for inmates to continue their education within the Windham Independent School District which serves the prison system. It is estimated that the recidivism rate of those who have received their GED or High School diploma from Windham is only twenty percent. At one time all state prison facilities were in the southeast quadrant of Texas since Hunstville was the headquarters but now there are units scattered all around Texas. A quite disturbing statistic, gleaned from a recent issue of *U.S. News and World Report*, says that Texas has the highest proportion of, its population behind bars of any of the fifty states with 6.53 Texans per 1,000 behind bars. Next highest is Louisiana with 5.68 per 1,000 with North Dakota being the lowest with .85 per 1,000. Actually, there is one area that is higher than Texas: Washington D.C., with 16.5 per 1,000 in jail.

Parks and Wildlife Commission operates the more than one hundred state parks located in all parts of Texas. Some of these parks have full facilities for utilities while others are bare of facilities but are still very acceptable for camping or simply a day outing. The Commission is also responsible for issuing hunting and fishing licenses and enforcing the state's hunting and fishing laws.

The **Texas Lottery Commission** is responsible for operating the various lottery games that we have in Texas such as Lotto Texas, Cash 5, Pick 3, Texas Million and the Instant Games (or "scratch off.") Courtesy of Ms. Marcy Goodfleish, Communications Director for the Texas Lottery Commission, it is estimated that for calendar year 1998 total lottery sales, for all games, was $2,900,000,000 with the State's share being $1,090,000,000 all of which now goes to the State's education fund which adds up to about 35% of total lottery sales. Approximately 53% goes to winners, 7% goes for administrative costs and the remaining 5% goes to the retailers who sell the lottery to customers.

There are, of course, many other state-level agencies, departments, bureaus, boards, etc. but those covered here are the ones headed by elected officials along with the Secretary of State, the Texas Higher Education Coordinating Board, the Texas Department of Public Safety, the Texas Department of Transportation, the Texas Department of Human Services, the Texas Department of Criminal Justice and the Parks and Wildlife Commission. There are, in total, more than two-hundred state-level agencies.

On-Line: The Executive

For the **Governor of the State of Texas**,

> http://www.governor.state.tx.us/

Master List of all **State of Texas Agencies**:

> http://www.texas/gov/agency/agencies.html

Window on State Government is one of the best sites on state government on the Web.

> http://www.cpa.state.tx.us/

Chapter 9

The Judiciary

Learning Objectives:

After reading this chapter, the student should be able to:

- Explain the functions of the judicial system
- Outline the court system of Texas, naming all the courts that comprise it; define the jurisdiction of each court, including the route of appeals; and describe the method of selection and replacement of judges, their tenure and qualifications

The court system in Texas—and all America—reflects hundreds of years of evolution, dating back to England of the Middle Ages. United States courts assume an *adversarial* quality: From the contest of opposing views, "justice" emerges. Centuries ago, if a subject of the throne had a personal dispute, the matter might be resolved on the playing field, where appointed knights would do battle. The "winner" of the contest reflected the "truth," and was regarded by most as a sign from God. This practice was known as *Trial by Combat*. Today the battle is in the courtroom, but the "champions" have law degrees rather than white steeds and heavy armor.

The Texas court system also reflects its particular place in American history. As noted in Chapter Two, the framers of the Texas Constitution in 1875 were reacting to Reconstruction, when the defeated South was compelled to change its ways. Once the federal troops were gone, however, things reverted back to "normal," as the Texas leadership saw it. Furthermore, public opinion then displayed a prominent frontier ethic that included a distrust of appointed officials. The only way to control judges, they reasoned, was to elect them. Only eight states elect judges on a partisan ballot.

Trial by jury is another hallmark of the Texas judicial system. All people in the United States have the Constitutional right to a jury trial in cases of a serious crime. But the Texas system goes much further. People who receive a traffic citation are entitled to a jury verdict. Furthermore, even in **civil** cases (law suits in which no crime is alleged), either side in the adversary process can demand a jury trial. As for costs, the "loser" often is compelled to pay, but there is no guarantee this arrangement will occur.

The nature of our elected judiciary and the jury system will be explored later. First, a brief overview of the structure of the Texas Court system is required.

The Trial Courts of Texas

Municipal Courts

These courts are often labeled "traffic courts" because most of their responsibilities relate to the prosecution of offenders driving motor vehicles. It is important to note, however, that municipalities only involve "incorporated" areas—places within a city boundary. Hence these courts are sometimes also called "corporation courts." Traffic violations outside a city limit are probably taken care of in a Justice of the Peace Court (see below). Municipal courts have no *civil* jurisdiction, meaning no lawsuits are conducted there. All cases therefore are criminal and involve Class C Misdemeanors (carrying a maximum penalty of $500 in fines) or violation of city ordinances, with fines of up to $2000. Cities are allowed under a 1989 statute to derive up to 30 per cent of their budgets from unhappy motorists. This particular law was directed at infamous "speed traps" such as Patton Village in Southeast Texas. However, some cities evade the law by placing defendants on "deferred adjudication" and charging only court costs, thus by-passing the state. The motorist is of course generally happy to oblige, to keep the violation off his or her record.

Usually municipal judges are appointed by the city council. They may be full-time, part-time, paid or unpaid, depending generally on the population of the city. As of 1999 there were 17 Municipal Judges in Houston, for instance, with 34 Associate (part-time) Judges. In small ("general law") cities, the mayor typically serves as sole municipal judge. Jury trials are rare and attorneys almost never appear, since the maximum fine for a Class C offense is above what most lawyers would charge anyway. Most trials in these courts last a few minutes and appeals are few. In addition to the accused, the police officer issuing the citation presumably testifies.

It is common to hear people talk of how they "beat" a traffic ticket. Usually this is accomplished by "falling through the cracks" in an overcrowded system. Perhaps the police officer was unable to appear, causing the judge to dismiss the case. Technical errors, at the discretion of the judge, may also merit dismissal. Similarly, defendants who are convicted can appeal to County Court, where judges sometimes never get around to it, and the original verdict is eventually suspended. This is especially likely in small cities where they have no "Court of Record," or transcript, of the trial. In these instances the County Court must conduct a trial *de novo*, or new trial, which is harder to fit into a crowded docket. Appealing a case usually involves a filing fee, which defendants gladly pay if their conviction would result in losing their driver's license or a hike in insurance premiums.

The most common remedy is simply to pay the fine. Increasingly, municipal and other courts allow defendants to pay through the mail by checking off the appropriate plea. If the defendant pleads "guilty" or "*nolo contendere*" (no contest), a handy chart on the citation often indicates the appropriate fine. To plead "not guilty" requires a trip to see the judge.

Justice of the Peace Court

Texas lore traces the local Justice of the Peace to the days of Judge Roy Bean and the infamous "Law West of the Pecos." Such law officers were often virtual dictators, especially in rural areas. Bean reportedly once shot a man as punishment, then charged "court costs" in the amount found in the dead man's pocket.

Although J.P.'s, as they are called, frequently perform marriages, certify deaths, and do other general duties, the job of a Justice varies tremendously with the population of the county. Each of the 842 J.P.'s represents a precinct, and is elected to a four-year term. The Texas Constitution does not require them to be attorneys, but newly elected judges must attend special training sessions. Some in rural areas are paid a token one dollar in salary. Others (in the urban areas primarily) receive compensation of over $60,000.

J.P. Courts share criminal jurisdiction with Municipal Court in the matter of Class C Misdemeanors. In a practical sense, this means mostly traffic citations issued *outside* city limits. Hence J.P. Court becomes the "traffic court" of many Texans. J.P.'s are assisted by Constables who perform a wide range of services, depending upon the population of the county. In the unincorporated suburban areas outside Houston, for example, Constables and their deputies are the chief law enforcement officers, though their court jurisdiction technically extends only to Class C Misdemeanors. The Sheriff's Department generally handles serious cases originating outside city limits. In most areas, Constables mainly serve court orders (subpoenas, summonses, etc.) and help the J.P. keep order. Inner city J.P.'s typically devote themselves to non-traffic matters, since municipalities handle all traffic violations within city limits.

Unlike Municipal Court Judges, Justices of the Peace have *civil jurisdiction*, which involves the dispensation of lawsuits. While it is possible under its concurrent (shared with County Courts) authority to try cases involving as much as $5,000, most cases involve disputes under $500. If less than $20 is at stake, no appeal is allowed unless it involves a federal question and attracts the attention of the United States Supreme Court, which is very unlikely.

Justices of the Peace have another important function regarding their civil jurisdiction: *Small Claims Court*. Certain kinds of cases involving disputes of under $5,000 may be filed in J.P. Court for a token fee. These procedures resemble the "People's Court" of television. There are generally no lawyers and cases are decided on the spot, quickly and informally. While the Court charges extra for jury trials, subpoenas, and other court costs, the key purpose of Small Claims is easy access by those who can't afford to get into court otherwise. Not all complaints by plaintiffs in Small Claims Court are permissible, with jurisdiction generally devoted to the collection of unpaid debts and landlord/tenant disputes.

County Courts

Texas has a County Court, presided over by a County Judge, in each of the 254 counties, as required by the Texas Constitution. As one might expect, the responsibilities of this court vary tremendously, depending upon the population of the county. Only one-fourth of County Judges are attorneys, and are merely required to be "well informed of the laws of the state." This stipulation is generally met by special training courses. The jurisdiction of these courts runs the entire range: *criminal* (Class A and B Misdemeanors), *civil* (between $200 and $5,000), and *appeals* from J.P. and Municipal Courts within the county.

Historically in rural counties, the County Judge could be expected to handle all these matters. Obviously this is impossible in counties with large populations. Therefore, the Legislature has responded over the years in 71 Counties with the creation of special courts, usually called *County Courts at Law*, to relieve the County Judge of many—if not all—judicial responsibilities. The law setting up these courts requires that judges be licensed attorneys. Harris County, for instance, has nineteen of these "statutory" courts, four of which deal exclusively with civil cases and fifteen with criminal matters in which the fine exceeds $500 or where a jail sentence may be imposed. Special *probate* courts also have been created in several urban counties to deal with wills, estates, and guardians when people die. The salaries of these judges vary, but all are elected to a four year terms on partisan ballots.

District Courts

District Courts are the chief trial courts of Texas, handling felonies and civil cases involving the largest amounts of money, as well as divorces, contested elections, and land title disputes. At the trial level, there is no higher state court. The Legislature has created 396 District Courts as of 1998, some of which are labeled "Criminal District Court." In rural areas their jurisdiction extends to more than one county, creating a confusing system in which district lines overlap, shunting some counties into more than one judicial district. As the chief trial court, District Courts are where citizens are most likely to be called for jury service. District Judges are elected to four-year terms and their salary is set at a minimum of $85,217, with county supplements approved locally.

Texas Appeals Courts

When judges exercise *appellate jurisdiction*, they review a trial that has already been held. An old legal maxim declares that *trial* courts "find the facts" of a case. (Did the defendant, for instance, shoot her husband?) Appellate courts, on the other hand, "find the law." In practical terms this means appeals are chiefly concerned with *procedural* matters. Technically, appeals judges are not concerned in a criminal case with guilt or innocence or, in a civil case whether the plaintiff or defendant is correct in his or her claims. Their job is to review the transcript of the trial, looking for errors of procedure that may conflict with the law, the Constitution, or established *precedent* (a previous case dealing with a similar matter). They also consider oral and written arguments from both sides in the adversary process.

Court Structure of Texas

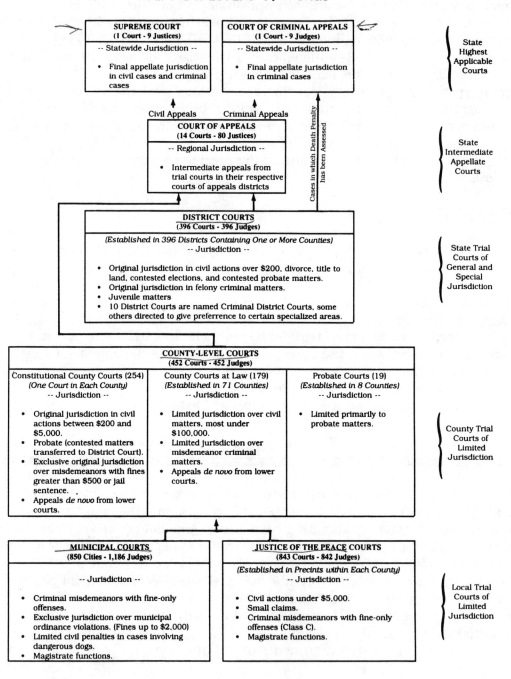

SUPREME COURT
(1 Court - 9 Justices)

-- Statewide Jurisdiction --

- Final appellate jurisdiction in civil cases and criminal cases

COURT OF CRIMINAL APPEALS
(1 Court - 9 Judges)

-- Statewide Jurisdiction --

- Final appellate jurisdiction in criminal cases

State Highest Applicable Courts

Civil Appeals   Criminal Appeals

COURT OF APPEALS
(14 Courts - 80 Justices)

-- Regional Jurisdiction --

- Intermediate appeals from trial courts in their respective courts of appeals districts

Cases in which Death Penalty has been Assessed

State Intermediate Appellate Courts

DISTRICT COURTS
(396 Courts - 396 Judges)

(Established in 396 Districts Containing One or More Counties)
-- Jurisdiction --

- Original jurisdiction in civil actions over $200, divorce, title to land, contested elections, and contested probate matters.
- Original jurisdiction in felony criminal matters.
- Juvenile matters
- 10 District Courts are named Criminal District Courts, some others directed to give preference to certain specialized areas.

State Trial Courts of General and Special Jurisdiction

COUNTY-LEVEL COURTS
(452 Courts - 452 Judges)

Constitutional County Courts (254)	County Courts at Law (179)	Probate Courts (19)
(One Court in Each County)	*(Established in 71 Counties)*	*(Established in 8 Counties)*
-- Jurisdiction --	-- Jurisdiction --	-- Jurisdiction --
• Original jurisdiction in civil actions between $200 and $5,000. • Probate (contested matters transferred to District Court). • Exclusive original jurisdiction over misdemeanors with fines greater than $500 or jail sentence. • Appeals *de novo* from lower courts.	• Limited jurisdiction over civil matters, most under $100,000. • Limited jurisdiction over misdemeanor criminal matters. • Appeals *de novo* from lower courts.	• Limited primarily to probate matters.

County Trial Courts of Limited Jurisdiction

MUNICIPAL COURTS
(850 Cities - 1,186 Judges)

-- Jurisdiction --

- Criminal misdemeanors with fine-only offenses.
- Exclusive jurisdiction over municipal ordinance violations. (Fines up to $2,000)
- Limited civil penalties in cases involving dangerous dogs.
- Magistrate functions.

JUSTICE OF THE PEACE COURTS
(843 Courts - 842 Judges)

(Established in Precincts within Each County)
-- Jurisdiction --

- Civil actions under $5,000.
- Small claims.
- Criminal misdemeanors with fine-only offenses (Class C).
- Magistrate functions.

Local Trial Courts of Limited Jurisdiction

Source: *Houston Community Newspapers.* Reprinted by permission. Updated by author.

Appellate judges in Texas serve six-year terms. Every two years, roughly a third of these jurists come up for election on partisan ballots, adding to the list of judicial posts voters are expected to evaluate. Virtually all of them could walk down a crowded street unrecognized, but they make decisions that affect ordinary people every day. Appellate judges must be at least thirty-five years old with at least ten years of legal experience. The Governor is authorized to fill vacancies (with Senate consent) until the next election. Decisions on appeals courts are made by majority vote of the judges (who are called "justices" on appellate tribunals) sitting either in panels or *en banc*, in which the entire membership sits together. Juries are not used in appeals, but oral and written arguments are presented by attorneys for both sides.

The Texas Courts of Appeal

Eighty Justices in these courts are elected from fourteen districts in Texas. Each court has a minimum of three Justices (a chief and two associates) and a maximum of twelve. The largest court is in Dallas, while two courts are in Houston alone. Salaries are set by law at 95 per cent of what a Texas Supreme Court Justice earns. The Courts of Appeals hear both civil and criminal cases, except for capital punishment review. These courts are "final" (barring any federal questions) in matters of divorce, slander, and boundary disputes.

The Texas Court of Criminal Appeals

The Court of Criminal Appeals is called the "court of last resort" in criminal cases. Except in rare instances when the United States Supreme Court gets involved, convicted defendants have exhausted all alternatives when this court rules. Typically the caseload (there is a backlog of over two years) consists of appeals from the Courts of Appeal and death penalty cases, which come directly from District Court. Approximately 200 capital murder cases typically await appeal.

One reason for the delay is simple. This is a single court, with nine members, in the second largest state in the U.S.—and a state with a very high crime and conviction rate. In spite of the public's concern over crime, the Justices enjoy relative anonymity, with incumbents usually getting re-elected with little difficulty. Large campaign contributions generating media advertising are rare in criminal court elections.

The Supreme Court of Texas

In terms of appellate jurisdiction there is nothing particularly "supreme" about the Texas Supreme Court, which is a court of "last resort" for **civil** cases only. Consequently its specific decisions attract less attention from the general public than the *other* court of "last resort," the Court of Criminal Appeals.

The Supreme Court of Texas is composed of nine members elected statewide: one Chief and eight Associate Justices. High-stakes lawsuits are appealed here. Consequently, attorneys who represent plaintiffs and defendants are very interested in the results of elections to the Supreme Court. The Justices also rule upon matters of law and constitutionality, particularly when Courts of Appeals have contradicted the Supreme Court's precedent or each other. If four Justices favor it, a case involving an "error" on the part of the Courts of Appeal can be scheduled for oral argument, or such an error may be corrected by a *per curiam* (a brief, unpublished) opinion without argument. The Supreme Court also has administrative responsibilities such as designing the rules for civil procedure and adjusting the workload for various lower courts.

Judicial Politics

Theoretically, electing judges gives the people a voice in the administration of justice. According to public opinion polls Texans are universally agreed that judges *should* be elected rather than appointed, as in many states and the entire federal court system. Few citizens, however, can name a single judge out of the almost 2,000 jurists in the state. Harris County, for example, has 56 District Judges, 23 County Courts-at-Law and probate judges and 16 Justices of the Peace—all on the ballot. In the old days, most folks only had a few judges to remember. Today, in all but the most rural counties, this is no longer the case.

In elections of low visibility, voters make choices using the fuzzy criteria of **name recognition**. There are rarely any issues in a judicial race, despite the public's concern over crime and justice issues. Name recognition can only be achieved in the metropolitan areas of Texas through media advertising, and this costs money of course. Attorneys whose interests are potentially at stake are often obliged to cough up campaign contributions supporting judicial candidates. This even applies in the trial courts. Lawyers who might frequently appeal in Judge Smith's court, for instance, feel compelled to contribute to Smith, lest there be some form of retribution later. One never knows what motions can be approved or delays granted when the wheels have been lubricated with a hefty display of friendship.

Similarly, incumbent judges usually do not draw strong opponents. It is not difficult to figure out why. Imagine running against a sitting District Judge, and losing—as most challengers do—then appearing in the same judge's court, filing a motion or asking for a delay. Even the most upright judge might be tempted to dish out a little "justice" on his or her own. Courthouse discussions abound with such tales of woe.

Another by-product of the low level of public awareness is what some have called the "familiar name syndrome." In the confusion of candidates, strange things have happened. In 1976 a man named Don Yarbrough was elected to the Texas Supreme Court, chiefly because his last name was spelled similarly to a popular former U.S. Senator. Shortly thereafter, Mr. Yarbrough was forced to resign due to public charges of fraud and bail jumping. He was arrested on the Caribbean island of Grenada where he had enrolled in medical school, amidst a flurry of embarrassing publicity. Recent judicial races have seen the likes of Sam Houston Clinton, Daniel Boone, and Ron Chapman (who also happened to be a popular radio announcer in Dallas). In 1994 a perennial candidate named Gene Kelly (not the famous actor and dancer) made it to a Democratic primary runoff spot for the Texas Court of Criminal Appeals. On the Republican side, a political newcomer named George Busch once got 42 per cent of the primary vote for the Supreme Court.

Some insiders argue that Texas does *not* elect most judges. When a District Judge or higher is considering retirement, there is often an unspoken agreement to leave office *during* the term rather than at the end. This allows the Governor to fill the vacancy until the next election, in which the incumbent has the edge. When the Governor makes appointments affecting a local Senator's district, the practice of **Senatorial Courtesy** also applies. The Governor must clear the name with the affected Senator or the Senator will get his or her colleagues to kill the appointment when the nominee comes up for approval. What is the moral of the story? Anyone who wants to be a judge had better have political connections (including, perhaps, campaign support) with her or her State Senator.

Occasionally, in spite of a reported decline in identification with political parties among citizens, partisan sweeps are increasingly common. In the 1998 elections, the Democrats suffered most, losing almost all of the contested seats for District Judge in Harris County alone. Katie Kennedy as of 1999 is the only Democratic judge in Harris County (and notice her last name). Texas has voted Republican for President in every election since 1976, affecting "down-ballot" judicial posts in many counties. Abolishing "straight ticket" voting would be an obvious alternative, but incumbents—Democrats and Republicans—are reluctant to abandon a practice from which they could benefit.

The issue of *race* is of paramount importance in urban counties where large proportions of ethnic minorities reside. Although Harris County, for instance, currently contains forty per cent ethnic minorities, as of 1999 there was only one African American judge—and he (Levi J. Benton) was appointed by Governor Bush to take the place of another African American who resigned to practice law. In all counties the judges in the courthouse are, for the most part, white males. While judges presumably render decisions regardless of factors such as race, the *perception* of fairness is something else. Racial minorities increasingly perceive that the system is stacked against them, especially since jails and prisons typically have an over-preponderance of minorities. Studies have shown that it is usually whites who get out on bail and receive probated sentences in far greater proportions than their share of the population. And blacks who kill whites are statistically more likely to receive the death penalty than whites who kill blacks.

Proposals for Change

Almost no one is happy with the method of electing judges in Texas. The problem, however, is finding an acceptable alternative—and one agreeable to the voters who insist on having a voice.

On the issue of minority representation, a recent proposal has received the most attention. It involves the potential election of District Judges from **single member districts**. Such a plan would treat judicial elections like those for legislative or city council seats in large cities. Minority representation would presumably be guaranteed, assuming the districts were drawn to reflect targeted neighborhoods. Despite the fact that political scientists have been unable to detect *any* policy differences with the use of single-member districts, minority Texans often press for such a change.

The United States Supreme Court ruled in 1991 that the Voting Rights Act, which was designed to empower racial minorities, applies to judicial races too. But the high court also held that the Texas system of judicial selection was *not* discriminatory. Legally speaking, race isn't supposed to matter. As a matter of fact, the Court in 1996 overturned the practice of "racial gerrymandering" (drawing district lines using race as the key factor) in Congressional districts.

Ideas to inject more diversity on the bench can get downright exotic. Supreme Court Chief Justice Tom Phillips once proposed a highly controversial approach called "cumulative voting." Cumulative voting, which has mainly been advocated by liberal civil rights advocates, allows voters to cast *more than one vote* for the same candidate. Hispanics or blacks, for example, might wish to cast all their votes for candidates of their race. This approach to getting more minorities into judicial positions (which is used in some cities and school districts in the United States) has often been considered "too radical" to be practical. Ironically, Chief Justice Phillips is a conservative Republican. Perhaps his proposal reflects the desperation of many officials to try something—*anything*—to make changes.

Some reformers argue that "merit selection" of judges is the proper path. Most of these proposals are variations of the so-called **Missouri Plan**, which many states have adopted in one form or another. One variation calls for judges to be appointed by the Governor from a list of three nominees named by a representative commission. At the end of a specified period (say four years) the appointed judge would face the voters in a "retention" election in which voters would simply choose whether to keep or remove the incumbent. The Governor would then appoint a new one if he or she were tossed out of office. The presumed result of this approach would be to eliminate partisanship, campaign contributions, and the perils of the "familiar name syndrome." Naturally, the "politics" of judicial posts would shift to the nominating commission, where various special interests and perspectives would come forth. Political scientists have been unable to detect any measurable advantage of this method, partly because the qualities of a "good" judge are so subject to individual interpretation. One study discovered that 99 percent of "retention elections" in ten states over twenty years resulted in the re-election of incumbents anyway. Hence the appointive-elective combination, even if adopted, would hardly result in anything drastic.

Both major political parties are skeptical of changes that would weaken their potential influence on judicial politics. Any variation of the current method would require a Constitutional Amendment, which takes a two-thirds vote of both chambers of the Legislature and voter approval. It must be remembered that most Texans vehemently oppose any alternatives that purport to take away their voice at the ballot box. To complicate matters even further, any change would have to find a way between the 1965 Voting Rights Act, which prohibits changes in elections that might endanger the chances of minorities, and 1996 U.S. Supreme Court decisions banning race-based political units.

Justice For Sale—*Again?*

On November 11, 1998 the popular television program "60 Minutes" broadcast a segment about the Texas court system. Actually it was a "follow-up" to an earlier program several years ago. In both the original broadcast and its successor, the profile of the Lone Star State was not flattering. The specific topic concerned elections for the Supreme Court of Texas. By way of background, one of the principal financial contributors to candidates for the Court years ago was a plaintiff's lawyer, Houston's Joe Jamail. Jamail had successfully represented the Pennzoil Corporation in a suit against Texaco. The suit resulted in a multi-billion dollar award, the largest jury verdict of its kind in recorded history. When Texaco routinely appealed to the Supreme Court, the Justices refused to take a serious look at it. Critics charged that the Justices who voted not to hear the appeal had been influenced by their contributions from Jamail and other plaintiff-oriented lawyers. While the case was eventually "settled" with a reported one billion dollars, howls of criticism resulted. As might be expected, lawyers who traditionally represent *defendants* in civil cases were the principal complainers. The recent "60-Minutes" follow-up portrayed the Texas Supreme Court just as unfavorably. However, this time the Court (which is now very different in makeup) was elected reportedly with money from corporate interests rather than plaintiff's attorneys. In other words, the same thing is going on now, but the Court just switched sides. What's going on here?

Political scientists have learned to track the votes of appeals court judges, placing them (somewhat arbitrarily) into the categories of "**underdog**" and "**upperdog**." (More than one scholar has sarcastically dubbed this approach the *canine* theory of judicial behavior.) In civil cases, when a Justice votes for the plaintiff, it is generally recorded as an "underdog" vote, meaning the beneficiary is presumably someone who has been wrongfully injured. The classic "underdog," for instance, would be the patient in a medical malpractice case. Under this view, the "upperdog" would be the defendant. This broad category would include insurance companies, doctors, and corporations who tend to get sued.

Simply put, these scholars have been able to measure the extent to which appeals judges tend to be "pro-plaintiff" or "pro-defendant." (Trial judges are more difficult to assess because they don't "vote," except in the case of motions.) This under/upperdog split is also apparent in what kinds of people tend to support which candidates for office. Sometimes it is easy to see. Millionaire rancher Clinton Manges once admittedly poured over $350,000 into judicial campaigns in an attempt to get judges sympathetic to ranchers in a dispute with oil companies. "Pro-plaintiff" money is often funneled through the Texas Trial Lawyers Association (known in Austin as the "Trials.") The "defendant" side is slippery to identify, but doctors, hospitals, insurance companies, and large businesses supply generous contributions to judicial candidates through their Political Action Committees.

Two points need to be emphasized about the "Justice for Sale" perspective. First, Justices rarely fit neatly into upperdog/underdog compartments. Perhaps the most significant case decided by the Texas Supreme Court in the last generation was the **Edgewood v. Kirby** case of 1989, ordering a massive overhaul of the state's system of school finance. It was a classic "underdog" decision, benefiting the poorer school districts against the wealthier ones. But the decision was unanimous, nine to zero. Underdogs, upperdogs, liberals, conservatives, Democrats and Republicans all voted alike—at least on this important case.

The second point to remember is that judicial politics is not much different from all politics. We would hardly be shocked if a legislator voted consistently for the interests that helped him or her get elected. Such obligations are perhaps inherent in an elected judiciary too. Maybe the people of Texas understand this. According to the respected Texas Poll, 72 per cent of the public believes judges' decisions are "somewhat influenced" by political pressure from campaign contributors. Yet 71 per cent favor keeping the current system of elected judges.

Trial by Jury

Most criminal and civil cases never reach the trial stage. Civil cases are generally settled "out of court," and criminal cases usually result in a **"plea bargain,"** when the defendant pleads guilty in exchange for more favorable treatment. Hence the popular image of American justice (enhanced by television dramas and in celebrated cases such as that of O.J. Simpson) is inaccurate to the degree that it projects a full-blown trial as the way matters are typically settled. In fact the picture one should have is of private conversations between attorneys, prosecutors, and judges, feverishly engaged in the task of *avoiding* a trial. This image is less dramatic, perhaps, but more rooted in reality.

Grand Juries

Grand juries have a rich history dating back to England of the Middle Ages. Their purpose has traditionally been to decide if enough evidence exists for a criminal trial. Philosophically, the idea is that one's fellow citizens—*peers*—should evaluate such matters, not an agency of the government.

Texas Grand Juries are composed of twelve citizens who meet the qualifications for trial juries (see below). They are used primarily for felony investigations, though they are not limited as such. Misdemeanors usually are prosecuted through the use of an **information**, which involves documents filed by the District or County Attorney, based on a complaint by any creditable person, often a police officer.

Though any qualified juror can legally serve on a Grand Jury, and some counties use random selection, the selection process is often far more complicated. The District Judge becomes what tradition calls the **"key man."** He or she appoints a Jury Commission, composed of three to five citizens from different parts of the county. The Commission prepares a list of prospective Grand Jurors, using unspecified criteria. The Judge then narrows the list down to twelve and appoints a "foreman" (male or female, of course). Needless to say, the District Judge can get the sort of jurors he or she thinks necessary to do the job. Judges and prosecutors defend the "key man" selection process, claiming it is not biased jurors they are seeking, but dependable and conscientious people who can find the time to serve. Jurors typically are "on call" during a three to six month term, sometimes serving as often as two days a week in urban areas.

Grand jury proceedings are secret: Press and public are not allowed. Presumably this protects witnesses from embarrassment or intimidation, but in celebrated cases, television cameras often record the witness entering and leaving the jury chambers. Participants are instructed not to discuss their deliberations, and witnesses can not bring their attorneys into the chambers with them. As a result, Grand Jury proceedings are one-sided investigations (**"ex-parte"** is the legal term) in which evidence comes solely from the District Attorney's office prosecuting the case. Not surprisingly, jurors generally agree with the D.A. in deciding whether to accuse someone. "Runaway" Grand Juries, striking out on their own to investigate, are rare.

If at least nine members of the Grand Jury agree, they adopt what is known as a **Bill of Indictment** (called a "True Bill") and the defendant stands accused officially. If the Grand Jury lacks the votes to indict someone, it is called a "No bill," (in legal terms, *ignoramus*—literally from the Latin, "We don't know.") If the deck seems stacked in favor of the prosecution in Grand Juries, it must be remembered that the trial is yet to come, where the presumption remains "innocent until proven guilty beyond a reasonable doubt." The burden of proof is ultimately on the state.

Trial Juries

While service on Grand Juries is a rare occurrence for the average person, most adult Texans are quite likely to receive a summons for service on a trial (or "**petit**") jury. The qualifications are minimal, according to Chapter 23 of the Government Code: Jurors must be at least 18, of "sound mind," citizens, able to read and write, and not convicted or under indictment for a felony. Automatic exemptions are allowed for those over 70, people with custody of children under ten, caretakers of the disabled, those with physical or mental impairments, or students "in class." Everyone else is legally expected to appear when called, but courts often make exceptions when contacted about emergencies or delays.

The Texas Secretary of State provides a list of potential jurors, taken from voter registration, licensed drivers and ID cards issued by the Department of Public Safety. Computers are used to choose prospective jurors (called "veniremen") by random selection. District Court juries consist of twelve persons; all other trial courts have six-person juries. People who have been called up for jury duty generally convene at the specified time and begin a process of sorting and eliminating, depending upon the case load and pending trials. A judge listens and rules upon requests by those who wish, for personal reasons, to be excused. An oath is given. Most experienced veniremen recommend bringing along reading material, as the selection process is often lengthy and somewhat unpredictable. Many perplexed citizens have waited for hours, even days, only to be sent home with a polite thank you. Why? Perhaps the pending case was settled "out of court," or resolved with a plea bargain. Or simply perhaps more people were called up than needed.

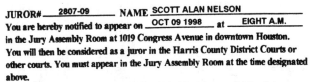
The system is designed to produce an impartial jury. Before the trial jurors are seated, they must escape successful **challenges** by the opposing attorneys, in the form of an interview process known as **voir dire** (literally "to say truly"). Prospective jurors are asked individually and collectively about any prejudices they may have. It is common in criminal trials for citizens to be asked whether they have been the victim of a crime recently, for instance. Jurors must fully understand such concepts as "burden of proof," and "self-incrimination." Sometimes citizens openly admit to prejudices of one kind or another and are routinely thanked and excused.

A **challenge for cause** is requested by one of the attorneys and ruled upon by the judge if a reason can be found for a prospective juror to be eliminated from consideration. These challenges are unlimited in number. **Peremptory** challenges, known around the courthouse as "strikes," are opportunities to eliminate a juror for no *apparent* reason. Appearance, body language, occupation, religion, and general attitude are all fair game, but race and gender have been ruled out by the United States Supreme Court. Each side has a specified number of "strikes," depending upon the nature of the case. Generally more peremptories are allowed in criminal cases than in lawsuits. Skillful attorneys use their "strikes" wisely to fashion a jury that will listen favorably to their side.

Judicial Procedure: Criminal Cases

Thanks to television and movies, most Americans have a general sense of what a criminal trial is like. Most of us can cite *verbatim* the rights of suspects at the time of arrest *("You have the right to remain silent . . . ")*. Over the last fifty years the United States Supreme Court has enforced rigid standards upon the states, resulting in a great deal of uniformity. Suspects are entitled to these rights whether they are in California or Mississippi.

In Texas, trial by jury is an entitlement in all criminal cases, even the smallest of misdemeanors. Defendants can waive a jury trial if they wish, whereupon the case is decided by a judge (except for capital murder cases, which must be decided by a jury). The verdict must be unanimous in a Texas criminal trial. One must constantly remember, however, that in all states the vast majority of cases are settled through guilty pleas by plea bargaining. This avoids a trial altogether except for a brief hearing. The general public disapproves of plea bargains, probably because they result in punishments that are less severe than what may befit the crime. But most professionals (police, judges, attorneys, probation officers, etc.) insist that plea bargains are indispensable. A trial in every case is virtually impossible given the limited resources of the real world.

For almost forty years the United States Supreme Court has required that states provide attorneys for people who can't afford one. This only applies, however, to persons accused of serious crimes (those prescribing prison or a jail sentence). Some states have fully-funded Public Defenders' offices whose sole responsibility is defending accused people who need it. Texas, however, provides court-appointed counsel, in a manner that varies from county to county. Often this takes the form of a rotating list of attorneys. Typically they are paid according to the services they perform. A jury trial would involve more time—and hence more money.

Civil Procedure

A law suit begins with a **plaintiff**, the party who "complains" by filing a **petition** with the clerk of the court of original jurisdiction (which depends upon the money involved and the nature of the complaint). A filing fee must generally be paid. Divorces, for instance, are filed in the District Clerk's office. The clerk issues a **citation**, which is **served** (delivered by mail or in person) to the **defendant**. The petition also includes the **remedy** that is sought, which usually involves money but could also direct a change in behavior on the part of the defendant. If the defendant wants to contest the suit, a written **answer** is filed with the same clerk, explaining why the plaintiff is not entitled to the stipulated remedy.

Judges have authority to dismiss lawsuits, according to precedent or common sense. (Imagine hypothetically a suit filed by a plaintiff who claims his neighbor has been communicating with flying saucers in a conspiracy to kill his azalea bushes. Obviously this should go no further in clogging the overcrowded dockets of the court system.) Usually the filing fee takes care of most frivolous matters, but the judge may step in to stop a proceeding before it goes any further.

A trial date will be set once all the paperwork is in place. The waiting period could be weeks or months, depending upon how many delays either side asks for and how efficient the court is in expediting its caseload. It is during this period that *discovery* occurs, in which each side is obligated to share its evidence with the other. (Unlike television portrayals, "surprise" witnesses and documents are generally not allowed.) The long waiting period serves a useful purpose in encouraging settlements "out of court."

As noted earlier, Texas allows trial by jury in all cases, including law suits—a relatively rare practice among the states. Either side in the adversary process can demand a jury by right. This entitlement adds an important dynamic to Texas justice, and has perhaps contributed to the Lone Star State's reputation as a suit-happy haven for plaintiffs and their lawyers. Typically it is the plaintiff who requests a jury trial. Most controversy involves expensive "tort" claims (cases of wrongful personal injury), such as the recent highly publicized jury awards involving breast implants in Houston. Nationwide, a recent book on the implant cases by Dr. Marcia Angell called **Science on Trial**, reports that from 25 to 40% of tort claims go to plaintiff's attorneys. In recent years an organization in Texas called Citizens Against Lawsuit Abuse has enlisted 17,000 members statewide in an effort to forestall what they see as "frivolous" suits. On the other hand, a 1996 study by the Pennsylvania-based Jury Verdict Research, a national clearinghouse on civil law suit statistics, indicates that, at least in Harris County, plaintiffs are more likely to *lose* than elsewhere in the country. The whole concept of "frivolousness" is definitely a matter of perspective.

Whatever their alleged generosity, juries are very unpredictable. Attorneys often advise their clients to settle out of court to avoid the "wild card" of trial. Lawyers can use the threat of a jury trial to intimidate opponents into a better deal. Naturally the "game" becomes political as well. Although the Supreme Court of Texas makes the rules for civil procedure, statutes passed by the Legislature can modify them. Interest groups representing the two principal sides in the adversary process (the plaintiff's and defendant's attorneys, insurance companies, etc.) lobby energetically to stack the cards in their favor. In recent years, for instance, a bitter fight has waged over the issue of trial by jury in workers' compensation claims. Business lobbyists obviously have a point of view quite different from plaintiff's lawyers, who are ably represented in the Legislature by the Texas Trial Lawyers Association.

If a settlement does not occur, the trial date eventually arrives. After brief opening statements, the plaintiff's case is presented, subject to cross-examination by the opponent's lawyer. The jury may be escorted to the private jury room from time to time, as the adversaries argue the admissibility of evidence according to precedent. The defendant's case is presented next, and cross-examined by the opposing attorney. Throughout the trial objections are commonly raised, either to convince the judge to disallow certain testimony or establish a basis for appeal later. An important distinction between a criminal and a civil case is that criminal cases involve rights guaranteed by the United States Constitution, while a civil case generally does not.

Once the testimony is complete, a "**charge**" to the jury is prepared by the judge and attorneys for both sides. This "charge" is very important. It is a set of written instructions defining precisely what the jury is to decide. Civil juries do not rule upon questions of guilt or innocence. Rather, they might be instructed to answer a series of "yes" or "no" questions and deliberate on the proper remedy if the defendant is found negligent. After reading the charge to the jury, the two sides make closing arguments. Finally the jurors retire with their instructions to the jury room.

In the jury room, the foreman (who is selected by his or her fellow jurors) attempts to obtain responses to the questions. Unlike criminal juries, civil juries do not require unanimity. Only ten votes out of twelve (five out of six in County and Justice of the Peace Court) are necessary to render a decision. Anything less represents a "hung jury," or mistrial, whereupon a new trial can be ordered with a new panel of jurors. Jurors are typically given a list of items they are not to discuss during their deliberations or outside the courtroom during any breaks. If the case involves an automobile accident, for instance, jurors are not allowed to speculate whether the defendant has insurance. Such rules are designed for fundamental fairness, but also reflect the "card stacking" by interest groups (in this case, insurance companies) in the formulation of rules by the Texas Supreme Court and the Legislature.

If the jury can reach a verdict, they send word to the judge, court is called back into session, and the verdict is announced. In our adversarial system, it will be recalled, there are "winners" and "losers." However, it is often difficult to tell which is which in a complicated case. "Losing" a case with a small remedy might be very pleasing to the defendant.

Getting a lawyer in the first place could potentially be the most serious practical dilemma. The "right to counsel" only applies to criminal cases, and those without funds often have little entry into the court system. Plaintiff's lawyers often take cases on "contingency," in which a portion of any monetary award is taken as payment. Under this approach, the plaintiff pays little or nothing until a favorable verdict or settlement is announced. The attorney takes the risk of losing.

The State Bar of Texas in 1992 recommended that all attorneys donate fifty hours of work each year for poor people who need a lawyer. Indeed, large law firms often donate portions of their caseload **pro bono publico** ("for the good of the public"), but this has not been enough to meet increasing demand (there are around 90 million suits filed annually in the United States). While the Bar Association guidelines remain only voluntary, it is hoped the halls of justice will remain open to all Texans, rich or poor.

On-Line: The Judiciary

Texas Judiciary Online for all your state legal needs, including links to state courts.

http://www.courts.state.tx.us/

Texas Supreme Court

http://www.supreme.courts.state.tx.us/

Office of Attorney General of Texas has extensive information for consumer rights, child support, victims' rights, and much more.

http://www.oag.state.tx.us/

National Center for State Courts is an information clearinghouse for state legal affairs.

http://www.ncsc.dni.us/ncsc.htm

Find Law is a huge online resource for legal matters.

http://www.findlaw.com/

State Bar Association of Texas

http://www.martindale.com/profession/statebar/tx99.html

Tarlton Law Library

http://tarlton.law.utexas.edu/

Justice For All is a Houston-based advocate for victims' rights.

http://www2.jfa.net/jfa/

Court TV

http://www.courttv.com/

Chapter 10

Texas Fiscal and Budget Policies

Learning Objectives

After reading this chapter the student should be able to:

- ✪ Discuss the impact of conservative ideas on Texas budget practices
- ✪ Describe the constitutional rules and constraints on the Texas budget and budgeting practices
- ✪ Describe the major economic forces shaping the Texas budget
- ✪ Discuss how legal actions affect the Texas budget
- ✪ List and summarize the major sources of state revenue
- ✪ List and summarize the major components of state spending
- ✪ Understand the roles of the major budget players in Texas
- ✪ Discuss trends affecting state finances
- ✪ Summarize the controversial issues raised by state budgeting practices

The fiscal and budget policies of Texas government are the most important outcomes of Texas politics. How much money should the government raise? What kind of tax system should we have? Who should benefit from for state spending? Who should bear the burden of state taxes? What are the spending priorities and unmet needs of the citizens of Texas? What is the proper size (and responsibility) of government? These matters are ultimately settled by the fiscal and budgetary decisions public officials make on behalf of the citizens of Texas.

Budgets are more than the numbers of dollars required for financing government operations. Budgets are blueprints for the moral and civic responsibilities of individuals and their governments. They are an accounting list for our collective values. In so far as budgets show us who will pay and who will benefit by state taxing and spending policies, they are also scorecards showing who is winning and who is losing the grand struggle for power that is political life. For these reasons, the state's fiscal and budgetary policies deserve our close consideration.

TEXAS BUDGETS: CULTURAL, POLITICAL, AND ECONOMIC BACKGROUND

The fiscal and budget policies of Texas are the product of six interactive forces rooted in the cultural, economic and political dynamics of a complex state.

1. The "economic conservatism" of a broad range of Texans;
2. The legal requirements of the Texas Constitution;
3. The demographic characteristics and needs of the citizens;
4. Past and current court orders restricting legislative discretion about state spending;
5. The level of Federal Government spending in Texas;
6. The performance of the Texas economy.

Fiscal Conservatism in Texas

Fiscal conservatism is a set of values and attitudes held by both citizens and lawmakers in Texas about individual responsibility, capitalism, and the proper role of government in the lives of individuals! (See Figure 10.1).

Figure 10-1. Fiscal Conservatism

Economic Individualism. A strong sense of individual freedom of choice *and* accountability rooted in private property, individual hard work, and self-sufficiency.

Limited Government. The belief that government intrusion into the private lives of citizens should be kept to a minimum. Taxes should be kept low and services limited so individuals have the maximum of opportunities to exercise their liberty.

Capitalist Enhancement Strategy. Government can be selectively used to support the capitalist infrastructure for individuals and businesses in the private sector. Providing qualified citizens with access to public education and businesses with tax breaks is part of this strategy.[2]

Opposition to Welfare. Most Texans are skeptical about welfare. Many believe it morally bankrupts individuals by nurturing an attitude of "welfare dependency."

Good Business Climate. Government should promote business formation and operations by keeping taxes low and regulations on business at a minimum.

It should be noted that all citizens in Texas do not share the core beliefs of fiscal conservatism. Liberals believe that government spending should focus more on the needs of the poor, the wealthy should pay a greater share of the taxes, and businesses should be regulated to protect the public good. Most Texans, however, believe in the core conservative principles. Fiscal conservatism thus defines the economic and cultural basis for budgeting in state government.[3]

Constitutional and Statutory Constraints On Fiscal Policy

All democratic constitutions establish procedural guidelines and place substantive limits on the economic powers of government. As a general rule, state constitutions place more limitations on the fiscal operations of state government than the U.S. Constitution places on the fiscal operations of the federal government. The Texas Constitution fits this pattern.[4] As Chapter Two indicated, the generation of Texans who wrote and supported the 1876 Texas Constitution tried to limit the powers of state government. This is especially evident in the wide number of constitutional provisions they placed on the fiscal operations of Texas government. Since 1876 numerous statutes have been added to further define and constrain the fiscal operations and policies of Texas. Figure 10.2 and Figure 10.3 summarize the most significant procedural and substantive fiscal rules in Texas.[5]

Figure 10-2. Important Fiscal Procedures in Texas

Biennial Budget. The Texas Constitution requires that the Legislature to convene **biennially** (every other year) and adopt a biennial budget (one lasting for two years). The Legislature meets in odd-numbered years (2001) and during the 140 day session makes a budget to be implemented for two fiscal years. The fiscal year begins September 1 and ends August 31.

Comptroller of Public Accounts. The Comptroller must certify that adequate tax revenues exist to meet projected expenditures during the forthcoming biennium. The Comptroller also serves as the state's tax collector.

Line-Item Veto. The Constitution gives the governor the authority to remove a specific line of spending from the budget bill. (The simple threat of a veto is sometimes sufficient to alter the Legislature's appropriation.)

Earmarked or Dedicated Fund. This type of fund limits the legislature from shifting major amounts of state funds from one program to another. Dedicated funds legally require that specific tax revenues can only be spent on the programs indicated by the Constitution or by statute. An example of a dedicated fund is the "Permanent University Fund." Presently Texas utilizes 360 dedicated funds. The governor has been given limited "emergency" powers to shift the surplus from one fund to another during a declared fiscal emergency.

General Services Commission. This board oversees the purchases of state agencies. It generally requires a competitive bidding process for purchases in amounts greater than $1,000. The six board members are appointed by the governor to serve overlapping six-year terms.

Cash-Accounting. Cash-accounting means that expenditures are entered when money is paid rather than when obligations for spending are incurred.

Biennial Budget. Budgeting for the nation's second most populated state is more or less a full-time undertaking. To address the need for a full-time budgeting process and to accommodate the constitutional requirement for a part-time Legislature and a biennial budget, the **Legislative Budget Board (LBB)** was created in 1949 to deal with the growing demand for more professionalism in state budgeting practices. As we shall see, the LBB writes the budget for Texas in a practical sense.

Comptroller of Public Accounts. Part of the checks and balances system of the Texas Constitution, the Comptroller of Public Accounts must certify the presence of funds before the legislature can actually appropriate money to any state agency or program. The biennial budget process requires the Comptroller to make an estimate of the state's financial resources. The estimate depends, of course, on the projected amount of revenues that will be generated by the Texas economy. Former Comptroller, John Sharp and present Comptroller, Carole Rylander, played major roles in shaping the state's recent budgets. In recent years the Comptroller's forecasts have been sufficiently cautious so as to leave surpluses in the State's General Revenue Fund. In 1988 the voters authorized a constitutional amendment requiring any surpluses to be placed in an **Economic Stabilization Fund.** The surplus in this fund would to be used in the event that future projections fall short of balancing revenues and expenditures. During the budget process in the legislature, demands for spending usually exceed the availability of funds. The Comptroller's forecast about the "size of the pie" thus sets the fiscal parameters for the budgetary process in the legislature.

Dedicated Funds. The use of dedicated or "earmarked" funds has a long-standing history in Texas. These funds require legislators to spend tax revenues in the manner required by law. Defenders of dedicated funds counter that the funds allow the public to "see where the taxpayers' dollars are going," and thus prevents the legislature from "playing politics" with the public's money. Critics of dedicated funds argue that the funds essentially "tie the hands" of state officials. By "locking-in" how the money can be used, the legislature is unable to make adjustments in spending as the needs of Texans change from one generation to the next. This in turn prevents the legislature from creatively fashioning responses to emerging problems. During the 1980s a public outcry for more prison construction arose in Texas. Because state spending was "locked-in" by dedicated funds, the legislature had limited alternatives for constructing and operating additional prisons. Largely in response to this problem, the legislature passed a statute in 1987 that allows the governor to declare a financial "emergency." Once declared, an emergency prevents an agency from spending part of its appropriation in order to transfer "savings" from one agency to another. In 1987 the Texas Department of Corrections was able to obtain an additional $50 million for prison construction and maintenance.

Low Business Taxes. Texas is only one of three states that does not tax corporate or business profits. By keeping corporate taxes low, however, state officials inevitably have to raise money elsewhere—typically from individual citizens. Many business leaders and state legislators believe this arrangement works for the benefit of average Texans. They believe that high business taxes discourage employers from relocating to Texas and may even drive away employers from the state.

Figure 10-3. Important Limits on Texas Fiscal Policy

Balanced Budget. In 1942 the voters adopted a constitutional amendment requiring the state to operate with a balanced budget.

No Income Tax. In 1993 the voters adopted a constitutional amendment which, in effect, bans the state from using a state. (Technically speaking, the amendment did not ban the income tax outright. The amendment requires that any action by the Legislature to adopt an income tax must be approved by a majority of the electorate, which is the procedure similar to adopting a constitutional amendment. The amendment further requires any adoption of an income tax to be linked to a proportional rollback in local property taxes.)

No Statewide Property Tax. Texans adopted a constitutional ban on a state property tax in 1985.

No Corporate Profits Tax. Currently Texas does not tax the profits of corporations operating in the state.

Limit on Welfare Spending. In 1992 the Legislature and the voters passed a constitutional amendment that limits state spending for *Aid to Families with Dependent Children* (cash subsidies for poor, single-parents with children) to 1 percent of total state spending per biennium.

Limit on Growth of Spending. Article VIII, Section 22 of the Texas Constitution prevents the growth of spending from exceeding the rate of growth in the state's economy.

In an effort to sidestep the tax ban on corporate profits, the state turned in 1992 to its long-standing **corporate franchise tax** to raise additional revenues. The cooperate franchise tax is paid at a rate of $0.25 on the taxable capital (net worth) and 4.5% on earned surplus (after-tax surplus). Many business leaders contend that this is slipping a form of a corporate tax in the back door, as it were. Instead of taxing profits *per se, only* the net worth of the company is taxed. Inevitably such a tax will fall more heavily on industrial-type businesses that have large investments in plants and facilities. Service-based businesses such as law firms, accounting firms, and the like, generally do not have large or expensive physical assets and thus escape much of the tax burden.

Needs of the Citizens

Popularly elected governments make fiscal policies and enact budgets to fund programs that address the needs and demands of the citizens. Budgeting is not always about "politics." In spite of the *inevitable* conflict over taxing/spending priorities there are objective conditions that create a need for public services. Regardless of their political philosophy or party alliances popularly elected leaders are elected in order to fashion responses to these objective conditions. Approximately twenty-nine percent (29%) of Texans are ages 1 to 17. The relative youth and low incomes of Texans create a demand for access to public education. A "younger" state can generally expect to have a higher crime rate that in turn creates a greater demand for law enforcement. Fully one-third of the poor in Texas is youth with special needs for nutrition, education, and access to health care. Geography, too, enters the budgeting picture. The surge in youth-related crime in the past decade has created a particular need for reform and increased financing in the state's criminal justice system. The immense size of Texas (long distances between population centers) creates a particular need for funding of highways that other states simply do not confront on so vast a scale. Figure 10.4 provides an overview of some of the budget-sensitive characteristics of Texas. (What other direct and indirect political consequences can be linked to the data in Figure 10.4?)

Figure 10-4. Texas Demographic Facts

General Population Data

Population	20.1 million (84.2% metropolitan area residents).
Age: 0-18:	4.2 million (29% of population is school age, #2 in nation).
Age: 65 older	1.7 million (10.2%).
Birth Rate:	18 per 1,000 population.
Teenage Birth Rate:	16.2 % of births to teenage mothers (# 11 in the nation).
Income:	$25,920 per capita (1999), $33,072 per household (1997).
Unemployment Rate:	5.0%.

Welfare Data

Poverty Rate:	Poverty—$16,400 for a family of four, 1997.
	16.6% (3.2 million people).
	1.1 Million Children Under 18 live in poverty.
Public Aid Recipients:	6.3% of Texans.
Food Stamp Recipients:	14.7% of Texans.

Educational Data

Teacher Salary:	$33,038 (#35 in nation).
Hi School Grad Rate:	59% (#48 in nation).
Expenditures per Student:	$4,894 (#31 in nation).
Illiteracy Rate:	16%.

Geographic Data

Area:	266,000 square miles.
Roads\Drivers:	275,000 miles, 12 million licensed drivers, 12,777 miles traveled per vehicle.

Crime Data

Police:	24.4 per 10,000 population.
Crime Rate:	644 per 100,000 population.
Inmates:	100,136 (#2 in nation).
Inmate Rate:	69.3 per 10,000 population.
Police Expenditures:	$110 per capita (1992).
Correctional Expenditures:	$103 per capita (1992).

Sources: U.S. Bureau of Census, *Statistical Abstract of the United States: 1998.*
<http://www.census.gov/statab/www/>

Legislative Budget Board, *1998 Texas Factbook.*
<http://www.lbb.state.tx.us/>

The impact of these Texas characteristics on the budget is not always immediate. Civic leaders must balance the present costs of addressing the legitimate needs of citizens with the long-term social and financial costs of failing to act. They must weigh the *opportunity costs* of failing to act. It is a commonplace fact that prison populations and criminals come from backgrounds where illiteracy, poverty, child abuse and broken families, are ever-present conditions. With the annual cost of housing an individual in the Texas Department of Corrections now exceeding $40,000, Texans are increasingly confronted with the unenviable choice of paying now or paying later. The failure to address the present-day needs of youth may only postpone the time of reckoning but not the expense of doing so. One can only speculate about the private sector costs incurred by citizens as they attempt to deal with the social consequences of these conditions. How much social and economic cost is incurred to society, for example, by the fear of crime? Fear to move about freely in public areas, increased racial and ethnic tensions, and the vast expenditure of money for home security devices, personal weapons, and private security forces are only some of the indirect social and financial costs associated with crime.

Legal Actions

Legal actions also impinge on the budget process in Texas. During the past decade three court cases challenging the constitutionality of state budget policies have been tried and successfully won by the plaintiffs against the State of Texas (and its local-governments). One estimate calculates that more than 50% of the budget has been under the influence of a judicial mandate at one time or other during 1980s and 90s.

School Funding. In *Edgewood v. Kirby* a State District Court in Austin (reaffirmed by the State Supreme Court in 1989) the method for funding public education was declared unconstitutional. Plaintiffs for the San Antonio-area school district challenged the *equity* of school financing in Texas. This case set in motion a six year struggle by the voters, the legislature, and three governors to design a fair system for financing public schools. From 1987 to 1991 the voters rejected three constitutional amendment proposals intended to resolve the matter[6] In 1995 the legislature allowed a "tiered system" whereby property rich school districts could contribute to a "recapture" fund to be distributed to property poor school districts. This plan, known as *Senate Bill #7,* completely rewrote the basic education code for Texas. It also required an immediate allocation of an additional $1.6 Billion for public education. Although the immediate crisis passed, the struggle to find a fair system for funding Texas schools will continue to challenge future sessions of the Legislature.

Prison Operations. In *Ruiz v. Estelle* (1980) a federal district court in Tyler ordered drastic changes in Texas prison operations. Along with requiring many internal changes in prison system practices, the court action forced the legislature to relieve prison overcrowding. As a result, older prisons have been modernized and newer units have been added. In 1992 an agreement between Attorney General Dan Morales and attorneys for prisoners withdrew the matter of prison conditions from immediate court supervision. Following this agreement, the voters approved a plan to borrow money for prison construction.

Immigrant Services. In *Plyer v. Doe* Texas schools were required to allow the children of illegal immigrants to enroll in public schools and participate in special education programs. The decision in *Plyer v. Doe* sparked a national debate on immigration. In 1997 voters in California approved Proposition 187 that is designed to roll-back many of the state-funded social services provided to *illegal* immigrants. The large number of immigrants in Texas, both legal and illegal, will keep this legislative-judicial skirmish alive in the years ahead.

Tobacco Settlement. Legal actions do not always cost the state money. Texas joined many other states in legal actions against cigarette manufacturers. In essence, these cases sought to retrieve medical expenses the state had incurred for providing medical services to smokers. Faced with the prospect of fighting numerous legal battles in the states, cigarette manufacturers asked Congress to intervene. In 1997 Congress established a Comprehensive Tobacco Settlement Agreement and Release fund. The central provision of this settlement was an arrangement whereby states would not seek additional damages in return for a cash settlement from the manufacturers. Attorney General Dan Morales agreed and Texas expects to receive $1.8 Billion for the 2000-01 biennium and an estimated $17 Billion for the period 2000-25.

Federal Contributions to Texas Spending

The federal government will contribute approximately $27.7 billion (approximately 29.4%) of the state's projected 2000/01 budget (See Figure 10.5). Most of these federal funds are received through a process known as *Grants in Aid* whereby *both* the state and federal governments contribute to the financing of selected programs. In general the federal government provides a proportionate level of funding based upon the state's base funding for a particular program. Thus, there is an incentive for states to increase the level of funding for a program in order to gain more federal support. Most federal spending in Texas is provided to supplement welfare programs in Texas. Federal spending contributes approximately 58% of the budget for Health and Human Services spending. The largest of these jointly funded programs are the Temporary Assistance for Needy Families (formerly Aid to Families with Dependent Children), Medicaid (medical for needy citizens), and Woman and Infant Childcare (a nutritional program).

Figure 10-5. 2000/01 Federal Funds

Function	Amount in Millions	% Change
General Government Total	$ 443	1.3
Health and Human Services	$15,630	.8
Education	$ 4,340	1.6
Public Safety and Corrections	$ 176	-27
Natural Resources	$ 197	-6
Business & Economic Development (Includes Transportation)	$ 5,300	8.1
Regulatory Agencies	$ 4.8	4.2
Total Federal Expenditures	$ 27.7 Billion	1.9

Source: Legislative Budget Board, *Summary of Budget Estimates for the 200/01 Biennium*, January 1999.
<http://www.lbb.state.tx.us>

Federal Cutbacks. In the early 1980s the conservative Republican President, Ronald Reagan, and his conservative allies in the Congress launched an effort to reform what they regarded as excessive and runaway "welfare spending." By consolidating various programs and cutting the combined funding, by straightforward cuts, and by substituting **block grants** (broad, general-purpose-funding) for **categorical grants** (program-specific-funding) the Reagan forces were initially successful in curtailing federal spending for welfare programs administered by the states. As a result, the percentage of total state spending provided by federal revenues began to fall in Texas and other states.

This loss of federal revenues ushered in an era of both budget cuts for human services and tax increases for citizens as state leaders moved to replace some of the lost federal revenues. Following electoral gains during the 1986 election cycle, Democrats in Congress were successful in replacing some of the funding "lost" in the early 1980s. As a result, federal contributions to the state rose during the 1986-1996 period.

Following the 1994/96 congressional elections, Republicans gained a majority in both houses of Congress for the first time since 1953. Part of the House Republican's *Contract with America* called for cutting federal support for many welfare programs. The major federal welfare program, Aid to Families with Dependent Children (AFDC) was renamed the Temporary Assistance for Needy Families (TANF) and the administration of the program's fund was moved from the Department of Human Services to the Texas Employment Commission. The new funding rules for TANF are complex. In effect, the federal guarantee of a cash subsidy for the needy was removed. In its place, states were given temporary block grants to replace the loss of AFDC monies. In addition, new rules for qualifying for aid were implemented. In order to qualify for TANF support, individuals must be actively seeking employment or engaged in some form of training to acquire job skills. After an initial increase in funding during the 2000/01 biennium, federal welfare funding in Texas is projected to decrease. This recent history seems to suggest that the state's budget will continue to be affected by the yo-yo of federal spending.

Performance of the Economy

Of course, the ability of state government to fund programs to meet public needs and demands ultimately depends on the state's economic basis and the skills of its citizens. Three historic forces have shaped the Texas economy in recent years:

1. The transformation of the economy from one mostly dependent on the oil and gas industry to a more diversified economic base.
2. The rapid growth during the 1970s and early 1980s has been replaced by more stable growth in the 1990s.
3. The emergence of global markets and competition for both workers and employers.

Economic Diversification. In the 1970s Texas experienced unprecedented economic growth due in large part to the rapid increase in oil prices. International military conflicts and market actions taken by the Organization of Petroleum Exporting Countries (OPEC) figured greatly in this period of spiraling energy costs. Following the collapse of oil prices in the early 1980s, and the subsequent downturn in the state's energy sector, the legislature was confronted with a biennial struggle to make revenues balance with expenditures. Former Comptroller Bob Bullock estimated that for every $1 decline in the price of oil, Texas government lost revenues of $100 Million as overall economic activity declined in the state.[7]

The decline of the energy industry during the 1980s had a dramatic impact on Texas politics and government. During an economic downturn, the demand for vital public services continues. Citizens expect the state to provide quality education for children and to build roads and prisons, for example, regardless of economic cycles. Because of these and other financial pressures the legislature enacted a series of four successive tax increases in the 1980s and early 1990s. The last increase was estimated to be the largest single tax increase in *any* state's history. Political fallout from rising taxes was predictable and immediate. Voices in opposition to taxes were organized and pressure was brought to bear on elected officials to limit the size of government (see *conservatism* above). Voters approved a constitutional amendment in 1994 to limit increases in state spending to *no more* than the underlying increase in the state's economic growth.

The downturn in the energy sector set-off a near collapse in property values in the state. And this decline in property values started a nationwide collapse of the savings and loan industry. As a result of these near-calamities, business and government leaders hastened their efforts to diversify the state's economy. Part of this strategy required local government officials to provide property tax exemptions and other tax breaks for firms willing to relocate to Texas. Hi-technology industries were particularly targeted for expanding the state's economic profile. The efforts to diversify the economy of Texas have been successful. The Legislative Budget Board estimates that service sector employment will provide 32% of all jobs in Texas by 2007.

Stable Growth. Most sectors of the Texas economy survived the recession of the late 1980s in good fashion. The overall picture for the state's economy shows the agricultural, manufacturing, financial services, transportation, and wholesale and retail industries all experiencing growth from 1984 to 1999. The construction industry has rebounded. The energy sector, however, continues to decline. Gas prices in mid-1999 were at the lowest level in a generation. In spite of this historic decline in the energy sector, economic growth in Texas is strong as the state enters the next century. The 1999 projected Gross State Product is $697 Billion. Per capita income stands at $20,900 in 1999 and is expected to grow at an annual rate of 6.7% through the year 2007. Not all the economic news has been good, however. On average, Texans earn nearly $5,000 less than the national average per capita income. In all but three of the past ten years, the unemployment rate in Texas has exceeded the national average. Projections for the future, however, show a strong expansion for jobs through 2007 with significant increases in both employment and personal income.

International Economy. International markets will shape the development of the Texas economy in the years to come. The passage of the North American Free Trade Agreement (NAFTA) in 1994 raised early expectations that trade with Mexico and other Latin American countries would hold tremendous growth potential for Texas. The collapse of the Mexican stock market and fall of the peso in 1995 dampened early optimism of an economic bonanza, but the long-term prospects for continued economic expansion remain. Shipping and transportation, manufacturing, and the consumer electronics industry expect to see increased economic activity as a result of more trade. Talks involving Mexican and American officials have begun regarding building a "free trade" super-highway that would stretch from Mexico to Canada. International markets, however, come with increased competition and the attendant risks for workers and employers. Workers in the higher skilled enterprises may benefit from international trade, but workers in lower-skilled jobs may face wage pressure as they compete with the lower-paid workers in Central America

Each of the preceding factors shapes the overall structure of the Texas revenue stream and the priorities for state spending. In recent years, several trends are evident in these matters. First, the economic base of the state has grown. Second, the selective sales tax was raised periodically and remains the primary revenue source for the state. Third, the state's revenue stream no longer depends on oil and gas taxes. Figure 10.6 summarizes the key trends regarding the Texas budget.

Figure 10-6. Financial Trends

	1995	2000 (Proj.)	Annual % Change
Per Capita Income	$21,100	$27,290	3.5%
Total Personal Income	$395 Billion	$555	7.2%
Gross State Product	$523 Billion	$750 Billion	8.0%
Tax Collection Per Capita	$1007	$1,132	2.5%
Total Expenditures	$37 Billion	$49 Billion	2.2%

Source: Legislative Budget Board, *Trends in Texas Government Finance*.
<http://www.lbb.state.tx.us>

THE BUDGETING PROCESS: PLAYERS, PROCEDURES, AND POLITICS

The Texas Constitution, Legislative Rules, and political interests determine the players and define the "rules of the game" for writing budgets for state government.

Budgeting and Politics

In an ideal world appropriating the taxpayers' dollars for needed state services would proceed in a "rational" manner. Spending priorities would be carefully and fairly established, revenues would be generated in an equitable manner, and those responsible for spending the public's money would be held accountable for the public trust. The real world is a far cry from the realm of theory. Political differences frequently inhibit the formation of consensus about priorities, tax equality is a goal, and inadequate time, knowledge, and money make oversight procedures largely inadequate to the task of holding state agencies accountable.

In the words of one Political Scientist, budgeting is an incremental process of "muddling through."[6] Budgeting in democracies is a slow, often laborious process in which continuity rather than revolution is the norm. Last year's budget is the best guide for understanding next year's in spite of the rhetoric of candidates to "clean house" and re-order or "re-invent government." Budgetary incrementalism is especially prevalent in Texas where the use of numerous constitutional provisions, a brief (140 day) biennial legislative session, and the previously-mentioned court orders virtually "lock-in" considerations about spending priorities. (These features guarantee that power over planning the budget will be exercised by a few, key legislators and their professional staff.) Individual legislators typically want to be re-elected or move-up to a higher office, secure benefits for their districts, and voters sometimes demand more services *and* lower taxes. Geography also shapes the budgeting process. Any budget will almost certainly contain **pork barrel** spending. These are spending items in the budget that benefit a specific legislative district (and the reelection chances of the legislator) but are of questionable value for advancing the general interests of the state. Every democratic budget in the world shows some evidence of pork barrel spending. Budgetary decisions are also affected by genuine philosophical differences about the very purpose and nature of government itself. Some citizens, interests, and legislators want to spend more money on law enforcement in order to prevent crime. Others would like to see more money spent on alleviating the social conditions of crime—poverty, poor education, and failed socialization. All of these factors make writing a budget the *culmination* of politics in Texas. Budgeting is the point in the governing of society where all of the political forces gather at once. Average citizens (and most students) often see "politics" as corrupting the process of writing a budget, but to the trained observer of political life, writing a budget is the quintessential political act.

Writing the Texas Budget

Writing and passing the budget into law requires the joint effort of the Legislative and the Executive branches of state government. Budgets, like all laws, must be passed by the House and Senate and signed into law by the Governor of Texas. The Texas Constitution gives the Governor the additional power to use a line-item veto over specific spending items in the budget. The Comptroller of Public Accounts must certify the presence of sufficient funds for the Legislature to make appropriations. The following is an overview of the major players in the budget process.

Legislative Budget Board (LBB). The Legislative Budget Board assembles a preliminary budget for the full legislature to consider once the regular legislative session convenes. The LBB was created in 1949 to handle the growing complexity of the state's budget. The LBB employs full-time professionals to assist key legislators in drafting a budget for the state. (The Governor may also prepare and submit a budget of with the aid of the Office of Budget and Planning [OBP]. The Legislature has historically used its budget in the appropriations process, so the OBP will not be discussed here.) Ten legislators serve on the LBB (See Figure 10.7).

Figure 10-7. Members of the Legislative Budget Board

The Lieutenant Governor	The Speaker of the House
Senate Chair of the Finance Committee	House Chair of the Appropriations Committee
Senate Chair of the State Affairs Committee	House Chair of the Ways and Means Committee
Two Legislators Appointed by the Lt. Governor	Two Legislators Appointed by the Speaker.

All organs of state government—state agencies, boards, and commissions—must make requests for appropriations before the LBB. The LBB *begins* the budget process by issuing general guidelines or *spending targets* that each agency must meet. To establish these targets the LBB studies financial forecasts provided by the Comptroller of Public Accounts and other economists. Specific units of government must in turn make requests for funding before their appropriate oversight agencies. This college, for example, must submit a budget to the Coordinating Board of Higher Education. The Coordinating Board assembles the requests from all colleges and universities in the state and then presents an overall higher education budget before the LBB. After the LBB reviews and assembles all the specific requests for funding, the preliminary budget is submitted to the House and the Senate. The House and Senate then conduct hearings on the budget proposal. Both the House and the Senate make adjustments to the LBB version, but generally stay within the overall parameters set forth in the preliminary proposal. The legislative session, then, is more a culmination of events than it is a beginning. As a general rule, the legislative session focuses on making subtle shifts at the margins of the proposal rather than making wholesale revisions in the LBB proposal.

House and Senate Hearings. The LBB proposal is submitted during the first five days of the legislative session. Following its introduction, both the House and the Senate initiate independent hearings on the appropriations bill. In the House, the LBB prepared budget is sent to each of the substantive committees (Education Committee, for example) for review. Most of the substantive committees have established sub-committees with oversight responsibilities for the state agencies under their guidance. These sub-committees conduct hearings and are in turn asked to appear before the Appropriations Committee to comment on the proposed LBB budget. The Appropriations Committee can increase or reduce the substantive sub-committee request. An increase requires a two-thirds vote of the Appropriations Committee, a decrease occurs by simple-majority vote. Because of its smaller size (31 members as opposed to 150) the budgetary review process in the Senate is primarily the responsibility of the Senate Finance Committee. The budget proposals that emerge from the House and Senate rarely agree and a conference committee must reconcile the differences. Generally speaking, the conferees are working at the margins of appropriations and no dramatic changes are likely to occur in the proposals. Figure 10.10 provides an overview of the budget process in Texas.

Comptroller of Public Accounts. As mentioned above, the Comptroller of Public Accounts must certify that tax revenues are available to meet projected spending. The Comptroller's Office has over 2,800 employees to assist with the tasks of economic forecasting, the administration and collection of taxes, and budget review. Over 90% of all taxes in Texas are collected by the Comptroller's Office.

Governor. The Governor of Texas has the authority to veto specific items in the budget and must sign the overall budget into law. Often the threat of a veto is sufficient to force the legislature to accommodate the governor's intention. In response to the previously discussed court orders and budgetary constraints of the 1980s, the governor was given the ability by a 1987 statute to prevent a state agency from spending part of its appropriation. The governor can now shift funds from one agency to another within a range of a 5% increase to a 10% decrease.

TAXES, REVENUES, AND SPENDING

The funding for the 2000/2001 biennium comes from four basic sources[9]:

1. State Taxes $48.7 Billion
2. State Fees and Other Revenue $14.4 Billion
3. Federal funds $27.7 Billion
4. Lottery Proceeds $ 3.3 Billion
       Total $ 94 Billion

State funds contribute about seventy percent (70%) of all spending in Texas with most of this amount coming from various taxes. Federal contributions to Texas are somewhat higher for the biennium because of tobacco settlement (see above). Most of the federal contributions to the state are for federal welfare programs administered by the state.

State Taxes

True to their spirit of independence and conservatism, Texans don't like taxes. In 1997 Texas was ranked 48th out of 50 states in its per capita taxation rates.[10] Projections from the State Comptroller show that per capita taxation will continue decline during the next ten years. By any measure, Texas is a low tax state! However, this ranking is based on taxes levied by state governments only. When local governments are added to the state totals, however, Texas' rank jumps to 31st. Because Texas uses neither a personal income tax nor a comprehensive business profits tax, it must rely on the _general sales_ tax to generate the bulk of its revenues. Originally adopted as a 4% tax on basic goods, the rate has grown steadily to its present figure of 6.25%. (Local governments have additional taxing authority and can add up to 1 cent or 1% to the state sales tax. As many urban areas of the state have approved a _transit authority tax_, this raises the effective sales tax to 8.25% of purchased goods.) All the major taxes in Texas have been increased in recent years. Figure 10.8 provides an overview of the tax structure of Texas.

The sales tax in Texas is a *selective sales* tax. In general, it applies mostly to the sale of personal property or goods (*resale* of property is exempt). Thus, the most notable feature of the sales tax is what it *does not tax*. The major exemptions to the sales tax include food, most services such as legal fees and advertising, medical prescriptions, and supplies used in agricultural production. (For a complete list of the tax exemptions in Texas, see Tax Exemptions & Tax Incidence.) <http://www.window.texas.gov/taxinfo/incidence/lsaut.html> Efforts to diversify the revenue stream have included legislative proposals to expand the sales tax to cover more services, especially legal, financial, and advertising services. Lobbyists for these industries, however, have been successful in blocking these efforts in recent legislative sessions.

Figure 10-8. Major Texas Taxes with Revenues Generated for 2000-01 Biennium

Source	Rate	Amount in $ Millions	% of Total*
Selective Sales Tax	6.25 %	27,530	62
Motor Vehicle Taxes	6.25 %	4952	11
Franchise Taxes	.25 % net worth	4,200	9.6
	4.5 % earned surplus		
Oil Production and	4.6 % of value	1587	3.6
Natural Gas Production	7.5 % of value		
Motor Fuels	20 cents gallon	1,116**	2.5
Tobacco/Cigarette and	41 cents pack	1,959	4.4
Alcoholic Beverage	$6 barrel on beer		
Insurance	vary 1.6 % — 3.5 %	1,574	3.5
(Other Taxes Include)			
Inheritance	same as federal (first 600K exempt)		
Hotel\Motel	6 % under 30 days		
Utility	vary		
Total Other Taxes		1,495	3.3
Total Tax Collections		44,401	100
		($44.4 Billion)	

Source: Carole Keyton Rylander, Texas Comptroller of Public Accounts, *2000-2001 Biennial Revenue Estimate.*
<http://www.window.texas.gov/taxbud/bre99/re1098b.html>
*Percentages based on Tax Collections, Lottery Proceeds, and State Fees, only—percentages do not include federal funding in Texas.
**Legislative action delayed the release of motor fuels tax from the previous biennium, thus producing a smaller than usual revenue for this biennium.

Other Sources of Revenue

The Comptroller of Public Accounts estimates that in the 2000/01 biennium, an additional $27.7 Billion in federal funding will be available to the state. Federal contributions to the state generate 29.5% of all state revenues. A variety of state fees, permits, fines, and lottery proceeds and dividends make up the remaining $17.7 Billion in revenue. Figure 10.9 provides an overview of the 2000/01 revenue stream, excluding any new bonds that may be issued.

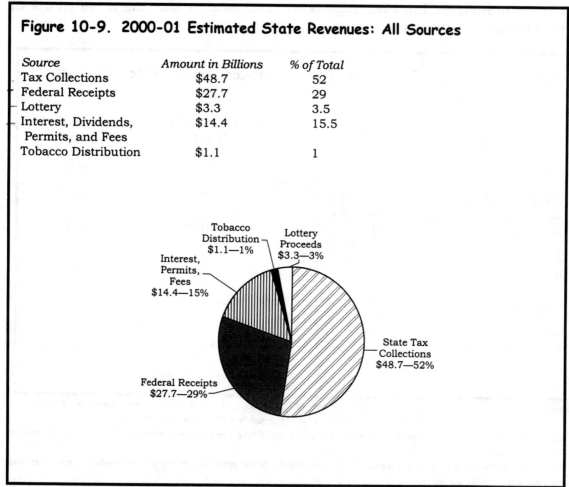

Figure 10-9. 2000-01 Estimated State Revenues: All Sources

Source	Amount in Billions	% of Total
Tax Collections	$48.7	52
Federal Receipts	$27.7	29
Lottery	$3.3	3.5
Interest, Dividends, Permits, and Fees	$14.4	15.5
Tobacco Distribution	$1.1	1

Source: Carole Keyton Rylander, Texas Comptroller of Public Accounts, *2000-2001 Biennial Revenue Estimate.*
<http://www.window.texas.gov/taxbud/bre99/re1098b.html>

Spending

Most state spending is dedicated to financing four basic functions of state government: public education, public welfare, highways and transportation, and correctional institutions (prisons) and public safety. Public education and public welfare together account for *more than 80%* of state spending. Spending by state government has grown in recent years. As discussed above, reforms in public school funding have created most of the increase. Changes in federal rules and revenues have caused a dramatic increase in welfare spending, especially in medical-care programs, unemployment compensation, and nutritional programs. Increased public pressure for new prisons created a two and one-half fold increase in money spent on public safety. Figure 10.10 provides an overview of state spending.

ISSUES IN TEXAS FINANCES

Budgeting in Texas is a dynamic process. Economic cycles, pressure groups, changing demographics, and national politics create an environment in which legislators must creatively respond to evolving conditions. Because they raise fundamental questions about budgeting, the following issues consistently return to the legislative agenda.

Changing Tax Structure

The tax structure in Texas is slowly changing. In 1962 the sales tax was 2 % and generated 20% of all tax-related receipts. Today, the sales tax is 6.25 % and generates 62% of state tax receipts. This transformation has been due largely to a (relative) decrease in revenues generated by natural resources taxes and an increase in spending for education. Severance taxes are levied on the removal of raw materials (oil, gas, uranium, iron, etc.) from Texas. The combined projection for Oil Production and Natural Gas Production taxes for the 2000/01 biennium $1.6 Billion or only 4.2% of state-generated revenues. In 1978 this combined figure contributed 12% of *all revenues*. As oil and gas production declined, the state raised taxes in other areas to offset lost revenues from these industries. The political impact of this transformation has been significant on Texans. Typically, severance taxes are "passed along" by the producers to the end-consumers of the product(s).

Figure 10-10. 2000-01 Biennium Spending in Texas: All Funds

Function	Amount in Billions	% of Total	% Change
General Government Total	$2.2	2.4	7.4
Health and Human Services	$26.9	28.7	2.1
Education	$41.8	44.6	7.3
Public Education	*$29.2*	*31.5*	*8.7*
Higher Education	*$12.5*	*13*	*4.2*
Judiciary	$0.32	.3	1.7
Public Safety and Criminal Justice	$7.4	7.8	1.5
Natural Resources/ Recreation	$1.6	1.7	-3.0
Business & Economic Development	$10.8	11.5	-1.5
Regulatory Agencies	$0.44	0.5	3.8
The Legislature	$0.25	0.2	1.7
Total Net Expenditures	$91.7	100	3.8
Tobacco Settlement Disbursements*	$1.8	1.9	N/A
Grand Total Expenditures	$94	100	5.8

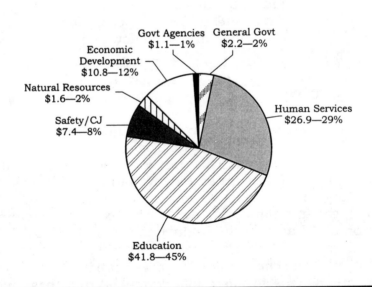

Source: Legislative Budget Board, *Summary of the Legislative Budget Estimates for the 2000-01 Biennium.* < http://www.lbb.state.tx.us/>

*The Tobacco Fund is a dedicated fund subject to different distribution rules. It is included here to make the Grand Total Expenditures accurate.

Texas Fiscal and Budget Policies

Producers regard severance taxes as a cost of doing business and raise prices accordingly. As many of the end-line consumers of Texas oil and gas are out-of-state consumers, the state was able to reap a tax bonanza. Out of state consumers, in effect, contributed to state revenues and state officials were able to keep other state taxes lower. This "free lunch" is now at an end and Texans are paying more to maintain the services of state government.

Tax Pinch and Tax Reform

Reliance on the sales tax as the primary source of state revenue was made possible because of the large energy and natural resource industries in the state. The dwindling tax base led to repeated efforts to find new sources of revenue. Throughout the 1980s and 1990s the legislature has sought additional ways to generate revenues. Most often this led to significant increases in the state sales tax. Texas currently has the *fourth* highest sales tax in the nation. It seems unlikely that lawmakers will increase sales taxes *rates* any further. Various proposals have been made to *broaden the tax base* by making additional products and services subject to the sales tax. To date these efforts have been resisted. In 1995 voters adopted the lottery in order to generate additional monies for the state. Faced with an exploding school-age population, numerous local governments have raised local property tax rates. Local property tax rates place Texas *seventeenth* in national rankings. Not surprisingly, calls for "tax relief" are most often directed at reducing local property taxes and the state sales tax. Many observers contend, however, that so long as the adoption of an income tax remains "off the table," real reform of the state's tax system will remain a hope rather than a reality.

Tax Justice

The reliance on the sales tax in Texas raises a fundamental question about the *fairness* of taxes as they are structured in Texas. State and national income taxes are, generally speaking, **progressive taxes.** Sales taxes are often **regressive taxes.** Progressive taxes work by requiring people in higher income categories to pay a higher *rate* of taxation. Progressive taxes are based on the principle that *civic justice* requires individuals who make more *from* their communities to return more *to* their communities. Regressive taxes work in the opposite manner. Regressive taxes require people in lower income categories to pay higher rates of taxation on their available income. *Lower* income citizens thus put *more* of their available incomes back into the community. Consider the example of two individuals where one makes $10,000 a year and the other makes $100,000 a year. Assume that both individuals make general purchases during the year for $5,000 at a 5% tax rate. It appears both pay the same or equal tax of 5% x $5,000 = $250. Yet the **tax**

burden on the lower income individual is greater than on the higher income individual—$250 is 2.5% of the $10,000 income but only .25% of the $100,000 income. Thus, a far *greater percentage of the available income* of the lower-income person must be set aside to pay the same tax. The overall regressive structure of the sales tax is diminished somewhat because many commodities essential for living are not subject to the sales tax. For example, food, drugs, and medical services are not subject to the sales tax. Because a large portion of a lower income family's income will go for these items, the overall tax burden on these families may be somewhat diminished.

Tax Cuts

After the 1996/98 elections, the Republican Party maintained majorities in both houses of the United States Congress. Republicans also gained legislative seats in the Texas Legislature in 1998 and scored impressive victories in all of the statewide elections. As a result, tax cuts will likely be an important legislative topic for Texas lawmakers in the near future. In 1997, Governor Bush proposed a plan to reduce local property taxes by allocating additional state monies to local school districts. The legislature agreed to allocate $1 Billion for property tax relief, but no requirement was made for local school boards to lower property taxes by the equivalent amount of money each district received from the state. As a result, many local school boards accepted the additional state money but did not cut local taxes. Early in the 1999 session Governor Bush again proposed cutting local property taxes by $3 Billion. (As this book went to press, the Bush proposal had not been resolved. To follow-up on the tax cut plan, see the Austin American Statesman.) <http://austin360.com/news/>

On-Line: Texas Fiscal and Budget Policies

The Legislative Budget Board is a major source for state financial and budget data.

http://www.lbb.state.tx.us/

Window on State Government is a rich source for state financial and tax data.

http://www.window.texas.gov/

State of Texas Government Information: You will find a link for the official Appropriations Bill for the 2000/01 Biennium here.

http://www.state.tx.us/

State and Local Government on the Net is a master list of links to other states and organizations specializing in state budget politics.

http://www.piperinfo.com/state/states.html

National Association of State Budget Officers provides comparative data, trends, and issues facing state budgeting.

http://www.nasbo.org/

Map Stats is a massive site from the U.S. Census Bureau contains resources for all fifty states.

http://www.census.gov/datamap/www/index.html

Statistical Abstract of the United States. If it's numbers you need, this is the place to start.

http://www.census.gov/statab/www/

Economic Statistics Briefing Room. Easy to use charts and graphs with more links.

http://www.whitehouse.gov/fsbr/esbr.html

ENDNOTES

1. Many economic and political theorists have noted the mutual interaction between political and economic freedom. Market-style economies thrive in liberal-democracies and liberal-democracies require market-style economies. See Charles Lindbloom, *Politics and Markets* (Basic Books, 1977). For a critical analysis of how the loss of market freedom erodes personal liberty *and* democracy, see Friedrich Von Hayek, *The Road to Serfdom* (Chicago: University of Chicago Press, 1944).

2. For an excellent discussion on the interaction between deeply held public attitudes about property, taxes, and personal responsibility and government policies, see Herbert Gans, *Middle American Individualism: Political Participation and Liberal Democracy* (Oxford University Press, 1988.)

3. For the classic discussion on the interaction of material forces (economics) and moral ideas (personal responsibility) in society, see Max Weber, *The Protestant Ethic and the Spirit of Capitalism*, translated by Talcott Parsons (New York: Charles Scribners Press, 1958). Also, see Milton Friedman, *Capitalism and Freedom* (Chicago: University of Chicago Press, 1962) and *Free to Choose* (Chicago: University of Chicago Press, 1978).

4. House Research Organization, State Finance Report: *Writing the State Budget*, Texas House of Representatives, Austin, February 19, 1999.

5. For a brief and informative overview of the fiscal rules in Texas, see Senate Research Center. *Budget 101: A Guide to the Budget Process in Texas*, Texas Senate Publications, Austin, 1999.

6. Thomas Whatley, Editor, *Texas Government Newsletter*, Vol. 22, Number 28, September 19, 1994 (Austin: Texas).

7. Lt. Governor Bob Bullock, "Texas' Fiscal Future—Time to See Realities," *Houston Chronicle*, March 8, 1992.

8. Charles Lindbloom, "The Science of 'Muddling Through,'" *Public Administration Review*, vol. 19 (Spring 1959).

9. Unless otherwise indicated, all data for revenue projections and tax sources may be found in Carole Keyton Rylander, Texas Comptroller of Public Accounts, *2000-2001 Biennial Revenue Estimate*.
   <http://www.window.texas.gov/taxbud/bre99/re1098b.html>

10. U.S. Census Bureau, State Government Tax Collections: Fiscal Year 1996-97.
    <http://www.census.gov/govs/statetax/97tax.txt>

Index